MONDAY MORNING
ETHICS

The Lessons Sports Ethics Scandals Can Teach
Athletes, Coaches, Sports Executives and Fans

LEADERSHIP
BOOKS
Thoughtful, Relevant Leaders
From Around The World

Chuck Gallagher and Bruce H. Wolk

FOREWORD

Ruby Newell-Legner, CSP www.7StarService.com

Daily we are confronted with decisions that reveal our integrity, our character. Sometimes we pause long enough to reflect on the possible repercussions of our actions and in most of the examples in this book, I wonder if they had a moment of reflection at all. Did any of them contemplate the consequences, or did they just think they wouldn't get caught?

Did they sleep well the night before? Did they realize that their seemingly unimportant decisions would change the rest of their lives? Or do they not have any conscience at all? Did they not hear that inner voice warning them or did they just turn down the volume so low that it could not be heard?

As a fan experience expert, consultant, and trainer, I frequently encounter situations that give me pause, like the stories you are about to read. I can't help but wonder how the individuals affected by the scandals referenced in this book felt on Monday morning.

As I read each chapter, I couldn't help but reflect on their selfish decisions, some perhaps made in the spur of the moment and others contemplated for months. Did any of these individuals realize the impact their decisions would have on their family members, colleagues, teammates and organizations?

Did they desire to have a "bad boy" reputation or was it an accident? Or were their actions just a rebellious act of discontent? Were the scandals just skeletons in the closet that they thought would never get out?

Was that one decision just a slip of integrity where their values weren't strong enough to use good judgment? Was their moral code weakened by circumstances beyond their control?

Perhaps they saw no light at the end of the tunnel and felt the decision they made was their only option.

As you read the thirty-one stories, I encourage you to reflect on the wisdom and insight offered by Chuck and Bruce. Remember that your reputation is a gift you give yourself. The choices that you make every day reflect on how you are perceived...not what you think of yourself. As people interact and do business with you, they are constantly evaluating your character. Those around you are sizing up your honesty, integrity, and trustworthiness.

Colleagues, clients, and complete strangers are observing your behavior and forming theories about your competence, character, and commitment. Your actions are constantly under scrutiny and your motives are being judged.

Take full responsibility for creating the reputation you want for a lifetime. You are your own publicist, so take charge of your own public relations, respect, integrity, and significance. Those are the character traits I have watched Chuck Gallagher demonstrate through his daily actions. His reputation is solid, and his life is filled with opportunities to make a difference.

I met Chuck through our leadership roles in the National Speakers Association. Through our work together, I came to respect Chuck's character and perseverance. During many conversations, his passion for helping people became very clear as one of his strongest values. I watched him make decisions and take action to honor and help others avoid the painful lessons he had learned early in his career. These are the same insights he offers to everyone he encounters through his speaking and in everyday life. This second-chance wisdom offers invaluable lessons for all of us.

Thank you for showing us transparency and vulnerability, Chuck. As a consultant and trainer in the world of sports and entertainment, I will use these stories to start conversations. I will help others reflect, gain insights...and teachings, to save others from going down the wrong road.

PREFACE

What is time? Well, time can be a funny thing. Events that happen in the moment don't seem to have any real significance until we look back and put them into perspective.

As I write this, I reach back to an important moment in 1990. I didn't know it would be significant then, but it must have been one of those occasions when a seed was planted that took a long while to harvest.

My son was just six at the time, and I was a "road warrior" speaking around the country on various topics, none of which had to do with sports. But as a sports fan, I kept up with what was going on, especially in baseball. On one trip, I decided I wanted to buy a team pennant and bring it home to Rob (my oldest) as a gift. Team pennants, along with baseball cards, were the collectible of the day. Ah, those baseball cards! Each one had a story. Rob and I would spend hours rearranging the cards and talking about the sports stars featured on them.

I recall when Rob and I were sorting through baseball cards in March of 1990, and my son held up a card and said, "Well, Dad, I guess this one's no good now."

I looked. He was pulling out a Pete Rose card from its protective plastic sleeve.

"Why do you say that, Rob?" I asked. "He's got more hits than anyone!"

"Yeah, Dad, but he's been banned. He's a cheat!"

I was surprised to hear my son share this opinion, one that he'd gotten from watching sports news.

"Guess he blew it," he said. "Hey, Dad, wonder what would have happened if he had not cheated?"

Now Rob wasn't clear on exactly what Pete Rose had done – I guess he figured if you got banned, you must have cheated somehow. But the question asked in the innocence of youth stuck with me and became the foundation of this book.

At that point, more than thirty years ago, I had no thought that I'd be writing a book on sports ethics with my good friend Bruce H. Wolk. Heck, I didn't even know Bruce then. But the idea of what would have happened if those of us who had made stupid choices had not made them continued to intrigue me.

What if Pete had never chosen the short-term gain from gambling and instead bet on the long game – his reputation and future career?

Questions like that have perplexed me for decades. You see, I made some stupid choices of my own, choices that would forever change the trajectory of my life.

Nine months after my son and I talked, after I'd already put it out of my head, my misdeeds came to light. My unethical choices would change my life, the lives of my two boys, and my career.

Just like Pete Rose, one poor choice I made led me to another and then to another. My financial crime choices became a pattern of behavior that, over time and with no immediate consequences in sight, eventually crushed me as I stood before a judge and the people I hurt.

I emerged from a hell of my own, making me wiser, stronger, and more compassionate, but not without a period of soul-searching, humility, contrition, and gratitude for a second chance.

So, as Bruce and I embarked on this journey to explore ethics in sports, I have a unique perspective not only on the action but, more importantly, on what may have motivated the unethical choices that resulted in shame.

It is my fervent hope that this book will help prevent someone from making an unethical choice. If we can reach that person, or hopefully, many people, this effort will have meaning to me beyond words.

-- Chuck Gallagher

In Monday Morning Ethics, we have included thirty-one well-known sports scandals — professional and amateur sports alike — covering a period of about seventy-five years. The scandals are *intentionally condensed.* We're aware that much more could have been said about the thirty-one incidents.

Every scandal could be made into a book of its own. Each scandal has its heroes, victims, and villains. We encourage readers to spend time researching the cases they find interesting.

That said, we intentionally wrote the cases in such a way so as to make great ethics teaching tools, whether you are involved in athletics, business, nonprofit organizations, any aspect of healthcare or simply as conversational points for those of us who like sports.

Chuck Gallagher is one of the most inciteful and concerned people I have had the pleasure of meeting. He lives his ethical conviction daily. As an ethics motivational speaker and consultant, he deeply cares about individuals making good choices for themselves and is an inspiration for those in need of a second chance.

Think of Chuck's Ethics Review as the jumping-off point for your own conversations within your teams, conferences, associations, classrooms, community groups, or with your friends.

Not surprisingly, no one involved in any scandal we present has ever fully recovered their reputations as a result of their unethical actions. There was some point in each scandal when effective sports ethics training might have changed the personal course of history for the wrongdoers. Even the most flawed of people in these scandals, the most psychologically damaged, were surrounded by enablers who made their behavior possible.

Time has marched on for almost everyone involved in these disgraces. However, the wrongful acts they committed will live on as well.

-- Bruce H. Wolk

CONTENTS

INTRODUCTION..1

THREE COMPONENTS OF AN ETHICAL LAPSE............3

SECTION I THE GAMBLERS 7

    CHAPTER 1..9
    PETE ROSE BETS ON BASEBALL AND LOSES HIS REPUTATION

    CHAPTER 2..17
    THE BASKETBALL POINT-SHAVING SCANDAL OF THE 1950S

    CHAPTER 3..27
    THE "OPERATION SLAP SHOT" GAMBLING SCANDAL

    CHAPTER 4..35
    HOUSTON ASTROS SIGN STEALING SCANDAL

SECTION II HIGHER EDUCATION...................................43

    CHAPTER 5..45
    SOUTHERN METHODIST UNIVERSITY (SMU) FOOTBALL SCANDAL OF 1987

    CHAPTER 6..53
    KATIE HNIDA AND THE UNIVERSITY OF COLORADO

    CHAPTER 7..63
    DUKE LACROSSE SCANDAL OF 2006

    CHAPTER 8..73
    1993 FLORIDA STATE UNIVERSITY SHOE SCANDAL

    CHAPTER 9..83
    MICHELE SHARP, KEAN UNIVERSITY AND TRIPS TO SPAIN

    CHAPTER 10 93
    CLEM HASKINS, THE UNIVERSITY OF MINNESOTA AND BLIND AMBITION

SECTION III THE CONSPIRACIES 101

CHAPTER 11..................103
The Winter Olympics Vote-Trading Scandal

CHAPTER 12 113
The Salt Lake City IOC Scandal

CHAPTER 13 123
Alan Eagleson and the NHL Players Scandal

CHAPTER 14 131
The Danny Almonte Story

SECTION IV THE SPORTS LEADERS? 141

CHAPTER 15 143
Spygate: It Was All about The Win

CHAPTER 16 153
Deshaun Watson – So Much Promise, So Little Time

CHAPTER 17 161
George O'Leary, Almost the Mountain-top

CHAPTER 18 169
Donald Sterling – "I Own a Team, You Don't"

SECTION V DRUGS OF ALL KINDS 177

CHAPTER 19 179
Alex Rodriguez and the Biogenesis of America Scandal

CHAPTER 20 189
The Pittsburgh Pirates Cocaine Trial of 1985

CHAPTER 21 199
Kamila Valiyeva Doping Scandal, 2022 Winter Olympics

SECTION VI VIOLENCE MOST FOUL 207

CHAPTER 22 209
The New Orleans Saints Bounty Scandal

CHAPTER 23..**217**

TODD BERTUZZI, STEVE MOORE, AND ON-ICE VIOLENCE

CHAPTER 24..**225**

RAY RICE AND THE ELEVATOR

CHAPTER 25..**235**

AARON HERNANDEZ DEALER, DUPE OR DEVIL?

SECTION VII ETHICAL FOOLS................................**241**

CHAPTER 26..**243**

A SHOT TO THE KNEES: NANCY KERRIGAN AND TONYA HARDING

CHAPTER 27..**251**

RYAN LOCHTE TRASHES BATHROOM, DANCES WITH STARS

CHAPTER 28..**259**

LORI LAUGHLIN – OPERATION VARSITY BLUES

CHAPTER 29..**270**

TERRENCE WILLIAMS SCAMS THE NBA

SECTION VIII THE MONSTERS................................**278**

CHAPTER 30..**280**

JERRY SANDUSKY AND PENN STATE UNIVERSITY

CHAPTER 31..**292**

LARRY NASSAR AND A CULTURE OF ABUSE

ABOUT THE AUTHORS.......................................**302**

CHUCK GALLAGHER

BRUCE H. WOLK

INTRODUCTION

The lessons that sports ethics should communicate to sports fans, athletes, coaches, and associations are critical teachings that can impact behavior both on and off the field. Yet, in addition to being educational, the lessons should be fun to debate and open to discussion and opinions. We should all encourage debates on sports ethics issues because it leads to greater understanding and positive action.

Bruce and I wrote Monday Morning Ethics to bring sports ethics to life. We took thirty-one of the most famous sports scandals in recent history, examined the actions that led up to each outcome, and then, from an ethical perspective, dissected each to look at what may have motivated these sports figures to act unethically.

Some of the scandals discussed are as well known today as they were when they happened – Pete Rose betting on baseball, for instance. Some of the cases were as outrageous then as they are now, such as Tonya Harding ordering her bodyguard to destroy Nancy Kerrigan's kneecaps. Some of the cases have faded into sports history – the 1950s City College of New York point-shaving basketball scandal or the Operation Slap Shot hockey scandal, for example.

Each of these thirty-one cases has something important to teach us. You can take any of these cases and think of a similar situation that has taken place in your professional, university, high school, or association setting.

TIMES CHANGE, PEOPLE DON'T.

While the settings may have changed, the same problems that affected athletes back in the day can easily happen today. Look at Terrence Williams scamming the NBA or Lori Loughlin using her privilege to get her daughter into the athletic program of a university. In fact, with social media, video surveillance, smartphone cameras, and even drones, many of the ethical dilemmas athletes faced then can be even more challenging in today's world.

What we want this book to convey is that every bad choice can lead to a bad consequence. We also want you to see that every one of these scandals could have been avoided.

Our passion is sports ethics because we love sports, but our ultimate goal is to help you make great ethical choices for yourself and your career.

THREE COMPONENTS
OF AN ETHICAL LAPSE

It's not just power or position that contributes to the fall of smart people. If you look at any ethical failure, three components are always present in some form or fashion: need, opportunity, and rationalization.

If one of these three components is missing, no ethical lapse occurs. Or, as I say often in my sports ethics consulting engagements, you can't stand on the three-legged stool with one leg missing. What was the need for Pete Rose, DeShaun Watson, Alex Rodriguez, Ryan Lochte, or Ray Rice to make bad choices? Perhaps position and power do provide a certain level of opportunity the average person lacks.

But the key question is: How did they rationalize their behavior?

Research has shown that these three behaviors are at the core of what would cause an otherwise ethical person to make unethical and potentially illegal choices. These behaviors are well documented for those charged with fraud, but – whether illegal or just plain wrong – all choices are founded on these three core components.

Need – Described as the perceived pressure a person experiences; need is the first critical component of what motivates a person to stray from ethical to unethical behavior. Need may come in a variety of forms. The person who is in too much debt, for example, likely experiences financial strain – the root of my need back then.

Pete Rose, by many standards, had a need for the adrenaline rush that gambling provided once he was off the field. Bill Belichick's need when it came to Spygate was certainly not money; likely, his actions were triggered by the need to win at all costs. Whatever the pressure, need is the core emotional state that starts the ball rolling with regard to making unethical choices.

Opportunity – It makes no difference what your need maybe if you don't have the opportunity to satisfy it with unethical and potentially illegal choices. Without opportunity, there's no fuel for the unethical fire. I was a trusted employee, and with that trust came opportunity. In order to meet my perceived need, I used the opportunity to create a way to find a short-term solution to solve the problem.

Dumb (and I mean really dumb) as it was, Tonya Harding believed she needed to beat Nancy Kerrigan and would stop at nothing to do so. The opportunity, of course, was to physically injure her chief rival. If successful, her need would be met.

Rationalization – Need combined with opportunity provides a firm foundation, but the glue that holds unethical activity together is the ability to rationalize that what's wrong is right. If you ask most people found guilty of unethical or illegal behavior, they'll tell you they felt their actions were legitimate at the time. I, for example, rationalized that I was not stealing money as long as my intent was to pay it back. Further, I solidified this mental game by paying back some of the money. Surely, I thought, I wasn't guilty of stealing money as long as I was paying it back.

That, of course, is a clear example of stinkin' thinkin'. The mind can be tricky, and when you combine need with opportunity and can rationalize bad behavior as good, you have the perfect storm to move from ethical to unethical, and potentially illegal, behavior.

The combination of need, opportunity, and rationalization creates an effective framework for discussing the cases that follow.

SECTION I
THE GAMBLERS

CHAPTER 1

PETE ROSE BETS ON BASEBALL AND LOSES HIS REPUTATION

Who: Pete Rose, MLB Hall of Fame Contender

Offense: Gambling on His Own Team

Result: Banned from Major League Baseball for life in 1989

The debate with regard to Pete Rose always begins with a simple question: Should Rose be in the Baseball Hall of Fame?

There is no end to the opinions, and, after all these years, nothing has been resolved.

Born April 14, 1941, Rose made his Major League Baseball debut with the Cincinnati Reds in 1963. He would end his playing career with the Reds in 1986. In between, he had stints with the Philadelphia Phillies and the now-defunct Montreal Expos. Over the course of his career, Rose played five positions: second base, right field, left field, third base, and first base.

His statistics remain amazing. He had a career .303 batting average. He also had 4,256 hits in more than 14,000 at-bats, and he played in 3,562 games — all of these are MLB records. He never took performance-enhancing drugs or steroids. No player has ever matched his production and, arguably, no player had his determination and drive. In fact, his nickname was "Charlie Hustle."

Pete Rose was so loved by the city of Cincinnati, and the Reds organization in particular, that in August 1984, he was hired to be a player/manager. Had he turned his back on baseball and completely left the game after the 1986 season — when he hung up his spikes as a player — Rose would have been a first-round Hall of Fame lock. But he didn't leave the game that year. He continued on as manager and posted a 412–373 record over the course of his managerial career.

For all of his baseball skills as a player and manager, Rose had a major weakness: He was a big-time gambler. It was no secret, either within baseball or outside it. He loved the thrill, and he loved the action. He would not be the only professional ball player to ever like gambling, but it was how he gambled that got him in trouble.

As a manager, his salary approached $1 million annually. That's more than $2.5 million in 2022 dollars. In addition to his salary, Rose raked in cash through commercials and endorsements, and he had the freedom to throw that cash around. It was common knowledge that he bet on horse racing, but over time there were strong and troubling suspicions that he was also betting on baseball. Bowing to suspicion and maybe a little pressure, Major League Baseball launched a behind-the-scenes investigation as to the extent of Rose's gambling.

On February 20, 1989, Rose was summoned to a meeting with then-outgoing Commissioner of Baseball Peter Ueberroth and his eventual replacement, Deputy Commissioner A. Bartlett "Bart" Giamatti. Giamatti previously had been the president of the National League. At the end of the discussion, those in attendance accused Rose of betting on baseball. Rose vehemently denied the charges, and the meeting ended in anger. For a week or two after the meeting, the accusations seemed to have been dropped, and all was quiet. As it unfolded, though, this turned out to be just a breather in the proceedings until MLB could finish its investigative work.

On March 6, 1989, Commissioner Ueberroth launched an in-depth investigation of Rose based on his discussion with Giamatti. As described in the eventual agreement Rose reached with Giamatti after he became commissioner, an inquiry was launched "concerning allegations that [Rose] engaged in conduct not in the best interests of baseball in violation of Major League Rule 21, including but not limited to betting on Major League Baseball games in connection with which he had a duty to perform."

Rose was accused not only of betting on baseball in general but on his own games while he was managing. He was betting both for and against his beloved Reds.

On March 25, 1989, as the story and the investigation were gathering steam, Rose was also forced to refute accusations that he was flashing "betting signals" during his games to his bookies. He described the allegations as being ridiculous. He kept denying any notion of gambling on baseball.

On April 3, 1989, two days after Giamatti officially took over the office of commissioner, Sports Illustrated magazine released an article detailing the gambling charges. The article was followed on April 9, 1989, by another damaging document. The Special Counsel to the Commissioner of Baseball turned in a 225-page report highlighting Rose's gambling involvement. On April 11, 1989, Commissioner Giamatti provided a copy of the report to Rose and his legal team, and a hearing was scheduled. The media sharks were circling.

There was the usual legal wrangling so common in these situations. For example, on April 19, 1989, Rose, through his legal team, requested an extension of the scheduled hearing. The extension was requested to give Rose "an opportunity to respond formally to the information in the report." The extension was granted, and the hearing was rescheduled for June 26, 1989.

About a week prior to the hearing, on June 19, 1989, Rose sued Giamatti. (By then, Bill White had become National League president.) in an effort to prevent him from deciding the case. It did little good.

On June 22, 1989, physical evidence was produced showing Rose's involvement in various bets. Despite Rose's posturing and denials, in August of 1989, Commissioner Giamatti banned Rose from baseball for life because of extensive evidence substantiating that he had bet on games. For the sake of history, we should mention that Giamatti died only eight days after banishing Rose. Conceivably, the stress of dealing with the issue had something to do with his passing.

Charlie Hustle was officially out of baseball, banished as though he had never existed.

In the 1990s, Rose repeatedly asked for reinstatement from commissioners Fay Vincent and Bud Selig, but his requests were shelved or denied.

As the years went by, a die-hard core of Pete Rose fans remained steadfast. They would continue to flock to baseball card and poster signings and would listen intently to Rose's interviews. He would step onto a Major League Baseball field in 1999 as a member of the All-Century Team. The appearance occurred before the second game of the World Series. Even on that occasion, when he was interviewed (some say aggressively) and asked whether he would admit to gambling on baseball, he admitted nothing. In 2016 at Great American Ball Park, he was inducted into the Cincinnati Reds Hall of Fame.

On January 8, 2004, Rose released his autobiography, entitled "My Prison Without Bars." In an effort to gain reinstatement, he finally and publicly admitted that he had bet on baseball. In the opinion of the public, though, he failed to clear his name with those admissions.

Rose was interviewed by ESPN radio on March 16, 2007. In that interview, he admitted to betting on "every" Cincinnati Reds game while he was manager. It was a curious admission because, at the time, there was controversy on that point as well. The media had reported that on some nights, Rose would not bet on his team. Nor would he bet when certain pitchers took the mound, meaning he was selective when he had doubts about the outcome of the game.

On August 12, 2013, Rose shared some controversial thoughts with the media, including CBS Sports, claiming: "I should have picked up alcohol or beat my wife [as opposed to gambling on baseball]." After that, he repeated similar sentiments. He talked about athletes who took performance-enhancing drugs as being far more dangerous to the game than gambling.

In an article appearing in USA Today Sports (June 15, 2014), Rose said he believed Selig might very well reinstate him before Selig left office in 2015. However, on June 22, 2015, ESPN acquired a copy of a gambling diary that had been confiscated as part of a fraud case back in the late 1980s when Rose was still a player. The released diary showed that Rose bet on his own team not just when he was a manager but when he was a player as well. Selig did not reinstate him, and current Commissioner of Baseball Rob Manfred refused to reinstate Rose in 2015. As of 2022, he has still not been reinstated.

As more of a publicity stunt than anything else, in 2014, Rose briefly became a coach for an independent semi-professional baseball team that had no official link to Major League Baseball. Meanwhile, Rose continues with signings and has several outside business interests, including an online gambling website.

CHUCK'S ETHICS REVIEW:

Pete Rose Should Never Be Admitted to the Baseball Hall of Fame

While I believe in second chances, to earn one, you have to tell the truth. Pete Rose hasn't told the truth. I'm not sure he ever will. Pete bet on the wrong thing. He bet for the short-term thrill instead of betting on the long-term game: his future and his legacy. Had he bet on the right thing, today, he'd not only be in the Hall of Fame but would likely have a higher net worth than he currently does. It's sad to see someone with such a stellar record being reduced to sitting at a 6-foot table in a Las Vegas sports memorabilia store, signing autographs and looking miserable.

You see, there is a challenge when we start down the slippery slope of making unethical decisions. Over time, we try to rationalize that what we've done has somehow become acceptable.

Rose has most recently taken the position that gambling is not like abusing steroids or PEDs. I disagree. They are both addictions that will eventually kill a career or a reputation. In Rose's case, he was inclined to deny it both in the past and now. Whenever there was irrefutable evidence to accuse him, he did change his mind and say the accusation was true, but he never came completely clean. He stopped at a point of his choosing but never fully admitted the extent of his gambling.

There is a great deal of value in being open, honest, and transparent. Had Rose done so, he could have changed sports history and been an example of good ethics to others. His rationalization in saying, "If I was a manager gambling and not a player, then it's somehow acceptable," makes for a clear justification in his mind, but it's just not an honest evaluation of the situation. I can make a good argument that a manager can impact any game. A catcher can have a bad day, certainly, but a manager who is scrupulous can fiddle with the entire team and push the odds ever so slightly toward a win or a loss.

Most anyone who thinks clearly on this issue can understand that a player or a manager doing something immoral, illegal, or unethical, such as betting on baseball, may not change the outcome or the integrity of the game, but that doesn't change the fact that they have still made an unethical choice.

It appears that Rose had a constant need to gamble. He had the opportunity and the money to gamble. All he needed was the rationalization to gamble.

I will always admire what Rose did on the field as a player. If you love the sport of baseball, you could not help but be amazed by his incredible stats.

However, there's a difference between an unethical choice a person makes in his professional career and the fact that he was a heck of a baseball player. He may have been good at his profession, but it doesn't change the fact that he was completely unethical in breaking the established rules. To be clear, I acted unethically in my chosen profession and, like Rose, was removed from that profession, stripped of my professional credential, and never again allowed to be recognized for the accomplishment of being a well-respected CPA.

To get the second chance he so desired, to have the possibility of being recognized by the Baseball Hall of Fame for his significant accomplishments, and to be a person someone would look up to, Pete Rose needed to be completely truthful. This should have happened years and years ago when he was first hauled before the MLB commissioner. At that meeting, when confronted with the issue of betting, Rose could have chosen to say, "I have a terrible problem. I made a terrible mistake."

It would have been much like alcoholics confessing their addiction. Then, as in a 12-step program, Rose could have asked for everyone's forgiveness. It required being truthful instead of trying to mitigate the situation by saying — many, many years later — something like, "Yeah, I was betting, but it was only when I was a manager." It's awfully hard to look up to someone who disgraced the profession and continues to lie in the face of the truth.

It's arguable, I suppose, that had Rose been forthcoming at the very beginning of his gambling addiction, showed contrition, and sought help, MLB might have had a greater willingness to forgive him for his actions and to consider the possibility of his being included in the Hall of Fame. That opportunity passed years ago.

THE "WHY" OF IT ALL...

Whether you sell free weights to health clubs or you play professional beach volleyball, if you're human, you can relate to Rose's issues. We've all known people with gambling, alcohol, or drug addictions, domestic violence issues, or other bad behaviors. These people are broken in some way. I'm not saying these bad behaviors can't be fixed or helped, but Rose needed help – and he refused to get it.

Rose had all the success in baseball any player could want. He was rich, popular and loved. There was something deeper within his soul that was missing, something he'd lost and maybe couldn't find. It's difficult to say what was missing, but there was something he needed to do to satisfy the success he was looking for.

For Pete Rose, the transition from player to manager might have been boring. Perhaps it didn't have the same spark that being a player once had, and he needed something to provide that spark and energy. That may not be the whole story, but I do know from personal experience that, when something is deeply lacking in our lives, some of us choose behavior that gives us a temporary rush. The rush momentarily drowns out what we really need to fulfill us. It may be having a string of affairs, getting drunk or high day after day, or stealing from the company, or simply goofing off at work for weeks at a time.

I seriously doubt if Rose can remember all the baseball teams he bet on while he was a player. It makes no difference. Stupid choices eventually destroy people and their legacies. No one gets away with anything forever. There are numerous examples of people in sports who had lofty positions or huge careers, but who chose to operate in an unethical manner and outside the law. Consequences will always take place. Look at the odyssey of Lance Armstrong or Ryan Leaf; the reputation of Ty Cobb; the downfall of Tiger Woods; or the activities of the guys at BALCO, for that matter. Rose will always be a superstar, but he will always be the superstar who bet on baseball and destroyed his reputation and career.

No matter Rose's thought processes or his lack of truthfulness, it is secondary to the fact that he tried to deceive everyone for years. I cannot predict human behavior or the pressures on someone like the commissioner of baseball, but if I were him, I would take the stance that Pete Rose should be forever banned from consideration for the Baseball Hall of Fame.

CHAPTER 2

THE BASKETBALL POINT-SHAVING SCANDAL OF THE 1950S

Who: Numerous Division I Basketball Players, Junius Kellogg

Offense: Point Shaving Against the Spread

Result: Losses of Reputation, Arrests, Banishment from NBA

Although there were isolated incidents of basketball point shaving (fixing games by intentionally beating the spread) documented in the 1930s, the first widespread scandals of this sort started on the basketball courts of the City College of New York and the University of Kentucky in 1947. But CCNY and Kentucky weren't alone in being investigated. The 1950s investigation also swept up players from Long Island University, New York University, Manhattan College, Bradley University, and the University of Toledo.

When all was said and done, the shocking scandal encompassed eighty-six games in twenty-three cities and seventeen states. Thirty-two players and gamblers were singled out for their involvement. It rocked a nation of sports lovers who had just come through the horrors of World War II.

In the spring of 1950, CCNY won the National Invitational Tournament and the NCAA Championship. This was the first and only time in history the same team would win both tournaments. It would also be the last time the Final Four would be played in New York.

For CCNY, its 1950 championship moment might have been a piece of memorable basketball lore except for a meeting that took place on January 11, 1951 that blew up the respectability of collegiate basketball. It started when former team co-captain Henry "Hank Poppe" of Manhattan College, who held the school's scoring record (1,027 points), met with the current Manhattan College center Junius Kellogg. Poppe was connected to big-time gamblers and petty crooks. He offered Kellogg $1,000 to play below his best in an upcoming game. Kellogg refused, but Poppe asked him to simply reconsider In that period the NCAA knew gamblers and game-fixers were influencing players but no athletes had the courage to report it.Poppe scheduled another meeting with Kellogg at a bar on January 14, 1951. Kellogg reported the conversation to his coach, who then informed Brother Bonaventure Thomas, Manhattan College's president. Kellogg was worried. He was Manhattan College's first African-American basketball scholarship athlete. He did not want anything to sully his reputation or that of his family.

Kellogg's obituary in The New York Times on September 18, 1998, recalls that "The gamblers told him to 'throw hook shots over the basket' and 'miss rebounds occasionally.' Kellogg declined."

Brother Thomas urged the coach and Junius Kellogg to report the bribe to the police The police told Kellogg to go along with the offer but not to accept any money. The police wired Kellogg with a recording device.

Kellogg then came back to Poppe and told him he would accept his offer and would throw the game against DePaul University. Before the start of the DePaul game (January 16, 1951), Poppe had the audacity to go to courtside during the warm-ups and tell Kellogg how many points the team needed to "give-away" to satisfy the gamblers and crooks. After the game, which Manhattan College unexpectedly won by a few points, Kellogg went to Gilhuly Brothers Bar & Restaurant on 8th Avenue to meet with Poppe as arranged. However, the detectives had already tailed Poppe outside the Garden immediately after the game's conclusion and arrested him.

Under questioning, Poppe shared everything with the police and named former teammate and co-captain Jack Byrnes as being in on the game fixing in 1949 and 1950. Byrnes was arrested, but, interestingly, Poppe was never charged with a crime because he was cooperative.

The same day Poppe was arrested, detectives booked three fixers on bribery and conspiracy charges, citing them for being in violation of New York's penal code, which made it illegal to attempt to bribe a participant in any sporting event. We have to remember that in those days, college basketball was a huge deal, as the NBA was still in its infancy. College basketball was the biggest show in town.

As the case unfolded, District Attorney Frank Hogan, a man known as "Mr. Integrity" because of the seriousness with which he pursued justice, broke the story. Several contacts, including Max Kase, sports editor of New York's Journal-American newspaper, ran with the story. Manhattan College's involvement also made the front page of The New York Times.

When the scandal exploded on February 18, 1951, three CCNY players, including Ed Warner, were arrested for accepting bribes. Also, that evening, an NYU player was arrested on bribery charges.

The next day, a game fixer named Salvatore "Tarto" Sollazzo and former Long Island University player Eddie Gard were arrested. This led to the arrest of LIU's Sherman White, the nation's leading scorer, along with two other teammates. White's records were taken away, and he was banned from ever playing in the NBA.

Despite what already seemed like a slew of arrests, the case kept expanding. Floyd Layne of CCNY and former LIU player

Natie Miller were arrested, followed by others from the LIU and CCNY teams. The scandal quickly widened beyond New York. Eli Klukofsky, a fixer who had been arrested for bribing City College players during the 1949 and 1950 seasons, also admitted to bribing Toledo University players. This led to Bradley University players admitting to taking bribes from gamblers to hold down scores in games against St. Joseph's in Philadelphia and against Oregon State.

In August 1951, Hogan's office charged more gamblers, game fixers, and players. The players could have faced jail time, but, because they cooperated, they were placed on indefinite probation and barred from all collegiate sports and the NBA. Hogan then arrested three University of Kentucky basketball players for accepting $500 in bribes to shave points in a 1949 NIT game against Loyola of Chicago at Madison Square Garden.

In the aftermath, several players served brief jail sentences. As 1951 drew to a close, a referee who was an accomplice of one of the bribe-taking players was suspended for arranging the outcome of six NBA games as well.

The NCAA would suspend the Kentucky basketball program for the 1953 season. Their All-American center would be barred from ever playing again. Kellogg was not convicted, but the NBA would never admit him into the league. By 1953, the scandal had largely faded. The players, gamblers, and game fixers would slip into obscurity and shame.

One name, however, should be remembered with honor.

The sports world celebrated Junius Kellogg across America. He graduated and became a member of the Harlem Globetrotters in 1953. Unfortunately, his playing days ended in 1954 after he was paralyzed in a car accident. He recovered to the point of being able to use a wheelchair and even coached wheelchair-bound athletes. He eventually became New York's first deputy commissioner and director of strategic planning for the Community Development Agency. Kellogg was awarded an honorary Doctor of Laws degree from Manhattan College — in gratitude for his lifetime achievements and service.

CHUCK'S ETHICS REVIEW:

Pay Me Enough, and I'll Make You a Lot of Dough

Bribery, fixing, and cheating are nothing new. I am sure these behaviors predate the Greek Olympics. There will always be gamblers and the unscrupulous who will try to influence athletes. Fortunately, there are also men and women of integrity who will stand up for what is right and noble. It has been more than 65 years since the point-shaving scandal, and yet some of the themes are as relevant now as they were then.

In 1951, given inflation, $500 was worth about $5,500 in 2022 dollars. Players threw away their possible NBA careers and reputations to shave points. So, was it worth it? No, not really. Anything unethical or illegal is never worth it in the long term.

While I'm not defending anyone or what they did, receiving $5,500 to throw away an NBA career doesn't make any sense. Of course, the NBA had just started at that time. It wasn't anywhere near what it is today. College basketball was still king. So, to some players, a bird in the hand ($500) was apparently worth two in the bush. How many of them were actually going to go from college to being an NBA star? Not many, and probably few of them, even cared about making it professionally back then. Still, their reputations got slammed. You don't get your reputation back that easily. Don't believe me? It's been 65 years. Most of the men involved in this scandal have passed away, and we're still talking about them in a negative light.

THE NBA SAVED ITSELF

I do believe that, when the NBA banned these players back in 1951, it really did save itself. Say anything you will about the NBA in 2022, in the early days of the league, officials chose a highly ethical road, and it paid big dividends. Had NBA officials not taken swift and decisive action, it would have sent a message to the gambling community that the NBA really wasn't a fair sporting competition and was just a way to create an illegal revenue source. So, yes, men of deep integrity sent a message, probably saved the league, and created a solid foundation going forward. It gave everyone hope that basketball could make it on a larger scale.

Junius Kellogg emerged from this scandal as a beacon of light amid all the ethical darkness. He was able to resist cheating when everyone else seemed to have folded, and although he never played in the NBA, I would argue he was one of its unsung heroes.

As humans, the quality of our character falls somewhere on a continuum between poor and great. Most of us, if we found a $100 bill in the parking lot of an airport, would take it. After all, how would we ever find the owner? If we left it there, we know someone else would just come along and take it. Some other people would not pick it up. It might be stealing, after all, and they would not take a dollar from someone if their life depended on it. They are persons of integrity and high character.

On a scale from one to ten, those with a one would not think twice about robbing you blind. Most of us would fall into the area around five. Kellogg's character and values were high enough and important enough to him that the bribe was not a significant enough temptation. He was a ten on the scale.

Also, let's not forget that, as its first African American scholarship athlete, Kellogg felt an obligation to Manhattan College. He didn't want to do anything that would hurt the chances of future African-American athletes receiving scholarship money. He was a person who felt an obligation to others, not just to himself. His example spoke to those associated with the early NBA, saying that integrity and strength of character were important in the formation of a credible league.

On the other hand, young men such as Manhattan College's Hank Poppe, the school's leading scorer up to that point, were much more enigmatic. Poppe approached Kellogg with a huge bribe. Although many people were prosecuted, Poppe was never charged, likely because, as the process started to unfold, he ended up cooperating.

Even today, a person accused of a crime can get a substantial reduction in penalties if they cooperate. Poppe chose the snitch route. My guess is that prosecutors looked at him as the key to fully exposing the scandal. Unfortunately for Poppe, this scandal killed his college reputation and scarred his name for life.

THE CROOKS AT PLAY

This scandal also teaches us something about organized crime and its undue influence on sports.

In the aftermath of the basketball point-shaving scandal, law enforcement didn't have the ability to do much of anything in the way of prosecuting crimes. Some petty mobsters got arrested but without many consequences. I would not be surprised if some of the crooks had their hands deeper in the pockets of law enforcement than they did those of the players. When the point-shaving scheme fell apart, some of the players suffered greater consequences than did the mobsters, especially when you consider the reputations they lost. But those behind the bribing suffered comparably less. To their minds, in that era, as long as they were making sure the prosecutors and judges were properly taken care of, the consequences of their behavior would be minimal.

Let's face facts: It took more than sixty years after the mob-influenced basketball point-shaving scandal for Las Vegas to get its first professional sports team (the Las Vegas Golden Knights of the NHL). I have no doubt that, despite the huge money in online gambling platforms, or maybe even because of it, there is still worry today about the undue influence organized crime can bring to bear on athletic contests. Backroom deals in Las Vegas will continue to be under suspicion.

To be clear, I don't think for a moment we can assume that all sporting events are pure and that cheating to benefit bettors won't take place again. I cannot believe that to be true. I would venture to say that we would be shocked to learn how many attempts to unduly influence games have been tried over the years, some very recently. Today's methods of cheating are probably more convoluted and covert than ever.

Does organized crime influence professional sports today? I would guess it does in the U.S. and, most likely, overseas as well. Just look at the breaking scandals and gambling accusations in professional tennis. It would be nanve to think it doesn't happen elsewhere and in other major sports.

What about the explosion in online gambling? Prior to internet gambling, most bettors had to take the extra step of contacting a bookie to make bets and to receive payments or to pay off debts. The personal nature of it made it a little harder for it to become addictive. Some bettors prefer to bet the sports books in Vegas casinos, and, when they lose, they merely walk away. It can be harmless entertainment. But once you introduce the ability to gamble online, all bets are off, so to speak. The fact that betting now takes place online makes it accessible to many more people. The impersonal nature of it makes online betting more addictive and less controlled. Is it hurtful? You're damn right it is — for certain people who get out of control.

Today, many gamblers are pouring major dollars into online sports betting. Given the high stakes, if gamblers can get close to players, they might try to influence them to cheat. Follow the money. When big bucks are involved, there are always people who are willing to cut corners to get what they feel they deserve, even if they have to commit a crime to do it.

TIME MACHINE...

If I could take a time machine back to 1951 and give sports ethics training to anyone, it would be to the players. They were the weakest link in this chain. They had the ability to shave the points, but, more importantly, they could be tempted by the dollars being thrown around. Remember that no one asked them to lose, only to avoid covering the spread by missing shots here and there. On the surface, that seems less egregious. In reality, it is still cheating.

The huge challenge of talking to players then, as now, would be that most of my advice would probably have fallen on deaf ears. Following World War II, the country was in lousy shape. Many people were starting over, and jobs were scarce. When you pit the immediate value of the money against the future possibility of playing in a new league, one that wasn't doing all that well, $500 sure must have looked attractive.

That makes what Junius Kellogg did seem all the more impressive.

CHAPTER 3

THE "OPERATION SLAP SHOT" GAMBLING SCANDAL

Who: Rick Tocchet and James Harney

Offense: NHL Betting Operation, Players, and Owners Charged with Gambling, Money Laundering, Conspiracy

Result: Some went to Prison; Others were Banned from Playing Hockey in the NHL; Others Paid Fines

Although "slap shot" is a hockey term, in the end, the Operation Slap Shot gambling scandal would turn out to have almost nothing to do with the sport of hockey. It had everything to do with gambling and the greed of the leeches who hang onto professional athletes. The reputations of several very prominent people were nearly destroyed and might have been destroyed for good were it not for one saving grace. We'll get to that shortly.

It was a chance meeting between a hockey player and a state trooper that would begin the incident. Rick Tocchet was an outstanding professional hockey player who played in the NHL for 18 seasons. He then switched to coaching, first as a minor league coach and then as an NHL coach. James Harney was a New Jersey state trooper.

The paths of the two strangers crossed in the mid-1990s. Like lots of people in law enforcement, Harney had an off-duty job to make ends meet: serving drinks at a sports bar in South Philadelphia. Tocchet would come into the bar from time to time, and the two men struck up a friendship. Then, as the decade came to a close, they developed a sort of business partnership. By 2001, an illegal sports-betting operation had been launched.

Fast forward to a New Jersey State Police press release dated February 7, 2006, entitled "State Police Investigation into Gambling Ring Yields Professional Sports Ties."

According to the release, the New Jersey State Police had begun to investigate Harney in late October 2005, when the New Jersey State Police Organized Crime Bureau uncovered information indicating that Harney, an eight-year veteran of the force, was a partner in a bookmaking ring. The ring operated in both south New Jersey and in Philadelphia.

At first, the investigation into the illegal bookmaking activities of Trooper Harney had nothing to do with athletes. As the investigation widened, it led to Tocchet, who was then a Phoenix Coyotes assistant coach.

Tocchet was charged with promoting gambling, money laundering, and conspiracy, while Harney was charged with official misconduct, promoting gambling, money laundering, and conspiracy. Charges were also made against a third man, James A. Ulmer, for promoting gambling, money laundering, and conspiracy. Ulmer was the go-between who funneled money back and forth from the operation.

Depending upon news sources, anywhere from five to 12 NHL players, coaches, and even team owners were identified as placing bets. In addition, it was alleged that Janet Jones, the model-actress wife of former NHL superstar Wayne Gretzky, was also placing bets. Rumors circulating in the media attempted to link Gretzky to illegal gambling with the ring, but no proof was ever uncovered to that effect, nor was there ever any link established to organized crime.

Tocchet had the money to build the operation, and he had many connections to athletes who liked to gamble. Harney, since he was a police officer, lent a certain cover of decency. It was not until the operation was finally dismantled that law enforcement realized just how major an operation the gambling ring was.

In the 40-day period leading up to the 2006 Super Bowl, the gambling ring had processed more than 1,000 wagers on professional and collegiate sporting events, the total of which exceeded $1.7 million. The operators would normally handle five to seven bets a day from high rollers. The New Jersey State Police made the scandal public on February 6, 2006. Two days later, Tocchet's lawyer released a statement, saying, "The allegation that Rick Tocchet financed an illegal gambling operation is categorically false."

Nevertheless, in the early days of August 2006, Tocchet admitted his guilt. The NHL gave him an indefinite leave of absence. NHL officials had apparently been conducting their own internal investigation, and it wasn't looking good for the coach.

An article that appeared on The Philadelphia Inquirer's website, philly.com, on August 4, 2006, reported:

"Former NHL star Rick Tocchet was an equal partner in the multimillion-dollar sports-betting ring led by a former New Jersey state trooper, the disgraced lawman asserted yesterday in pleading guilty.

Tocchet took wagers and cash from bettors and would cover losses. When bettors lost, Tocchet would be given 'a bag of cash' for his share of the profits."

Trooper Harney initially faced a possible jail sentence of up to twenty-five years. However, he agreed to testify against Tocchet in exchange for a lighter sentence. To the very end of the case, Tocchet's attorney felt he would be vindicated. In terms of actual jail time, Tocchet never saw prison but was sentenced to two years on probation. Vindication, however, is a word with many meanings.

THE AFTERMATH

The aftermath of this ethical scandal is more interesting than the week-to-week developments of the gambling ring. The saving grace for Tocchet and the NHL players who gambled with his illegal ring was that no link could ever be established that they bet on hockey. It was also the first time Tocchet had ever been in trouble with the law. He was just the money behind the endeavor and was not involved in day-to-day operations.

Despite Tocchet's two-year probation sentence, the NHL reinstated him on February 7, 2008, allowing him to go back to coaching. But even after such a tremendous playing and coaching career, he would always carry the stigma of having been involved in the scandal. He is prohibited by the NHL from ever gambling again, and he had to undergo psychological evaluations to ensure he was not a compulsive gambler.

On the other hand, Harney would lose virtually every possession he owned. On August 3, 2007, he was sentenced to a five-year prison term for illegal gambling and money laundering. He would be labeled a traitor to the police department.

Neither Wayne Gretzky nor his wife were charged. Placing bets with illicit or illegal bookmakers may not be the brightest of moves, but it is not a federal crime. Nevertheless, the scandal would be a permanent stain on the couple's reputation and on Wayne Gretzky's legacy as arguably the greatest hockey player of all time.

CHUCK'S ETHICS REVIEW:

Most Addictions Lead to Unethical Behavior

(The actions may not be illegal, but unethical is wrong no matter how you cut it!)

Sports ethics training is not a miracle cure for preventing criminal activity. It can certainly help, but it needs to be reinforced. Whenever new players, coaches or management are brought into any kind of athletic situation, a process of refreshing needs to take place. I'm sometimes asked: If the NHL had an ongoing ethical training initiative for coaches and players, could the outcome of this scandal have been changed?

Effective ethics training has the impact of making one more conscious of one's choices and the consequences that always follow. Had Rick Tocchet and the other players and coaches involved received ethics training, had they fully realized the impact and consequences of their actions, the outcome would likely have been different. That said, the question remains: If there's a dire need to commit certain acts, a need such as a severe gambling addiction, would the benefit of committing the unethical acts be greater than the concern over the certain consequences?

In some cases, the answer is yes. In other cases, the answer is no. All the NHL players involved were modestly wealthy in their own right. Their need wasn't so much the money as it was the thrill of it all. Was the thrill worth it? Hardly.

THE STATE TROOPER

The biggest loser in Operation Slap Shot was Trooper Harney. While Tocchet was able to go back to coaching, Harney lost his job and his reputation, and he served jail time. A seemingly uneven application of justice becomes apparent here once you realize that it took more than one person to create an effective betting ring. You examine the facts and figure that one responsible party has taken the fall while the other person goes back to his life. It would appear that both Tocchet and Harney had equal responsibilities in the creation of the ring, so they should have been treated equally by the justice system. Right?

The case, however, is not so simple. In this instance, the hockey coach was a public figure who had a reputation to maintain. He lost that reputation and, in fact, pled guilty to conspiracy and promoting gambling. He may or may not have been nanve about the consequences, but he did receive reasonable punishment.

The state trooper, on the other hand, represented the law. He completely understood where the consequences would lead. The hockey coach might have been involved for a certain thrill and even a sense of fun, but the trooper knew that it was illegal from the very beginning. Far better, it would have been for the trooper to say, "Why don't we start a hockey glove company?" There were many legitimate activities the two men could have considered. A gambling ring should not have been on the list.

Any outsiders who believe they can get close to a famous athlete in order to do something unethical should be forewarned: Justice is often applied unevenly. We see it over and over again. Professional athletes have an aura of celebrity. If they haven't done something incredibly stupid, like committing a capital offense or discharging an illegal weapon in a nightclub, celebrities will usually hold sway in our society. In this case, it was both the crooked cop and the celebrity hockey coach who made bad choices. The cop served time and lost almost everything he had. The celebrity coach suffered a loss of his reputation. While he did go back to coaching, I wonder how much endorsement money or sponsorships it might have cost him?

CHANGING TIDES

The coach's lawyer categorically denied the charges in February, but six months later, the lawyer admitted that the coach shared some guilt. This probably sounds like a case of "changing with the wind," but anyone who knows anything about the legal system will understand.

Lawyers have a responsibility to represent their clients to the best of their ability. So, ethically, even if their clients are guilty, they will still do the best they can. It is not surprising that a lawyer would profess a client's innocence until such a time when the client may be better served by admitting some guilt in this case.

Again, in this case, the celebrity had access to top lawyers, a supportive union, and team members who vouched for him. He enjoyed the benefits of public opinion and a good track record. The police officer, though, was a working stiff who had to take a part-time job pouring drinks. His fellow cops turned their backs on him. How else would this have unfolded the way it did?

GAMBLING, ADDICTION, AND SPORTS

Gambling represents different things to different people. Unfortunately, like alcohol or drugs, it often appeals to people with an addictive nature. I would also hazard a guess that professional card players are usually not heavy drinkers, especially during tournaments. It's a business. They have to be able to separate from addictive behavior to focus on what they're doing at the table.

For many hardcore amateur gamblers, though, placing bets becomes addictive. To them, it is not a business but a game. Professional athletes are often paid well, but they can also fall prey to gambling and get caught up in it. It is no different from any other addictive substance. The shame here is that many of these gambling-addicted athletes come from modest or impoverished backgrounds. They sign a multimillion-dollar contract, and all of a sudden, the money is like a magic spigot that gushes out an endless flow of cash. They don't know what to do with it, so they spend it. They may be good on the field, but they usually stink as gamblers, and, as often as not, they are urged on by their entourage — people just along for the ride.

The problem with spending so much on gambling is that most athletes have an extremely brief playing career, even if they don't get injured. Once they are out of the game the money flow abruptly stops, but the gambling goes on, and the debt may mount. The entourage goes away, and the music stops.

Then there is the gamble they take with their reputations. The coach would continue on in hockey and is now an assistant coach of the Pittsburgh Penguins. Still, every reference to his career includes the scandal. Was it worth it? Well, no, of course not. It's like Richard Nixon, who held the most powerful political office in the world, yet his name will always be associated with Watergate.

I hope I will always be remembered as an effective ethics speaker and as someone who tried to teach athletes and coaches about sports ethics because I really care about their lives. But I will also be reminded of my past when I made some mistakes that I regret. If you want to avoid being remembered in those ways, then don't make those choices. Bad choices will never leave you.

At the beginning of this case, we read about a number of people who had an interest in participating by betting in this ring. Why? It fed a multitude of needs. At the very basic level, some saw it as a way to help them supplement their income. Others saw it as a way to get closer to celebrity. It is also interesting to me that none of the hockey players bet on hockey. It is as though they thought, "Well, as long as I am not betting on hockey, I am not doing anything unethical." That is a rationalization, perhaps, but it fits in with an overall pattern.

This scandal is reflective of the human condition. It's about people trying to seek what they perceive to be a better life but going about it in an unproductive way. It is hard not to focus on the fact that most of the bettors probably regret throwing away all the money they did just because they thought they could make a fast buck and bring themselves thrills. Poor ethics cost them millions.

CHAPTER 4

HOUSTON ASTROS SIGN STEALING SCANDAL

Who: Houston Astros, A.J. Hinch, Jeff Luhnow, Alex Cora, Carlos Beltran

Offense: Sign stealing using pre-taped signals, relaying to batters

Results: Hinch, Luhnow suspended and fired

The 2017 Houston Astros were a force in Major League Baseball. All of the pieces were in place for a deep playoff run. The talent on Houston's roster was undeniable. Its lineup featured the eventual American League Most Valuable Player in diminutive second baseman José Altuve. Other big names included second-year third baseman Alex Bregman, shortstop Carlos Correa, outfielder George Springer and veteran catcher Brian McCann.

On the mound, the Astros deployed dual Cy Young Award winners in Dallas Keuchel and mid-season acquisition Justin Verlander. Houston also employed veteran designated hitter Carlos Beltran, who would come to play a prominent role in the now-infamous scheme the Astros developed that year.

Led by an all-star cast and buoyed by the addition of the oft-unhittable Verlander, the Astros charged through the regular season. Houston's 101-61 record earned it the second seed in the AL for the 2017 playoffs. Its first opponent was the Boston Red Sox.

In hindsight, Houston's dismantling of Red Sox starting pitcher Chris Sale in Game 1 at Minute Maid Park was suspicious. Boston's ace giving up seven earned runs on nine hits with three home runs in five innings was not impossible, but it was unlikely. He is too damn good.

Leading two games to none heading into Boston, Houston only needed one more win to advance. Boston trounced the Astros 10-3 in Game 3 at Fenway Park, but the Astros rebounded with a 5-4, series-clinching road win.

The New York Yankees presented a tougher obstacle in the AL Championship Series, but Houston advanced to its second World Series appearance. It is telling that the home team won each of the seven games in that ALCS. Home-field advantage, indeed.

THE SERIES

Houston's opponent in the 2017 World Series, the Los Angeles Dodgers, featured a starting pitcher on top of his game. Clayton Kershaw was a three-time Cy Young Award winner with an 18-4 record whose sit-down curveball was the envy of both leagues.

Kershaw was his usual self in Game 1 at Dodger Stadium, allowing just one run in seven innings of three-hit baseball. However, things were different in Kershaw's Game 5 start in Houston. In Houston, the Astros chased Kershaw in the fourth inning after hanging six earned runs on the Dodgers' ace.

In 2017, Houston was still reeling from Hurricane Harvey's devastating flooding. The city needed a boost, and when the Astros clinched its first World Series title in Game 7 on the road in LA, a feel-good story for the ages was complete. Yet, this tale is notorious, remembered not for the joy it brought to millions in a storm-ravaged region but for the stench of cheating that would tarnish it forever.

When everyone else is doing it, is it still cheating?

The news broke during the following MLB postseason. In an October 2018 piece for Yahoo! Sports, columnist Jeff Passan revealed that a low-tier Astros employee had been caught photographing opposing dugouts. While this information led nowhere, Passan also mentioned an incident during a 2018 regular-season series between the Astros and the Oakland A's.

According to Passan, the A's heard banging sounds coming from the Astros' dugout during the game. Believing the Astros were using electronic means to steal signs, the A's notified MLB officials, who promised an investigation. Other outlets reported a similar incident in 2017 when the Astros played the Chicago White Sox.

Passan also noted that unnamed players, including some 2017 Dodgers, said that the Astros were banging on a trash can to relay signals from the dugout to the batter.

We should note that stealing signs is a time-honored tradition in baseball. There is nothing inherently wrong or illegal about it. Runners on second base have a clear view of the catcher and are free to relay information to the hitter.

It is up to the opposing battery to combat this practice. Pitchers and catchers usually switch to more complicated signals with runners on second base. The difference with electronic surveillance is that no one needs to be on base for it to work, which is one reason MLB bans it.

The Astros weren't the first team to run afoul of this rule. In fact, MLB had already fined the Red Sox for using an Apple Watch to relay signs in the waning months of the 2017 regular season. The Yankees had a similar scheme, which involved the clubhouse phone, and paid a fine.

The Astros had won the World Series, though, and the appearance of an unfair advantage was untenable.

Let's backtrack a bit. When Beltran joined the Astros in 2017 as a 40-year-old, he brought with him 18 years of MLB experience. He was a journeyman with knowledge of other teams' methods.

As reported by Ken Rosenthal and Evan Drellich in a November 2019 exposü in The Athletic, the Astros believed other teams were using electronics to steal signs. One Houston coach, identified in other reports as bench coach Alex Cora, was ready to help Beltran devise a scheme to balance the playing field.

The Astros would use a camera in center field to record the catcher's signs. That camera fed to a monitor located in a hallway between the dugout and clubhouse. A player watching the live monitor would bang a trash can whenever an off-speed pitch was coming.

The scheme grew. Front office statisticians kept spreadsheets to organize the information they were gathering. In team emails, exposed by The Wall Street Journal's Jared Diamond, participants called the scheme "Codebreaker."

Former Astros pitcher Mike Fiers confirmed the Astros' methods, saying he warned his next teams about Codebreaker for the integrity of the game and to help his new teams' chances against the Astros.

"There are guys who are losing their jobs because they're going in there not knowing," Fiers told The Athletic. "Young guys getting hit around in the first couple of innings, and then they get sent down (to the minor leagues) ... I had to let my team know so that we were prepared when we went to go play them at Minute Maid."

The Athletic article led to an official MLB investigation. Commissioner Rob Manfred released his report on Codebreaker in January 2020, assigning both blame and consequences.

Houston manager A.J. Hinch received a one-year suspension and was fired by the Astros. Likewise for general manager Jeff Luhnow. Cora also received a one-year suspension and was fired as manager of the Red Sox. Beltran, who was named in the report but went unpunished, was fired as the Mets' manager before coaching a single game.

Manfred said that most of the Astros players had participated to some degree. Yet, save for Beltran, no Astros player from 2017 would pay a price. Manfred held Hinch and Luhnow ultimately responsible as leaders.

"Irrespective of Luhnow's knowledge of his Club's violations of the rules," stated Manfred, "I will hold him personally accountable for the conduct of his Club."

Despite the "player-driven" aspects of Codebreaker, Manfred assigned the most serious blame to the Astros' baseball operations department. It had become "an industry leader in its analytics," he said, but its culture was problematic.

"The baseball operations department's insular culture — one that valued and rewarded results over other considerations," had led, Manfred said, "to an environment that allowed the conduct described in this report to have occurred."

According to Manfred's report, the Astros abandoned the Codebreaker scheme in 2018, long before his investigation. The reason was simple: It didn't work.

CHUCK'S ETHICS REVIEW:

Comments

Trash Can Ethics in Houston

Winning. Losing. Competitive Advantage. All is fair in love and war. Everybody does it. The question is: What would motivate a team to break the rules knowing that getting caught is likely or even probable?

I'm not naive and it's not that absurd to think that any team might use the technical skills at hand to find a competitive advantage. But in this case, the "old school" banging on trash cans, now that's just funny. However, it gets less funny when careers, reputations, and huge amounts of money are involved.

There is, some might argue, a difference between using "legal" technological means to advantage your position and crossing the line of ethics to advance one's position in ways that could create outcomes or consequences that are less than desirable.

Most everyone with a cell phone has the ability to record a conversation. And, there have been highly unethical or invasive (even indecent) examples of cell phones recording unsuspecting individuals, presumably to gain an advantage. However, it does not mean those conversations are admissible in a court of law. In fact, the person recording might face severe penalties.

"Bugging" has been a sort of art form going back to Nixon's Watergate times, but since then, judges have consistently balked at such shenanigans when they occurred in law offices, divorce cases, board rooms, and divorce proceedings. Incidentally, the French had a bugging case of their own about twenty years after Watergate, and that was declared illegal as well.

There are characters who go into busy coffee shops and other venues with poorly secured Wi-Fi who literally intercept email. As an aside, it is why I warn clients against conducting business meetings such as real estate closings or involving credit card transactions at venues with questionable credentials. Regarding email, it is normally not illegal to send someone an email, however, it is illegal to send an email or text with an encrypted attachment to hack a computer system or to harass a student.

So, was Codebreaker the equivalent for the Houston Astros of illegal bugging or email interception? Of course, it was. The signs were captured and then used without permission.

Just because the technology is in place, that does not mean it can be used to gain an illegal advantage. Codebreaker was designed to gain unfair advantage using technology, just for baseball as opposed to politics.

Why would the Astros engage in this behavior? A theme you have read over and over in this book, but directly applies here, is the triangle of Need, Opportunity, and Rationalization needed for the creation of any case of fraud. While all three legs are important, for this discussion, I will concentrate on Need.

The power of Need, or perceived need, is amazing. Instead of playing on a level playing field with the pitcher and catcher knowing what is being thrown next and the hitter using his skill to meet the ball head-on, the Astros wanted to have the inside scoop. You see (here's where the Need comes in), if we knew what was going to be pitched, then we could better prepare to hit the ball, taking away the other team's advantage.

WERE THEY PROTESTING IN THE FRONT OFFICE?

I can just hear the Astros operations people saying, "I wonder how we could do that?" Some bright people might have mused about how to observe the calls between the pitcher and catcher. Observing calls isn't cheating, after all.

But if you can observe what is happening from afar, record it, then relay it from the clubhouse to the batter, you are more than observing; you are cheating.

Did anyone in the organization protest the technology being used that way? And I am not the first to think this, but were there cash bets being made? We know that bettors became wary of the team the following season. A tainted reputation will have that effect, but were insiders relaying to friends and associates to bet the Astros just because?

What I do know is that the Astros went from gathering data to using it "by banging on trashcans" to advantage their play.

Here's a question for you, the reader. Given the chance, would you use data that was not intended for you to advantage yourself or your team, or your organization, knowing that it was illegal and unfair?

YOUR ANSWER?

If you said yes, what if someone did that to you or your business? What if your neighbor could hack into your Amazon

Alexa account and hear what is spoken in your home? You know Alexa hears, right?

Or, what if a competitor hacked into your computer and knows your next business move? Is that acceptable? If you said yes, then I assume that you are fine with that being done to you. While the Astros say that the scheme failed and was stopped, it doesn't address the culture that allowed it in the first place.

That is where I continue to have the greatest concern.

SECTION II
HIGHER EDUCATION

CHAPTER 5

SOUTHERN METHODIST UNIVERSITY (SMU) FOOTBALL SCANDAL OF 1987

Who: SMU Players, Coaches, and Boosters

Offenses: Money, Gifts, and Bribes to Football Players

Result: NCAA Cancellation of Program, Firings, Program Suffered for Years

There is no worse consequence for a collegiate team than the NCAA imposing the so-called "death penalty." The death penalty means that an entire program has been shut down for committing serious infractions.

Let's go back to January 1976 when former Dallas Cowboys scout Ron Meyer was hired to be the head coach at Dallas-based Southern Methodist University. The university hadn't won a national championship since 1935, and the boosters had grown more than a little impatient. Everyone was clamoring for a change.

In February 1979, SMU managed to land two of the top high school running back prospects in the nation: Eric Dickerson and Craig James. On the surface, this appeared to be an amazing recruiting effort — these guys were dynamite on the field — but it was hardly by chance. The recruiting of both was shady at best. Dickerson, who had originally committed to a strong Texas A&M that went 8-4 in 1978 and was ranked 19th in the nation, later changed his mind to go to the floundering SMU Mustang program. Soon after, he was seen driving a new gold TransAm around the SMU campus. Rumors swirled, hinting that Texas A&M had given him the car illegally.

As for Craig James, he passed up football powerhouses Arkansas and Alabama for SMU soon after his girlfriend was given a full scholarship there. Thus, the famed "Pony Express" of Dickerson and James was formed. On October 25, 1980, before a national television audience, formerly lowly SMU beat No. 2 Texas 20-6.

While freak things have always happened in sports, as when a David beats a Goliath, the Texas beatdown just didn't seem right. We are talking about an SMU team that posted a 3-8 record in 1976, rising to become an 8-4 team in 1980, beating big-time programs, and becoming ranked 20th in the nation. Incidentally, in 1979, just one year previously, Texas had gone 9-2 and had beaten SMU 30-6.

Such a rapid advancement to major football heights raised a red flag. The NCAA looked into SMU's recruiting practices and found numerous recruiting violations, including questionable scholarships, dubious slush funds, and fancy cars given to some players.

On June 11, 1981, the NCAA placed SMU on two years of probation, prohibiting it from appearing on any nationally televised games or from participating in any bowl games for the 1981 season. Nevertheless, the program had become so magically loaded with talent that, on November 21, 1981, SMU beat Arkansas to finish the year 10-1 and capture the Southwest Conference title.

Then, early in 1982, Coach Ron Meyer bolted his promising SMU team to take the head coaching job with the New England Patriots. Several people interviewed on the ESPN documentary Pony Excess (ESPN Films: 30 for 30) believe

Meyer left a national championship contender because he foresaw additional sanctions coming from the NCAA.

Shortly after Meyer left, SMU hired former Southern Miss coach Bobby Collins to take the reins of the team. On January 1, 1983, Collins took SMU to an unbeaten season by topping Pittsburgh in the Cotton Bowl. However, SMU ended up in second place in the final national rankings behind Penn State.

In February 1983, offensive lineman Sean Stopperich signed on as part of the latest SMU recruiting class. Stopperich, a native of western Pennsylvania, had originally given an oral commitment to the University of Pittsburgh but then changed his mind.

On November 24, 1984, SMU won the Southwest Conference championship for the third time in four years. The next month, it would defeat Notre Dame in the Aloha Bowl and finish No. 8 in the nation. However, trouble was again brewing for this Cinderella team. Homesick and disgruntled by a lack of playing time, Stopperich left SMU not long after. Wary of what malpractices the school might be hiding, the NCAA began interviewing Stopperich about how he was recruited.

Meanwhile, toward the end of March 1985, Texas Governor and SMU booster Bill Clements (a former Mustang football player himself) conducted a private meeting with fellow boosters, including real estate mogul Sherwood Blount. The meeting centered on the SMU Board of Governors asking for boosters to put a halt to the school's recruiting tactics, which included improperly paying players.

Despite the meeting and the plea of the governor, it was not so easy for the university to completely stop the payments. Boosters were paying players on a weekly basis. In some instances, these promises to pay were in contractual form. If the payments were totally stopped and the contracts broken, someone was bound to blow the whistle. In the same meeting, Clements banned nine boosters from associating with SMU. He called them the "Naughty Nine" and said they were responsible for all the corruption of the program.

Clements' attempt to deflect the blame to the nine boosters didn't work. The NCAA was not impressed and laid down the harshest penalties to date. SMU was again placed on probation, this time for three years. Among the sanctions was a loss of 45 scholarships and a bowl ban for two seasons.

Crucial to the NCAA decision were the allegations Stopperich made. Stopperich claimed that SMU boosters paid him a $300 monthly allowance to play for the Mustangs. As if that wasn't enough, the boosters helped his father find a job in Dallas and assisted in moving the family near to the school to a rent-free apartment. This latest penalty marked the fifth time that SMU had been put on probation since 1974 and the seventh time overall.

On November 12, 1986, a new probe would come about as the result of former linebacker David Stanley. A member of the 1983 recruiting class, Stanley had been kicked off the team for drug problems. In an act of retaliation, Stanley talked about how he was recruited to a local news station and to sports anchor Dale Hansen.

Stanley revealed that SMU gave him $25,000 to play football for the school. In addition, he claimed that Assistant Athletic Director Henry Lee Parker paid him $400 a month as a living expense and paid his mother $350 a month.

When Hansen pressed them, Parker and Athletic Director Bob Hitch both denied they ever sent anything to Stanley or his mother. However, Hansen had the evidence with him in the interview: a letter suspected to have contained a payment to Stanley's mother, with the SMU seal on the left-hand corner and a postmark of October 1985, approximately two months after the school had gone on probation. With this report, SMU's fate was all but sealed.

On February 25, 1987, the NCAA gave SMU the death penalty. As a result, the 1987 season was canceled. In addition, there would be no home games in 1988, no television or bowl appearances until 1989, and only 15 scholarships per year through the 1988–89 academic year.

It was found that Governor Clements and others on the school board were aware of booster payments and the infamous slush fund, both of which had continued through 1985.

In January 1988, Pro Football Hall of Famer and Texas native Forrest Gregg was hired as head coach of SMU. Gregg was saddled with trying to restore the program's integrity and respectability both on and off the field.

In 1989, Gregg's first year, SMU was terrible. They went 2-9, including a 95-21 loss to the University of Houston. In Gregg's three seasons of manning the sidelines, the SMU Mustangs went 4-29. It was said that the team's walk-on players during that time weren't fit to play at the Division I level. Nevertheless, the team carried on as best it could. On December 24, 2009, SMU beat Nevada 45-10 in the Sheraton Hawaii Bowl for the program's first bowl victory since 1984. It had taken almost 33 years for the team to be consistently winning again in the ethically right way.

CHUCK'S ETHICS REVIEW:

Paid to Play, Paid to Win, Unethical Behavior Rampant at SMU

When a university football program goes from obscurity to national prominence in a short period of time, attracting quality players from all over the country, it would seem natural to ask, "How is this taking place?"

Normally, a blue-chip athlete wants to play for a national power, with a national program and a national winning reputation. As any fan of any team knows, things change. This year's NCAA basketball champion could be next year's goat. In regard to SMU, by the late 1970s, SMU had lost its football prestige. So certain university officials and coaches, with the help of wealthy alumni, gave themselves the mission of reclaiming that prestige. They reached out to athletes with an offer of a payday.

At first, a player being recruited might have thought, "I'm being heavily recruited to come to a nothing school with a losing reputation, and for what?" But before long, they realized, "Oh ... I get it. It's for the pay! For the goodies!" They were being recruited by a low-reputation school, but they got all the things they wanted even though they weren't eligible to receive them. Not a bad gig for playing football.

It seems SMU figured that, if enough athletes of talent were recruited and paid off, it could create a successful program. It literally bought a team. This pay-to-play formula, however, creates major risks for a university. When you begin to pay players for performing, it can all blow up on you — big time.

NO LOYALTY

When you have an unethical situation such as the one at SMU, most athletes are happy campers as long as they're being paid and have everything they want. But as soon as there's a wrinkle in the game plan, so to speak, the players become quickly disgruntled. Some who are not getting all the perks of others begin to think, "He got his and I'm not getting mine." This creates consternation among certain players. What's the recourse? One is to blow the whistle on the school.

Whistleblowing tends to fall into one of two categories: because it's the right thing to do (what you might call an ethical aha moment), or because the participants were promised something they didn't get (a greedy or selfish reaction). The rationalization in this second category is, on the face, completely unethical. The participant reasons, "I'll punish the SOB who didn't give me what I was promised."

This occurred at SMU, even though the participants must have known that what they were promised was against all NCAA rules. Their school paid them well, and they sold their integrity in return.

Once SMU's football program began having success and was enjoying newfound notoriety, it was hard to curtail the payoffs. Sure, it was sanctioned by the NCAA, but so what? It's too late to stop now. The notoriety was like a drug.

That's the problem with bad choices. Once you decide to make one, the next bad choice isn't far behind. At SMU, the coaching staff, the athletic director, and all of the assistants and associates participated to some degree. One bad decision bred dozens more.

EVERYONE IN ON THE ACTION

Just as the scandal appealed to the players' greed, it also appealed to the school's need to win. If I were part of the school's administration or coaching staff, or if I were the athletic director or any one of the numerous assistants and associates, and I knew we weren't playing by the rules, what would have motivated me to go along with the crowd? The underlying thought might have been this: If there's a winning team, and I'm associated with that winning team, there's an opportunity for me to get something out of it, like a better coaching job. There was motivation to commit unethical acts if, down the line, there was a potential reward.

As for the governor, he might have been smart enough to see the train wreck ahead. Election years will do that to a politician. The governor was an SMU graduate. He once played for the team. He probably wouldn't have gotten into the fray if he wasn't connected to the school, so he may have been trying to avoid political embarrassment by attempting to derail the payouts.

We have to remember that, at that time, the general public believed in the purity of amateur sports more so than it does now. In the 1980s, sports fans and athletic boosters were still clinging to the idea that amateur athletes shouldn't be paid. The hypocrisy of the sanctions against players taking money or gifts hadn't fully surfaced in those days, even though the players and coaches privately expressed that the policies were irrational. Why would the NCAA find the payments so offensive? Because payments stood for everything, we once found offensive in amateur athletics.

When Governor Clements got involved, he knew what they all knew: A successful athletic program means big bucks and fame to a school, often creating higher enrollment and greater national exposure. Nowadays, many in the public eye believe that college athletes should be fairly compensated for the services they provide to the school. A scholarship doesn't seem like enough when universities are raking in millions of dollars on games in which their athletes participate.

In the 1980s, though, the senior management at SMU turned a blind eye to the tough questions because they didn't want to answer the tough questions. They broke the NCAA rules to create the outcome they got.

THE ULTIMATE PENALTY

From an ethical perspective, every choice has a consequence, and what you do in the dark eventually gets brought to the light. When bad ethics come to light, you can run, but you cannot hide. SMU eventually paid the price for sticking its head in the sand.

The SMU scandal is an extreme but excellent example of the importance placed on winning above all other considerations. Once the wheels were set in motion, it really changed the focus of SMU. When you're not held seriously accountable and are eventually caught, the consequences can be awful. In the SMU case, they first had their hands slapped, but the initial consequences were not negative enough to stop the unethical behavior. The huge gains that came from the wins outweighed the consequences. Once the tipping point was reached, once everything came to light, all of the consequences burned them.

There was an added shame to this scandal that I think is worth talking about. At the start, people in power could have said, "We're Southern Methodist University. We're a religious institution. The concept of lying and cheating flies in the face of our core values, and the institution will not tolerate it." That never happened. Instead, the consequences kept building up until the program was shut down.

CHAPTER 6

KATIE HNIDA AND THE UNIVERSITY OF COLORADO

Who: Katie Hnida, Coach Gary Barnett, Numerous Players

Offense: Sexual Assault and Harassment

Result: Colorado Football Head Coach Gary Barnett was Fired

Katie Hnida was born in Denver on May 17, 1981. Even as a young girl, Katie loved sports and had aspirations of one day playing at the collegiate level. She was raised in a household where no limits were placed on dreams, even then-unheard-of dreams like playing Division I football at the University of Colorado.

While growing up in the 1980s, Hnida and almost everyone else in the Boulder/Denver area was aware that the Colorado program was experiencing problems. By 1989, twenty-four CU football players had been arrested over a three-year span under head coach Bill McCartney. The players were charged with offenses ranging from rape to night club assaults to animal abuse — for illegally skinning a rabbit.

In the spring of 1989, McCartney's daughter, Kristy, gave birth to his first grandson, Timothy. The child's father was CU quarterback Sal Aunese. Aunese would die of inoperable stomach cancer and lung cancer in September 1989, only nine months after leading his team in the 1988 Freedom Bowl. In November 1993, Kristy gave birth to another son, Derek, whose father was Shannon Clavelle, a CU defensive tackle.

Bill McCartney had had enough of football and resigned as head coach on January 2, 1995, stating he wanted to become more involved in religious activities. In 1995, Rick Neuheisel took over for McCartney, yet the football team's problems persisted. In December 1997, a Denver-area high school student reported she had been sexually assaulted by two CU recruits at a party. No charges were filed against the recruits, who left the program to go to another school.

In February 1998, Denver prosecutor Mary Keenan met with the CU administration about the 1997 sexual assault accusations. Keenan told the athletic office that she would be closely watching the school and its recruiting practices, which allegedly included providing prospective recruits with alcohol and sex.

To his credit, in 1998, Neuheisel invited a promising young placekicker by the name of Katie Hnida to try out for the team. Despite CU's problems, Hnida decided to commit to CU in 1999. She already had quite an impressive resume. She had graduated from Chatfield High School in Littleton, Colorado, where she played varsity football as a placekicker and had been named homecoming queen and Colorado Sportswoman of the Year. She was ranked first on Teen People magazine's annual "20 Teens Who Will Change the World" list. Who wouldn't want to at least give her a tryout? If nothing else, it would show CU as being progressive in equality issues.

On January 20, 1999, Gary Barnett was named CU head coach. That spring, Hnida began to practice with the team. During those spring drills, she was allegedly victimized by team members, who rubbed up against her, groped her, asked her for oral sex, exposed themselves, and carried out other forms of harassment. She could not go to Barnett with any complaints because he'd made it clear he did not want her on the team. Nevertheless, in mid-September 1999, Katie dressed for CU's game versus Kansas. She was only the second woman to ever dress for a Division I football game.

During her first year at CU (1999-2000), after continuing to fend off sexual comments and assaults by other members of the team, Hnida was allegedly raped by a teammate. Barnett had continued to make it clear he did not want her on the team, so she knew she couldn't tell her coach about it. Hnida has since said that she went to the police, but that the district attorney told her it was unlikely her alleged attacker would ever receive more than an ankle bracelet and house arrest. She did not pursue it further. In the summer of 2000, she said, she was again sexually assaulted, and it was then that she left CU.

In the fall of 2002, Hnida signed on with the University of New Mexico. She dressed for games and played as a kicker. Around the same time, Colorado received sanctions for recruiting violations during Neuheisel's tenure as coach. Though Neuheisel was by then coaching at the University of Washington, he was still punished for his recruiting methods.

On December 9, 2002, another CU student, Lisa Simpson, filed a suit against CU football players and recruits who had allegedly raped her. The suit accused CU of fostering an environment hostile to women. No charges were ever filed, though Simpson received $2.5 million when CU settled her Title IX claim in 2007.

On August 20, 2003, Hnida kicked two extra points during New Mexico's 78-2 victory versus Texas State. She became the first woman ever to score in an NCAA Division I football game.

A few days later, Hnida broke her silence and made allegations about being sexually harassed at CU. On October 27, 2003, prosecutors decided against filing sexual assault charges because the CU men had "third-party consent" to have sex with at least one woman at the party. On December 10, 2003, another student claimed she was raped by football players during the same party. A third woman, CU soccer player Monique

Gillaspie, also alleged she was raped by two football players after attending the party.

In January 2004, Keenan, the Denver prosecutor who had said she would be watching the program, released a deposition in which the CU athletic department was implicated to have used sex and alcohol as recruiting tools. Perhaps trying to salvage their image, Barnett and his wife, Mary, decided to begin the Gary Barnett Foundation to provide assistance for at-risk youth. Then, on February 7, 2004, Barnett sanctioned four players for their behavior with recruits, but his new attitude was short-lived. Three days later, an adult-entertainment company claimed it had been used by the CU football team for recruiting purposes.

Though CU officials denied this claim, the phone number of the entertainment company was found on the cell phone of CU football recruiter Nathan Maxcey. Maxcey denied ever using the number.

On February 17, 2004, Hnida made allegations about the CU football program to Rick Reilly of Sports Illustrated magazine. Barnett responded by insulting Hnida's kicking ability, stating, "Katie was not only a girl, she was terrible, OK? There's no other way to say it."

In February 2004, a female student told police that Barnett threatened to support his player one hundred percent if she came forward with her rape allegation. However, since Barnett was suspended by CU on February 19, 2004, police didn't follow up on the allegations. Barnett was put on paid administrative leave. Also, on that date, a seventh woman accused CU football players of sexual assault.

On February 23, 2004, an article by Rick Reilly appeared in Sports Illustrated about the Colorado football player who allegedly raped Hnida. In an interesting turn of events, on April 24, 2004, certain CU football players announced they had been receiving hate mail and claimed to have been harassed on campus.

In January 2005, Hnida appeared on the Today Show and claimed that Barnett said she kissed everyone on the team and had performed lap dances. At that time, CU officials had just initiated a get-tough policy, and so they issued a statement that seemed at best disingenuous: "The university has reached out to Katie to encourage her to provide information about her assault so that appropriate action could be taken. We remain steadfast in that we will not tolerate sexual harassment or exploitation in our athletic department or anywhere in the university."

In April 2005, Barnett received the Marinus Smith Award from the CU Parents Association. It was awarded to teachers, advisers, and staff who made a significant impact on the lives of undergraduate students. By December 2005, Barnett would be fired from CU. He received a $3 million severance package. The university cited a 70-3 loss to Texas in the Big 12 title game as the reason for the firing.

Barnett would not get another chance to coach in the years that followed. Instead, he became an analyst for Fox Sports Net. Hnida would write a book on her experiences and would briefly kick for a couple of arena football teams. She is now a motivational speaker and commentator, and to this day, she still occasionally gets death threats.

The Colorado football program went through a few more coaches before it started its slow return to national relevance. Unfortunately, the divisions between the university and the community over the transgressions of the football program persist.

CHUCK'S ETHICS REVIEW:

Gender Equality in Sports: Expect Ethical Action

Katie Hnida wanted to have a chance not only to play football but also to have a shot at kicking for a Division I men's football team. She was confident that she was qualified and would be competitive. Whether she was qualified was and remains subject to debate. It's an athletic question. What Katie experienced as a person, regardless of gender, was wrong. It should never have happened.

Certainly, there are those who say that men and women should compete equally in sports. The question has become even more complex with issues regarding transgender athletes.

The first classic case to raise this issue was in 1973 when twenty-nine-year-old Billie Jean King defeated fifty-five-year-old Bobby Riggs in a much-hyped Battle of the Sexes tennis match. That was tennis, of course, not tackle football. Without defending or demeaning King or Riggs, let's remember that one was in the playing prime of an outstanding career, and the other was a retired hustler. Not only were they separated by a net, but in recent years compelling evidence has surfaced that Riggs may have purposely thrown the match while betting against himself to pay off massive gambling debts.

Katie Hnida pushed the edge of that equality envelope. She was on the field to play, trying to become an equal. While Katie was on the cutting edge, she was also at the start of a long, uphill battle. It could be that her greatest contribution to sports history are the questions she raised rather than her on-field performance.

PUSHING ISSUES YIELDS CONVERSATION

First and foremost, every player, and indeed every person, has certain rights within the legal system. Felonies were committed against this young woman, and at every turn, she was discouraged from reporting them. Let me be clear that this was unacceptable on the part of the school and coaching staff. It appears she was thwarted all the way up the ladder.

The second issue here is one of ethically creating a level playing field. How is that best handled? Hnida was pushing that very issue. Though the NCAA rules allowed her to step onto a football field and compete equally, there was a culture in play that was difficult to change. She was right to say, "Just because I'm female, I shouldn't be banned from playing on the football team." Okay then, what's the next step? We need to talk about it because this is a complex issue.

Do we just accelerate any blurring of the line between the sexes and say, "It doesn't make any difference what sex you happen to be if you're good enough to make the team"? Or do we stay with the path we're on by recognizing that "girls are girls and guys are guys" and that's just the way it is always going to be? Again, regarding transgender athletes, I fully expect this will blossom into a national debate.

In terms of Hnida, I'm a strong proponent of all Title IX programs. Will those programs become obliterated in a mixed-gender free-for-all? Physically — and I do not state this with any sexual overtones — I can imagine very traumatic outcomes from a fully mixed-gender contact sport.

WHAT'S A LOGICAL MODEL?

Some of the answers might be addressed if we think about the questions that Hnida bravely raised from a sports ethics point of view. I have been asked, of course, what would have happened if Barnett had let her fairly compete for the job of being a kicker. All he had to do was to follow the rules, but he apparently wasn't ready to become a pioneer.

Again, I am fully aware of what Hnida was enduring, and I mean that word exactly, in terms of physical and emotional abuse that had nothing to do with football. Had Barnett given Hnida his endorsement and protection, the situation would have played itself out. I don't know if she would have made the team on her merits as a kicker, but that is not an ethical discussion so much as a football decision. The important discussion is why Barnett allowed her to be abused.

Chances are, had he just let her fairly compete, two things probably would have occurred: His bias would not have been there for everyone to see, and, absent his bias, some of the young men on the team might have responded differently toward Hnida.

That said, a team of young men playing a male-dominated sport in 1999 was not ready to accept a woman without a lot of intervention from the coaching staff. It would be like asking a southern bigot in 1947 to see Jackie Robinson differently. It's hard to go back in time using present-day values and correct what was wrong then. We don't have the benefit of time machines. I do agree, though, that had Barnett laid down the law and demanded absolute respect for Katie, the situation would have been resolved before it got out of hand.

On another level, let's be honest. More than twenty years later, how many females play Division I football? Football is a brutally hard, unforgiving sport. Placekickers do get hit, intentionally or incidentally. Should Barnett have allowed her to compete for a kicking job? If the answer is yes, then she should have been treated fairly, like any other walk-on competing for a job.

Let's also talk about biology and physiology. Yes, I know that parents and the media whoop and holler when an eight-year-old girl runs for five touchdowns against eight-year-old boys. However, I would not want to see the same girl compete as a sixteen-year-old running back against teenage boys.

Though kickers are seen as diminutive in the college and pro ranks, they still weigh an average of 200 pounds. They are relatively small players but not compared to most people. I wouldn't have discouraged Katie from competing, but I also wouldn't have shielded her from the reality of competition.

BAD BEHAVIOR CANNOT BE FORGIVEN

The lousy behavior of the CU team in that time period was largely ignored because there was an assumption that male athletes are simply beings who are competitive, driven, and full of testosterone. I do not mean steroids. I mean, you've got young men eighteen to twenty-four with a preconceived idea of who plays the game and what wins the game, and — unfortunately for those who must suffer the consequences — a misconception of what it's like to be a man.

Issues of bad behavior and, especially, sexual misconduct existed at CU a decade before Hnida's time, and it probably went back even further than that. The culture of sport is frequently that of a dominant male athlete who thinks he should have any woman in any way that he chooses. In no way do I think that's right. This is why we teach sports ethics. Young men can be as tough and competitive, and driven as they want, and they can also be taught to be ethical.

Bad ethics were out of control when Hnida played because Colorado had a bunch of guys who were held to no standard. If you go back to that period, it was not just a matter of not respecting women. There were also problems with bullying, animal abuse, and crimes against the community at large. In Hnida's case, it was complete objectification. They chose bad ethics over any semblance of proper behavior, and the coaching staff did nothing to help.

Barnett never coached again, and I am not surprised. There's so much that took place, so much baggage. The team was scarred, and Barnett didn't help. He promoted an environment that made it okay for players to abuse women and act out, and where it was clear, everyone would turn a blind eye to it.

The case uncovered the underside of collegiate sports, especially when it comes to stereotypes and the coaching of male athletes. The scandal exposed the truth of what goes on in a lot of programs. On a related but entirely separate topic, psychologists and educators have recently pointed out that young boys are falling behind girls academically and that boys and young men are being raised in an atmosphere of hostility and confusion as to their roles. If we want to elevate girls, we must also elevate boys and young men at the same time.

It was bold of Hnida to become a football player for a Division I university. At its simplest, this case should teach us to value those of all orientations and to not sexualize or trivialize them. I firmly believe that, with the perspective of time, at least some of the players from the team that year might be honest enough to admit that what happened was wrong and they should have protected Hnida. Others may be glad they were never prosecuted for their alleged crimes.

SECTION II

Most of them are now around fourty-five years of age, and some are fathers. They undoubtedly look in the mirror of time with a different perspective. The shortest route to achieving the goal of greater respect and equality in organized sports is through ethical training. Most college athletic programs have failed their athletes in that regard.

CHAPTER 7

DUKE LACROSSE SCANDAL OF 2006

Who: Duke University Lacrosse Team, Crystal Gail Mangum and Kim Roberts, DA Dennis Nifong

Offense: Alleged Rape

Result: Players Found Innocent, Nifong Disbarred, Loss of Reputation

While no sports scandal is pretty, the Duke Lacrosse scandal of 2006 is particularly unpleasant. It is a commentary on America's sad, racist past and also on what happens when political correctness runs amok.

This scandal took place from March 13, 2006, until around the end of June 2007, yet we're still dealing with some of the ugly issues the scandal raised. What follows is a highly condensed version of the events. The complete version could be offered as a full-semester college course and a textbook in its own right.

On March 13, 2006, a woman by the name of Crystal Gail Mangum and her coworker, Kim Roberts, was hired by the Allure Agency to dance at an off-campus house party in Durham, North Carolina. The house was one of those run-down, small, white-clapboard homes you can see at the edge of almost any college campus in America. The property was rented this particular year by the captains of the Duke lacrosse team.

Mangum was a student at North Carolina Central University. She also worked as a stripper. Mangum is African-American, and Kim Roberts is half African-American and half Asian. It is central to the scandal to note that, with the exception of one player, every member of the Duke lacrosse team that year was white.

Duke University is, by and large, a university of privilege. It has traditionally been a white university, though now about 10% of the students are Black. North Carolina Central University is a historically Black public university, and while there are white students at NCCU, they comprise only about 6% of the student body. Both schools are located in Durham.

The facts would later emerge that when Mangum arrived at the party, she was drunk and on drugs. The minute the two women walked through the door, the players — who had been partying stupidly hard as well — yelled at them that they had asked for whites and not ... well, you can guess what racial slur followed.

What ensued was a series of arguments that were racially charged and sexual in nature. The arguments escalated, and the two women decided they had had enough. As they left the dilapidated house, the taunts and drunken arguments continued. Roberts then called 911.

In the car, the two women got into a heated argument about the 911 call. Roberts tried to shove Mangum out of the vehicle, but Mangum wouldn't leave. Roberts then drove to a Kroger supermarket, where she asked a security guard for help in removing her passenger.

In an article for ABC News (April 16, 2006), Chris Cuomo and Lara Setrakian reported that Mangum told the security guard she had been held down by three members of the team who raped and robbed her. The security guard said Mangum did not smell of alcohol to him, but he said he suspected drugs might be involved.

When the police arrived, the alleged victim changed her story. When she was examined at the health center, there were some scratches and genital swelling consistent with sexual assault, but she would later admit to performing for money for another couple a few days earlier than the Duke incident. Nevertheless, the fact that she was in an altered state and had scratches and minor injuries was reason enough for the police to proceed with investigating her rape claim.

On the other side of the scandal, after the women had left the party, a team member sent out an offensive (both sexual and violent) email, making a joke of it all.

The police report and the victim's initial claim spurred the district attorney's office into action, and an aggressive prosecutor named Dennis Nifong saw this as a career-making opportunity. Of the forty-seven players on the team, forty-six were made to submit to DNA testing. As Mangum had identified her three attackers as white, the one African-American player was not tested.

On April 10, 2006, the lab results were returned, and there were no matches to the Duke players. The private lab had found numerous DNA traces from other men on the alleged victim, along with the DNA of her boyfriend. The rape case against the players should have been closed at that point, but Nifong never publicly disclosed that there were no DNA matches to the players. In fact, despite knowing that no matches existed, the private lab that worked with Nifong kept the case going on a fast track.

It was later determined that the director of the private laboratory had written a misleading report. He would eventually be fired in October 2007 for deliberately withholding evidence. Nevertheless, the alleged victim was asked to look at pictures of the team members on April 18, 2006. It would later emerge that she picked up to sixteen team members, then narrowed the list to five, then chose Collin Finnerty, age nineteen, and Reade Seligmann, age twenty, but with only about a 70% certainty.

The two were charged with first-degree forcible rape and other crimes.

Finnerty was no choir boy. He had a prior assault charge, and he did community service in November 2005. While committing the assault, he had shouted anti-gay epithets at his victim. Still, he ultimately cleared himself.

Seligmann's case was completely different. He had a solid alibi. He had left the party before the incident and even had records to show he wasn't there. On May 15, 2006, former team captain David Evans was indicted on similar charges.

The three men publicly voiced their innocence. Meanwhile, the drumbeat of media attention grew. Those who believed Mangum squared off against those who believed the young men. Nifong fueled the flames.

Ironically, during the photo lineup, Mangum initially identified only one player, a fourth man, with one hundred percent certainty as having raped her. That player supplied solid evidence he was with his girlfriend at North Carolina State University at the time of the alleged crime.

On June 8, 2006, Roberts testified that she doubted Mangum was raped. As the months passed, it became apparent that no rape had taken place. The charges against the players were finally dropped, but not until April 2007 — almost a year after the men had been charged.

Around the same time, ethics charges would be filed against Nifong for improper statements to the media, misinterpreting DNA evidence, and the prejudicial administration of justice. From the beginning of the case to the end, Nifong pursued the three young men with a passion. He seemingly believed only what he wanted to believe and was relentless in his prejudicial prosecution. Eventually, it would get him disbarred.

Mangum would not be prosecuted, either. It has been well-documented that she had a history of drug abuse and bipolar disorder. In fact, she had made a similar claim of rape in 1996. She also stole a car in 2002 and led the police on a high-speed chase. In 2011, Mangum was charged with the murder of her boyfriend. She is currently incarcerated. There are no winners in this scandal, not even the lacrosse players, who were charged and then declared innocent. It has remained a stain on Duke University to this day.

CHUCK'S ETHICS REVIEW:

A Tale of Two Piranhas: The Prosecutor and the Prostitute

While it's true that no one died and none of the accused saw jail time, this case involves some of the worst aspects of our society, from out-of-control kids to a stripper on drugs to a prosecutor who placed greed and notoriety above the law.

The universal ethical theme, in this case, is that every choice has a consequence. Of that, there can be little doubt. The Duke lacrosse players had choices. The women had choices. Certainly, the overzealous DA had choices — and not one of them made the right ones.

Boys Will Be … College Athletes?

Although they may at first blush seem like the victims here, the Duke lacrosse players need to shoulder their fair share of the blame. Every facet of this scandal illustrates the fact that what might seem irrelevant at the start has a consequence somewhere down the road. Combine a mix of drugs, alcohol, and sex, and add in a liberal dose of racism, and it's never going to end well.

Often, when we make choices, it is easy to be oblivious to the possible outcomes. But that does not excuse us from culpability. While they may not have deserved to be unjustly accused of felonies, the Duke lacrosse players nevertheless put themselves in a position where such allegations seemed plausible. By hiring strippers, drinking heavily, and treating the women disrespectfully, the players created an environment that placed their innocence in doubt.

I've been asked if ethics training could have changed the outcome of this case and if I would have included the Duke lacrosse coach in that training. Yes, it's possible ethical training could have helped. I would like to say that ethics training, whether formal or informal, is at the root of all good choices. Ethics training for the players and coach might have been a positive start and something beneficial or valuable later on. But I also think there was a systemic standard of "good ol' boy" entitlement that might have overridden any training I could have given these men.

There was something deeply ingrained here. I have no doubt that, while the parents of some of these kids might have felt a sense of deep shame, with others, there was a wink and a poke in the ribs. "Beer? Every kid parties. Strippers? Boys will be boys. Racial slurs? What's the big deal?" That's how some of the adults probably saw it.

Not to sound preachy, but 65 years prior to this scandal, young men of the ages of the Duke boys were heading off to war. They had no choice but to grow up quickly. Our society doesn't always encourage boys to be men, so we can expect the outcome we saw in the Duke scandal. I don't want to generalize and say that every kid will act this way, but I also don't want to minimize the consequences of what can happen when young people are not asked and expected to act like adults.

This scandal wasn't the first brush with the law for some of these kids. Only the year before, Collin Finnerty, one of the young men accused of rape, had assaulted a man and uttered anti-gay epithets. He was charged with that crime and had to perform community service. Now, would personalized ethical training have helped him? I don't know. I hate to say it, but my guess is not very much.

You see, if you ask most people whether or not they make ethical choices, they would likely say that they make them — until they don't. It's all relative. Finnerty is, in my opinion, a prime example of someone who wasn't properly taught how to make ethical choices and to realize the consequences of his actions.

On the other hand, after the young man's first experience with the law, he may have been somewhat more receptive to personalized training. We often see this with people in sports. Many collegiate or professional athletes have big egos. Sometimes the winning attitude takes on aspects of arrogance. Before they make a bad choice, their big egos may not always recognize potential adverse outcomes. But once they experience the consequences of a bad choice, they may be more susceptible to ethics training.

In Finnerty's case, the consequences were fairly insignificant: community service. I should also note that Finnerty's assault conviction was in 2005. Now, more than eighteen years later, people and the courts are more sensitive to what people say or how they act, especially in regard to gay or transgender issues. Today, he likely would have suffered greater consequences than he did then, as we are less tolerant of anti-gay behavior.

The Duke lacrosse scandal occurred in 2006, but the attitude of the players made it seem like it was 1956. Had the case been in just a little more doubt, had the DNA results been just the slightest bit in question, the consequences to the players could have been extremely severe. They might have rotted in jail cells.

Now, would I have offered ethics training to the coach? Yes. However, there's an old saying that goes, "The fish stinks from the head down." If the attitude for so many years was that wealth, privilege, and entitlement are all you need to get by, I don't think any short-term teaching provided to the coach and passed along to the players would have made much difference. I believe a bigger impact could have been engendered by the leadership at the very top of the university, who needed to make it crystal clear it did not support what happened, despite the ultimate outcome of the scandal.

The misguided idea that wealth and entitlement get you whatever you want without any consequences could have been harshly dealt with by the athletic director and on up. This was not just a men's lacrosse issue. It was a university and cultural issue.

DENNIS NIFONG, PIRANHA

The second question I'm frequently asked about this case involves that crusader for justice, Dennis Nifong, the district attorney. He concealed evidence from the court that revealed the players didn't rape the woman.

People have asked why this man, this supposed upholder of the law, would do such a thing. It's kind of like asking why Bernie Madoff created a massive Ponzi scheme or Elizabeth Holmes duped investors into putting money in a machine that didn't work.

In many cases, you don't know the deeper, underlying reasons, but many people would see that Nifong used this incident, which fell conveniently into his lap, as a way to bolster his political career. He saw it as an opportunity and was wooed by the possibility that this case would hold big promise for him. He failed to understand that Lady Justice wears a blindfold.

Nifong wanted to be the prosecutor who stood up for the oppressed little guy or, in this case, the lady, who also happened to be a minority in the state of North Carolina and who also happened to be female and underprivileged.

I'm sure the hard-charging Nifong felt that people with wealth or power or prestige needed to be brought down a notch or two. Again, if a person is going to make a bad choice, he needs to be aware that there will be all kinds of unforeseen traps. Had Nifong been successful, he could have had a clear pathway to fulfilling any political aspirations. Instead, he threw it all away by pressing a case that never should have been prosecuted.

RACE AND PRIVILEGE

There can be little denying that both race and privilege played a role in this case. We must tread very carefully, though, because privilege is all too often used as a scapegoat. If you consider all of the components of the case, there was more than enough unethical behavior to go around.

Here you have a young woman who was working her way through college, ostensibly as a stripper. I understand the need to make money, but that doesn't automatically mean she made a good choice. She made a series of terrible choices for her life. We know of petty crimes, drug abuse, alcohol abuse, and possibly untreated mental illness.

Then you have the prosecutor, who was overly ambitious. When the DNA testing results came back, he saw the case wasn't going to be the goose that laid the golden egg. But then he compounded one bad choice after another. He wanted to see if he could hide the truth and maybe try to get one of those eggs to hatch anyway. Additionally, both he and the woman played the same race card, though in different ways.

You also had kids of wealth and privilege who believed they could throw a party and hire strippers to perform sexual acts for them. When the strippers arrived, the kids realized they weren't the race they had requested, and so they decided to be jerks, which we all agree wasn't the brightest choice they could have made.

So everywhere around the circle, the scandal participants made dumb choices. Any way you look at it, there was a plethora of bad decisions that conspired to create negative consequences for all parties involved.

Skin color, wealth, and privilege do afford some the ability to make a different set of choices, ones that have less impactful consequences. Whether we like it or not, privilege does exist, and, in some cases, race does play a major factor in our justice system. If you look at the incarceration rate in the U.S., minorities are represented at a much higher percentage in prison than they are in the general population.

We look at that and ask, is it because they are a minority? We know that in some cases it's true. There are far too many stories of targeted car stops and racial profiling that led to arrests. Do some poor people, regardless of skin color, wind up making bad decisions because of their economic status? I think that can be true as well. Poverty can drive people of poor character to make very stupid choices. Notice that I said "people of poor character." The vast majority of poor people, of course, are ethical and of high moral character.

The wealthy often win the entitlement lottery and are not as affected by desperate, crippling economic conditions. The problem in present-day society is that celebrity often trumps everything, and this is especially true in athletics.

If a professional quarterback of an NFL team gets pulled over for a DUI, regardless of skin color, chances are the charges will be dropped. The problem with such a double standard is that aspiring young athletes will see it and believe they, too, are privileged.

If we loop back around to the Duke lacrosse team, there might possibly have been a little of that taking place. They saw life as a game of entitlement. "We're athletes," they seem to think. "We're rich, and we're entitled to our fun!" Little did they suspect that this same sense of entitlement would put them in some very hot water, where they would stay for almost a year.

As I said at the beginning of this ethics review, there's nothing pretty going on here. No winners, nothing triumphant — only a web woven by fools.

CHAPTER 8

1993 FLORIDA STATE UNIVERSITY SHOE SCANDAL

Who: Florida State University Basketball Team, Student Athletes, Nate Cebrun and Raul Bey

Offense: Influencing, Illegal Payouts

Result: Cebrun and Bey Sentenced to Jail, Losses of Reputation for Teams and Coaches

On the evening of November 7, 1993, as a Foot Locker sporting goods store in Tallahassee, Florida, was about to close, a man named Raul Bey showed up with anywhere from seven to eleven student-athletes from the Florida State University football team.

The players were encouraged to go on a buying spree. They bought $6,000 worth of merchandise, and Bey put the purchases on his credit card. However, the case was far more complex than a simple shoe sale.

Student-athletes are highly regulated by the NCAA. They may not accept gifts or cash from sports agents, whose job is to manage athletes in the signing of professional contracts. Sports agents are also highly regulated. Most register in the states in which they operate.

A "bird dog" or "runner" is a freelance go-between, a kind of semi-agent. Working in a large gray area between right and wrong, bird dogs cultivate players in hopes of steering them to a licensed sports agent. They may be employed by a particular agent or act as a kind of freelancer for multiple agents. It's a world based on greed. If a bird dog steers an outstanding athlete to an agent, it could mean a hefty cut.

To understand the Florida State shoe scandal is to know a bird dog named "Coach" Nate Cebrun. Cebrun is physically huge. His trademarks were his fine clothes and huge championship rings. His most impressive ring was from the University of Nevada at Las Vegas. One side of the ring read "Coach Nate." The other side displayed the score of a championship game. Cebrun never coached at UNLV. The ring was a replica.

Cebrun met Raul Bey in Las Vegas. Bey had struck it rich in the early days of the computer industry. Now he wanted to launch a sports equipment line, and he wanted to recruit a number of Division I athletes to help him endorse his products. Cebrun said that such a goal was right up his alley.

In October of 1993, Cebrun arrived at Florida State University to scout players, both for Bey's equipment line and for himself as a bird dog. However, he had no connections at FSU.

In a predatorial pattern that would repeat itself over and over again, Cebrun struck up a relationship with a woman who had a connection to the university. She was a widow, probably lonely and all too willing to try to help. The woman thought the son of a minister friend might be the connection Cebrun needed to approach the FSU team. The young man was a high school assistant football coach who knew a lot of people on campus. The assistant football coach was taken in by Cebrun's larger-than-life personality, and he subsequently introduced Cebrun to several student-athletes.

At the time, Cebrun told the athletes he was associated with a registered football agent. He wasn't. On October 10, 1993,

Cebrun held a more formal meeting with several athletes. He told the players that if they needed money for any reason, he'd be happy to help them.

According to Sports Illustrated magazine (May 16, 1994), on the day after that meeting, Cebrun had several players fill out questionnaires. Cebrun convinced his widow friend to loan him some money to give to the students as gifts. Cebrun denies this happened, but the young football coach later said he saw Cebrun hand out money. The loan Cebrun's girlfriend gave him was later replenished by Bey. Both Bey and Cebrun have denied ever giving money to players.

To further illustrate Cebrun's character, at nearly the same time of the FSU shoe incident, Cebrun was also involved in arranging illegal gambling trips for a University of Missouri basketball star and his mother.

Back at Florida State, on November 6, 1993, the day before the shoe store shopping spree, Bey flew to Tallahassee to use Cebrun's influence to get players to endorse his clothing line. Though Bey and Cebrun denied it, witnesses said they gave the student-athletes money at two area hotels and at the FSU football dormitory. Additional payouts were made later in November 1993 by Bey, Cebrun and the high school assistant coach.

A key question is this: Did Florida State University have any idea what was going on during that period? Apparently, the day after the shopping spree, an FSU assistant coach noticed several players wearing expensive sneakers and clothing. He questioned where the apparel had come from — indeed, coaches are supposed to look out for such purchases as an indicator of undue influencing — but just made a silly joke and let it go.

Another unnamed coach allegedly knew the amount of the purchases. Strangely and somewhat suspiciously, two days after the shopping spree, on November 9, 1993, FSU head coach Bobby Bowden called a team meeting to warn players about accepting gifts from agents.

On January 1, 1994, FSU beat Nebraska to win the national championship. Also, in January 1994, the widowed woman (now Cebrun's ex-girlfriend) told one of the FSU coaches what had happened. The coach largely ignored her, but he did a little investigating.

In May 1994, the high school assistant coach who had distributed money for Cebrun and Bey was grilled by the athletic committee faculty, the school's publicist, and others. This interview resulted in a press conference held a few days later. Florida State officials said two athletes had received cash gifts of about $40 and free merchandise. They blamed an unregistered recruiter working for an agent who was unlicensed in Florida.

On May 14, 1994, Bowden reported the infraction to the NCAA. Florida State officials claimed they had no knowledge of the incident until then. Had the NCAA learned of the scandal during the season, FSU could have been made to forfeit its season and been barred from playing for the national championship.

In February 1995, Bey was sentenced to one year in prison for failing to register as a sports agent.

In yet another indication of Cebrun's character, in April 2000, Auburn basketball star Chris Porter confessed to taking $2,500 from Cebrun. In late April of 2000, Cebrun would be arrested for making payments to Porter. He also allegedly coerced yet another woman to issue money orders used as payment.

Cebrun was also implicated in scandals at Fresno State and with SAT score fixing.

Cebrun eventually entered a plea deal wherein he pledged to work with the NCAA in exchange for his knowledge of all the scandals.

CHUCK'S ETHICS REVIEW:

On the Backs of the Innocent: Gaining Power, Influence, and Money

At the start of every season of almost every sport, but certainly, in Division I football and basketball, there are conversations about pushing for the NCAA to loosen its grip and allow players to be paid. Everyone talks about how good this would be because, after all, the players make money for their universities. A lot of money.

To be honest, though, if student-athletes were paid, I believe the scandals would get worse at the highest collegiate levels and would make the FSU shoe scandal seem like small potatoes. For example, suppose the NCAA decided to authorize Division I basketball players a payment of $30,000 a year. Okay, fair enough. But let's then say you're an athletic director, and you have a sophomore point guard who was on a team that made it to the Final Four. You know that he's a lock to get drafted by the NBA, probably for a multimillion-dollar contract. You tell him you're going to pay him a $ 30,000-a-year stipend, and he laughs in your face. He demands $160,000, or he's going to enter the draft. What will you do? Suppose the next guy who comes along wants more. Do you pay him, too? Where does it end?

As I said, at the time of this writing, the NCAA is loosening its grip on athletes being paid. I see this as a huge challenge in the years ahead.

Education is education; professional sports are professional sports. Despite all of the arguments to the contrary, I would keep the system pretty much the way it is. Student-athletes are still student-athletes. If they're on scholarship, they'll already receive an education that might cost non-athletes $100,000 or more. If student-athletes are struggling to make ends meet, as I know many are, then consider stipends to help them cover expenses but allow no negotiation above a set amount.

GOOD OLD CEBRUN!

Opportunists like Cebrun have always lurked in the dark corners of organized sports. We've seen examples throughout this book. Were we to look for similar cases in other countries, they would exist there as well.

Cebrun was an opportunist, the kind of character we see in all walks of life. He dressed big, had big fancy rings that meant absolutely nothing, and promised everyone around him the moon. In his wake, he left many people chewed up, beat up, and used. He represented a failed system. It is not so unusual for people of small-time influence to try to network their way to opportunity, fame, and fortune. The bird-dog scout wanted to be somebody. He wanted to connect with the players. While these characters often impress student-athletes with promises of riches and glory, they rarely deliver.

Also, understand that Cebrun was able to make people around him feel rich, powerful and needed. The widowed woman at FSU was able to fill a void in her life when Cebrun wheedled his way in. Bey wanted athletes to wear his clothes and quickly make him rich while riding the coattails of clothing powerhouses like Under Armour or Nike. Cebrun promised Bey he could do that. The so-so athletes had their egos massaged by a few bucks' worth of athletic shoes, making them think they were on their way to Easy Street. Life doesn't work that way.

Characters such as Cebrun are not rare in life. I've seen hundreds like him in the corporate world, and we certainly have our share of Cebruns in government. Athletes, though, are particularly vulnerable. They are young and naïve. They see an old guy come along and think they can outsmart the old guy with the smooth ways. He usually knows what they're thinking before they ever say anything. This is why ethics training is so important for student-athletes.

SQUIRMING AWAY FROM TRUTH

There is some question about what FSU coaches and administrators knew and when they knew it. If FSU had admitted prior to the national championship game that their students had been bribed, they likely would have had to forfeit. It probably wasn't a coincidence that just two days after the shoe gifts, head coach Bowden warned his players to refuse bribes. In my opinion, the team was covering its bases. If questioned, the coach could then say that he did his job and warned his players. Well, maybe he didn't.

In my opinion, Bowden likely knew something was going on and should have been more forceful about dealing with it. First, before the season even began, he should have established clear ethics training, underscoring the various rules and regulations student-athletes should know about. Then, once he learned about the shopping spree, he should have reprimanded the players involved and reported the incident to the NCAA, throwing his program on their mercy. Had he done so, it's possible the program might have gotten off with just a slap on the wrist. But the coach had a legacy to protect. By not saying anything, the legacy might have remained intact. The tradeoff would have been enormous, of course, and Bowden seemed unwilling to pay the price. His decision came down to this: $6,000 worth of sneakers and less than $1,000 in cash versus the national championship.

The time to apply good ethics was before the season started, and then it should have been reinforced from time to time throughout the year. Instead, by waiting until something actually happened, it was a case of too little / too late.

We can take the exact case above and alter just one little fact. A whistleblower — perhaps a scorned woman, a go-between, or even someone within the athletic department who has a chip on his or her shoulder — might go to the NCAA and anonymously report the bribes and the shoes. That's all. Just one anonymous tip to someone responsible for compliance, and this whole thing could have come down like a house of cards. As the investigation widened, everyone involved, including the seven to eleven athletes, could have seen the end to their collegiate careers and their futures in athletics, or even to their chances of success in business or medicine or whatever they had in mind outside of sports.

No one insulated these student-athletes against poor choices, brought to the test in the form of Nate Cebrun and Raul Bey.

The important lesson is this: Every choice, whether good or bad, matters. To a twenty-year-old athlete, a speech made by a droning official from the compliance department means little. Without proper education, these young people can't imagine how their choices at age twenty affect their forty- or fifty-year-old selves. Trust me; they will.

SPORTS ETHICS TRAINING

In terms of sports ethics training, could this scandal honestly have been avoided? It's a question I've been asked in different settings, and my response is that there are outcomes sports ethics training can accomplish and things it cannot. It's like attempting a field goal. A lot of factors must come into play to make that kick successful. If it's kicked properly, you'll see a trajectory that is true and accurate. It can't be blocked. You know the kick will give you your three points.

No matter what the announcers say up in the booth, a field goal is never automatic. Every player on the field must carry out their assignment. In a similar manner, if sports ethics training is effective, an athlete will be strong enough to look at a guy like Cebrun or Bey and say, "Absolutely not. Keep your lousy sneakers. Get away from me!" The athlete would probably report the shady character to the coaching staff, and the issue would be elevated up through the university from there.

From a sports ethics perspective, all collegiate athletes can learn from Florida State's mistakes, but those lessons can't be boiled down to the usual bull. The easy line, the stuff they pound into athletes at those once-a-year ethical training sessions led by an ex-athlete who messed up, goes something like this: "Don't screw up, and avoid temptations."

But it's so much more than that. Athletes at any level need to understand the full range of their choices, the consequences of those choices, and, ultimately, how those choices can affect their reputations long-term.

Can student-athletes do it all themselves? No, of course not. The Florida State shoe scandal took place in 1993. The internet was in its infancy, and the search engine had not been invented. The athletes didn't have the opportunity to do a search on this guy, which might have exposed him as a fraud. Also, understand that, as the ability to research a character like Cebrun improves, the degree to which unethical people can defraud and lie also improves. Cebrun could have created an entire online persona for himself, one that made it easier for him to prey on unsuspecting athletes. It's actually pretty easy to do.

The threat of a person of ill-intent taking unethical advantage of a situation is as valid now as it has ever been. Training must be in place. This is why ethics training done by a coaching staff, human resources officers or compliance staff from the athletic department is just not usually very effective. To be impactful, you want people speaking to the team who have experienced the consequences of bad decisions, people who know the ropes and are experienced in guiding sports ethics conversations in a practical way that will produce positive results. As you have seen from other scandals in this book, athletes who are ethically prepared have a strong sense of who they are and make good choices, no matter the era.

THEN THERE'S RAUL BEY

Bey seems like an interesting character, especially on the business side of sports. He wasn't afraid to toss his money around to gain power and influence. Bey had an idea, but in order for it to take hold, he had to have people running around wearing his stuff. He needed to find people to use.

Bey's critical connections were athletes who had influence, FSU guys in a big-time program. It was before social media and before an image of an athlete wearing apparel on Twitter or Snapchat could make sales skyrocket. He wasn't afraid to use these kids. This is the underbelly of sales; this is no man's land. Bey thought it was worth it to buy off some kids with a couple of bucks' worth of shoes and use them as stepping stones, but that is just a small part of this story.

The true story is the genius of a character like Cebrun. He used the widowed woman, who, through her friend's son, hooked him up with the student-athletes. The athletes liked the money and the prestige of getting a possible agent, and Cebrun didn't care what rules he was violating.

Everyone in this scandal was involved in making bad ethical choices, and no one was thinking about the consequences of their choices. Cebrun was a master puppeteer, and Bey was just another one of his puppets. Maybe Bey knew the kind of character Cebrun was, or maybe he knew he had to strike a deal with the devil for his business to take off. Regardless, Cebrun played him like a fiddle. Individually, each of the people Cebrun duped didn't have that much power, but Cebrun was able to take their collective influence and make it work. Together, they gave him the success he craved, at least until he lost it all.

In the end, those who were hurt the worst by Bey and Cebrun were the student-athletes, the coaches and, ultimately, the school. Just like good physical training, good sports ethics training could have prevented these injuries, or at least minimized the damages.

CHAPTER 9

MICHELE SHARP, KEAN UNIVERSITY AND TRIPS TO SPAIN

Who: Coach Michele Sharp, AD Glen Hedden, and Basketball Players

Offense: Illegal Solicitation of Funds, Fake Courses

Result: Four years' Probation, Firings, Termination of Scholarships

Kean University in Union, New Jersey, is an NCAA Division III school that has had more than its share of problems, specifically within the athletic department. Michele Sharp, former coach of the Kean women's basketball team, was at the very center of the storm.

Sharp was a basketball coach at Kean for 14 years. During the 2007–2008 academic year, and again in the 2010-2011 academic year, multiple convoluted violations were reported at Kean and within its sports programs, especially with regard to women's basketball.

A seemingly simple enough request began to raise suspicions. On January 29, 2010, Sharp sent an email to Kean's general counsel, Michael Tripodi. She asked his opinion about an opportunity to solicit funds to support a study class for athletes. In essence, the request was to fund a course that involved a trip to Spain. Sharp then proceeded, without any blessing from counsel and ultimately acting on her own, to solicit alumni donor funds, which was completely outside of the university's established procedures.

In the spring of 2010, Sharp managed to fashion a for-credit course on the history of Spain, an overseas learning class created exclusively for her basketball team. The university initially rejected the course, but Sharp resubmitted it in another format, and it was approved. The course, however, was a scam. It was camouflage for a scheme that allowed the team to play basketball overseas. The student-athletes received financial awards for the non-course in the amount of $7,075, plus university credits.

Then on November 22, 2010, Kean athletic director Glen Hedden learned that one of the players on the women's basketball team was not taking the proper number of credits to be eligible to play. This discovery led Hedden to conduct an investigation of the women's basketball team. In the process, he found out about the fraud regarding the history of Spain course, long after it had already happened. Hedden also learned the class didn't have enough students to be considered a class, a violation of the university registrar's standard. In fact, two of the players had another class scheduled at the same time they were supposed to be in the Spain course. On top of that, only student-athletes were allowed to register for the Spain course. As a side note, on January 4, 2011, a student-athletes "F" grade was changed to an "incomplete" so she could play the following day, an obvious NCAA violation.

Hedden had no choice but to do the right thing and report the violations he had discovered to the NCAA. He was initially considered a good-guy whistleblower, but then the NCAA and the university began to wonder just who had been minding the store.

On May 5, 2011, Hedden was fired by the university for not properly supervising the coaches, especially Sharp. The firing led to Hedden filing a wrongful termination suit against Kean

University on June 13. Hedden's lawsuit alleged that top administrators changed grades and created a course for members of the women's basketball team just so two players could meet eligibility requirements to play.

On September 28, 2011, Sharp was questioned by the NCAA for at least five infractions. But that didn't stop Sharp. On December 21, and again in the period from December 28-30, Sharp provided extra money for two of her players to take a trip to Florida. This was another NCAA violation.

After much deliberation, on April 19, 2012, the NCAA passed down a series of rulings. Kean was placed on four years of probation. All women's basketball student-athletes involved in the violations were declared ineligible, though the athletes could obtain restoration of their eligibility through the student-athlete reinstatement process.

The women's basketball team was forced to return per diem money to the NCAA that it had used to attend the Division III basketball tournament. Kean also had to return the 2011 honorarium for hosting the tournament.

Sharp was fired from her coaching position but was retained by the university and moved to a position as an athletic trainer. She would eventually resign. In 2013, Sharp would be hired as a high school basketball coach.

Some additional issues were brought out in the NCAA report. The inquiries indicated that a disproportionate number of student-athletes were receiving athletic scholarships over deserving academic students. According to the report, there was "impermissible financial aid and extra benefits for its student-athletes."

There were also strange academic manipulations with student-athletes who had suddenly qualified for a Dorsey scholarship, a non-athletic scholarship. The school had been penalized for many scholarship infractions during the period, and rather than addressing the more serious problems that had cropped up during Sharp's coaching tenure, they elected again to self-police and to show they were handling business. The university decided to disqualify athletes from receiving athletic scholarships who were also receiving academic scholarships. This decision imposed financial burdens on both those who qualified academically and on athletes who lacked the funds to attend school.

In an atmosphere where unsupervised coaches were free to change grades, fake courses, alter course loads, and provide disproportionate athletic scholarships and financial gifts, the university chose to remove opportunities for academic scholarships from good students and award them to athletes.

CHUCK'S ETHICS REVIEW:

I Want What I Want, and the Hell with the Rules

Sometimes those with unethical intentions are hell-bent on violating the rules because they simply think they have the right to do so. In regard to this case, I'm often asked why Coach Sharp didn't give up and let it go when the Spain course was initially denied. She must have known she was on thin ice, but apparently, she didn't care.

As to the why of it all, we have to examine the motivations of the coach at that time. I have to assume that she probably thought in terms of the following: Let's create a course that allows our athletes to receive credit and then let's make it such an easy grade that it helps them from an academic standpoint.

Sharp created a need for her athletes to take an easy course to boost their grades. Certainly, a course focusing on the history of Spain, held in Spain with all expenses paid, must have been intriguing to anyone! Second, in creating the course, she could have been thinking: I'd like to go to Spain and hang out for a week or ten days myself, so how do I get there, and how do I get it to be considered part of my job?

The question came down to need. Sharp needed to boost grades, and she needed to get out of Union, New Jersey, in the middle of winter. Why not beautiful Spain? It was — pun intended — a slam dunk.

As we discussed earlier, there are three components to every piece of unethical behavior: need, opportunity, and rationalization. Sharp's need was to create a trip for herself and the kids she coached. While she was at it, she let these student-athletes have an incredibly easy academic experience, all the while getting an all-expenses-paid vacation.

The problem, of course, was that it was a small club, open to only a handful of invited athletes. They got to play basketball and have fun at the expense of all established academic standards. It's the type of privilege that outrages those outside the athletic sphere. The coach had created a secret course within the university for herself and her athletes. It was a sweet yet totally unethical deal.

WHERE WAS THE ATHLETIC DIRECTOR?

We talked above about the three components necessary to create such a scandal. While the athletic director may not have had direct knowledge of the fictitious course, it was the athletic director's lack of monitoring that created the opportunity for this to happen.

In a great many cases, and certainly outside of athletics itself, having to monitor someone who works for you can be uncomfortable. It goes to the heart of the issue of trust. Yes, I may be an athletic director or university president, and, yes, I am responsible for the coach. However, unless something is brought to my attention or something is giving me great doubt, I'm going to believe that you're acting in the best interest of your program.

Let's say I am a Major League Baseball manager and a player on my team likes to play the ponies, and everyone knows it. He's a good player, and I need him. One day, I casually ask him if he ever bets on baseball. He tells me no. I believe him until I hear he also gambles on football, cricket, lacrosse, basketball, darts, bass fishing, and volleyball. I might be inclined to watch him a lot more closely and maybe get team security involved. Until my trust is broken, I may go along with it.

For the university athletic director, it all comes down to communication. If I have weekly scheduled meetings, procedures, and policies so that everyone understands my expectations and the rules of the university, then I am less likely to organize a fun-in-the-sun trip for my players.

The MLB scenario above is tougher. Players sometimes boss around coaches and managers, getting away with it because of their salaries and power. Still, if I were a manager and I knew a guy had a gambling problem, I would pull him aside and tell him that, if he's betting on baseball, the league is going to come down on him like a ton of bricks. I would also be obliged to tell my superiors that the player is betting on baseball. It's a matter of having rules and making them clearly defined and understood.

EVERYTHING IS CONNECTED TO EVERYTHING

The bigger problem with a case such as the Kean University scandal is that everything is connected to everything else, especially in a collegiate environment. In this scandal, athletes on athletic scholarships were tapping into the funds of needy students who had qualified for academic scholarships. To address this outrage, I need to go back to the justification of the coach in terms of one question: What's the greatest need of the university?

In an academic institution with an active athletic department, even for a Division III program, the need is always this: How do I attract the top athletes to my institution? What will it take? If the athletic scholarship only covers one-half of the costs of tuition, where will students get the other half? It then comes down to the institution raising the question of how much athletics contribute to the financial well-being of the institution. If I don't have the funds to acquire the top talent, what can I do to tap into another resource?

In this case, the story could have been a pretty easy one to make up. The justification might have been that many of the athletes came from disadvantaged financial backgrounds, and in the coach's mind, their need was greater. So, after the athletic scholarship money was used up, it was an easy reach to go after the academic hardship money.

I'm not saying I agree with this rationale because brilliant students who come from humble means must also be elevated. They shouldn't need to dribble a basketball or set a volleyball in order to get a scholarship. But it is entirely possible that the coach justified her actions in that fashion as the basketball players flew off to Spain.

From 2007 to 2011, no one at the highest levels of the university seemed to say anything when the percentage of athletes receiving scholarships doubled. Why would that have taken place?

A largely publicly funded university might find that public tax dollars or alumni contributions are dwindling. If that's the case, where does it make up the revenue? Athletics will certainly bear some of the weight of that revenue loss, at least indirectly. My apologies to those who hate sports, but alumni dollars usually don't come rushing into a school because the English department discovered a new Shakespeare play hidden in a dusty old book. The way dollars frequently come rushing into a school is through a scenario such as this: One crisp autumn day, a lowly Division II school (such as Appalachian State) is somehow able to beat a big-time Division I school (such as Michigan) in football. The media goes crazy! The Appalachian State student body and alumni go crazy! All of a sudden, the alumni dollars come rolling into the school, and there is a huge influx in enrollment. There is a clear relationship between the money that comes in through athletics and the money that's used to keep the institution alive.

From 2007 to 2011, why didn't anyone at Kean raise any questions? The simple answer: They didn't want to destroy the goose that laid the golden egg.

ETHICAL COUNSELING NEEDED!

Despite the money and promise a big-time basketball program holds, Kean University, or for that matter any other educational institution, has a more important consideration: the mission to educate.

Sports are important, but they are not more important than academics. Ethically, Kean's program was completely out of balance. Ethical counseling was needed, and, if I were called in, I would have definitely started at the administrative level. As for student-athletes, I think it's wonderful to teach them outstanding sports ethics skills. But students are not in a position to control those in higher authority. The ethical mindset needs to come from a higher level of authority first. Ideally, I would prefer to counsel all levels. But the real work must start at the top.

How much can we blame student-athletes for a program's ethical mindset? Coaches and recruiters often try to get student-athletes to believe the fantasy that if they come and play for a particular school, they'll hone their playing skills and become professional material. It is all well and good for athletes to have confidence in themselves, but, in 99% of cases, the fame and riches just won't materialize. These kids know that; they are not stupid. They know the score. Yet, even in this particular example, if the students realize a course is a sham, what are they going to do about it?

The cost of complaining is far too high, and no one likes a snitch. Student-athletes generally shut up to get by, even if they know they're getting a crap education — assuming they make it athletically for four or five years. It's far more reasonable to invite administrations and athletic departments to step up and lay down the ground rules for ethical behavior.

I have been asked if I'm surprised that this scandal happened at a Division III school and not a Division I school. No, I'm not. It is all about human behavior. It is like asking whether a mediocre basketball player who is unethical will be less likely to commit a sexual assault than an outstanding player who is also unethical. Bad ethics don't know school size or talent level.

The other question I am frequently asked is whether or not I find it unusual that a woman rather than a man was at the center of this controversy. After giving ethical training at many organizations and associations, both in the U.S. and overseas, I can say with assurance that I've seen no difference between the ethical behavior of men and women.

The reason you find more male examples in the sports world is because sports are currently more male-dominated. Men get more attention, but a need is a need. When a person's life gets so out of equilibrium, that person will do whatever it takes to put it back into balance. Male or female, we all want balance. If unethical coaches or athletic directors feel like all the other departments in the school are getting more attention, funding, or recognition, they might do something downright foolish or even illegal to bring things into balance.

Throughout the Kean scandal, Coach Sharp was largely benefitting herself. She had a need, and the need was fulfilled. While the scandal was rolling along, the chances of her getting caught were slim. Of course, it wasn't just the history of Spain course that got her into hot water. There were many other NCAA violations. It was not until the athletic director had enough of a suspicion to act that the whole train jumped the tracks. The coach's unethical behavior eventually had a huge negative impact on the school.

In this case, Sharp was able to achieve more international competition, higher GPAs for the athletes, and a bigger spotlight on her program. For a while, it succeeded, but then it all came crashing down.

CHAPTER 10

CLEM HASKINS, THE UNIVERSITY OF MINNESOTA AND BLIND AMBITION

Who: Coach Clem Haskins, Unethical Tutor, Numerous Athletes

Offense: Academic Cheating, Payoffs to Tutors and Athletes, Lying to Investigators,

Result: 7-year sanctions on Coach, end of Career

The Clem Haskins case is an example of the complexity of coaching, the possible pitfalls of university ambition, and the outcome of ill-defined ethics. Whether talking about Haskins' team practices or his coaching during games, former players molded under his tutelage speak highly of him. He was regarded as a tough taskmaster who got the most out of his players. His coaching ability was never in question.

Haskins was an outstanding high school and collegiate player who spent nine years in the NBA before becoming a coach at Western Kentucky, where he led the Hilltoppers to two 20-win seasons.

In 1986, Haskins stepped into the University of Minnesota program, arriving on the heels of numerous scandals at that school. Three Minnesota players had been accused of sexual assault, which led to the departure of the previous coach, even though the charges were later either reduced or dismissed. Haskins' reputation as a tough disciplinarian appealed to the university.

During the first years, Haskins coached at Minnesota, the team was abysmal. He had no choice but to build the team from the bottom up. Yet there was little in the way of controversy during those years.

In January 1991, the NCAA cited Haskins for a minor infraction, but the university fought it, saying it was covered during investigations that took place in the late 1980s. In February 1991, Haskins was reprimanded for his criticism of Big 10 officiating, but he received no penalties. Coaches often criticize officials, and it was easy to understand Haskins' ire. Perhaps some of it had been carried over from the 1989-1990 season when the program had a winning season in the Big 10 but did not receive an invitation to the NCAA tournament. Maybe that disrespect helped Haskins to really push the program.

Meanwhile, the team was really responding to Haskins' skills as a coach. With each season, the team steadily improved. The Gophers played so well that, by the 1996-1997 season, the team made an appearance in the Final Four. Haskins was named Coach of the Year in 1997 by The Associated Press.

On March 28, 1997, Los Angeles Times reporter Tim Kawakami wrote that Haskins, as he was preparing for the 1997 NCAA tournament, had said, "I have strong beliefs, very strong beliefs .... My philosophies have gotten me into trouble throughout the years, but that's fine, I'll take it because I will not waver from what I stand for or what I say or do in order to please anybody else."

The magic turnaround of this once-terrible team might have continued had a former tutor by the name of Jan Gangelhoff not stepped forward in March 1999. Gangelhoff told university executives that between 1993 and 1998, she had personally written more than 400 papers for as many as twenty basketball players.

The students were not doing their own work. Gangelhoff was not a freelance tutor or writer either; she worked for the university as the office manager for its academic counseling unit.

Haskins denied everything. Nevertheless, the university began to discuss a buyout of the coach. According to an article appearing on June 11, 1999, in the Los Angeles Times newspaper, "McKinley Boston, vice president of athletic and student affairs, signed Haskins' ten-year contract in 1994 when he was the men's athletic director. It includes an unusual clause that allows Haskins to receive $423,000 in deferred compensation even if his contract is terminated with just cause. If 'just cause' could not be shown, Haskins would be entitled to almost $1.2 million, plus benefits."

Upon further investigation, it was revealed on June 12, 1999, that Gangelhoff had been rewarded with a nine-day trip to Hawaii in 1995 in return not only for writing athletes' papers but also for doing their coursework beginning in the 1993 academic year. The investigation found a personal check Haskins wrote to a travel agency on behalf of Gangelhoff and one of her coworkers.

On June 26, 1999, Haskins agreed to a buyout totaling $1.5 million, even though investigators at the university found nothing directly linking him to the academic fraud. Nevertheless, university President Mark Yudof said it was very likely that fraud did occur. It would not be until November 20, 1999, that the AP would break the story of a 1,000-page report based on an in-depth investigation of Haskins.

The report revealed that Haskins had lied to investigators. It indicated that he knew of the academic fraud and that he also told his players to lie. These revelations spurred Boston and men's athletic director Mark Dienhart to resign. The academic counseling department and other faculty members were also implicated for their failure to recognize what was happening.

In addition, the AP piece stated: "The investigation also found that Haskins gave up to $200 in cash directly to three athletes and that he arranged a standing hotel discount for parents of athletes even though he had been cited by the NCAA for a similar violation at Western Kentucky ... [University President] Yudof said the team competed with one or more ineligible players in the last five seasons ..."

In a secret NCAA investigation conducted in August 2000, Haskins admitted he paid the former tutor $3,000, but he wouldn't acknowledge that the program had suffered from academic fraud.

Then on September 12, 2000, the University of Minnesota sued Haskins to recover part of the $1.5 million buyout, now contending that he lied about his student-athletes' cheating. Despite Haskins' repeated denials, on January 27, 2001, a judge ruled that the Haskins case could move forward. Almost a year later, it was ruled through arbitration that Haskins had to return $815,000 of the $1.5 million. University officials finally decided that they would have had trouble proving to a jury that Haskins had known academic fraud was occurring.

Haskins intimated that he wanted to be reinstated and allowed to coach. The NCAA said it would place sanctions on him such that he would not be able to coach for seven years. The stigma attached to Haskins during that time would pretty much assure no other program would touch him, and he never coached again.

CHUCK'S ETHICS REVIEW:

It's Not About What You Learn, It's That You Learn to Win

It is hard to blame the athletes in the University of Minnesota cheating scandal. The unethical actions were carried out by the head coach and other school officials around him. Maybe the young men believed that, if they followed the coach to the letter, it would have resulted in an NBA meal ticket. Such an unrealistic outcome almost never happens, though. The odds against it are astronomical. Instead, the coach likely saw this opportunity as just another stepping stone to personal success, while the athletes were apparently expendable.

As hard as it is to understand Haskins' actions, such as academic cheating, the behavior of the woman who worked as the office manager for the university's academic counseling unit is even more puzzling. This was the person who wrote papers and did coursework for the athletes. We see people like her, seemingly on the sidelines and holding little power, throughout the tapestry woven by many of these scandals.

In this administrator's case, there was something emotional or psychological she stood to gain that caused her to knowingly choose to do something wrong. How did she justify doing the academic work for the kids? There are several possible rationalizations. Perhaps she thought it was expected of her. Perhaps she was afraid she'd lose her job if she didn't do it. Or perhaps she felt it would elevate her in the eyes of superiors and ensure her long-term job stability. Her overriding mindset might have been: "If I'm a conspirator or co-conspirator or deliverer, and I'm doing it at the behest of the coach or the athletic department, I'm probably pretty secure in my job." But she may have also felt bitter about it, a feeling that may have come from a deep-seated realization that her behavior was wrong. It's reverse psychology that says, "If I go down, everybody goes down."

Now, we can ask if the trip to Hawaii she was given was enough of an incentive for her to do something wrong. No, it likely wasn't. Logically, it is unlikely someone would do something so unethical for seven years merely for a single trip to Hawaii, no matter how tempting the climate and beaches may be.

We can think of the trip like the sprinkles on the icing of a cupcake — something sweet that is added on after the fact. Maybe the guilt caught up to her, and she could no longer justify her behavior. She began to get cold feet. Maybe she went to the coach with her concerns, and maybe he said, "That's a shame. I just got tickets to Hawaii." All of a sudden, there was a short-term reward, one that enabled her to rationalize the activity and continue to do it. For a time, it stabilized the situation, but she was compromised.

THE WALL

It appears as though the Minnesota basketball team had put up an impenetrable wall around itself and the rest of the athletic department. It's not so difficult to see how that can happen. It's not right, no more than is the marketing or manufacturing department of a technology company finding ways to isolate itself from the CEO, but it can happen. This isolation almost always leads to major ethical problems.

If you are among your university's leadership, you want your school to be positively recognized. Any school would want that. You do not want to be seen as a loser school rife with scandal. So, you bring in a new coach to clean up the program.

The Minnesota basketball team was a woeful loser when coach Haskins arrived. In his first years at Minnesota, the team was abysmal. Then, Haskins started to turn the program around. He was a tough disciplinarian and got everything ship-shape. He had a lot of support and did whatever it took to win. The university responded to that.

Before Gangelhoff sounded the alarm, the basketball team that had been awful and riddled with challenges was climbing back into the sunlight. Remarkably, they made it all the way to the Final Four in the 1997 NCAA Tournament. Haskins was named AP Coach of the Year, and the program was firing on all cylinders.

Now, if you are among the university leaders, how much do you want to rock that boat? Not much. Even if you suspect something may be amiss, you do not want to quell the program's ongoing success. You were a loser, and now you're a winner. It feels damn good to win. You like the positive image and the publicity you get from that, and who wouldn't? Remember when Jim Valvano took a mediocre Cinderella team, North Carolina State, to national prominence? It was an amazing time. I'm not comparing Valvano to Haskins, as each case is radically different, but the excitement around a poor or mediocre team making it to national prominence is amazing; it's a drug. You crave the positives. Positives bring money, recognition, and all that goes along with it.

Haskins' actions were fine for a couple of years, but then he began to play it loose, just like he'd done at his previous coaching job. Gangelhoff received the vacation bribe in 1995, but it took her a couple of years to get religion, as they say. By 1997, the team's success was unmistakable, and it might have kept it going had it not been for the whistle-blower and her conscience.

There is, of course, a price to pay for unethical behavior, because every choice has a consequence. The scandal forced the resignation of the athletic director and vice president of athletic and student affairs. Had they not resigned, they likely would have been fired. The reality is that, under the leadership of those individuals, there was an ongoing, unethical, and inappropriate academic scam they failed to detect. Perhaps it's not fair to assume you can catch every cheater, but a systemic problem occurring within an athletic department that goes unnoticed for that long demonstrates that someone was asleep at the wheel.

NO SECOND CHANCE

While I believe in second chances, I cannot justify it in this case. No, not after Haskins had told his players to lie, bribed them, and gotten them cheap hotel rooms — not to mention all of the years of academic fraud committed with his full knowledge. Let's not forget that, after what had happened at Western Kentucky, Haskins had already had his second chance.

Haskins adopted a similar mode of operation at Minnesota. He proved that, given the opportunity, he would support fraud and deception as a means to an end rather than promote a solid foundation of academic and athletic excellence. If you're given a second chance, most of the time, there isn't a third.

There can be no mistaking the ethical message Haskins sent to his players: whatever it takes to win, that's what has to be done. Unfortunately and all too often, many young people, whether athletes or not, are taught that, if you're going to win, you've got to cheat, and that it is OK to do it.

The coach was "teaching" rationalization. In his mind, if your need is strong enough and if you have the opportunity to cheat, then that is just fine. Of course, the problem with rationalization is that it is fool's gold. Ultimately, you don't win. Your college degree becomes worthless, you do not get an education, and your credentials are without merit. When these graduates eventually try to compete in the marketplace, their inferior education becomes all too evident.

Amazingly, Haskins was given a buyout. Had I been in a leadership position at Minnesota, I would have fought against it. He should not have been awarded anything. For all I know, the university leaders might have based their final decision on the fact that they were embarrassed enough already and that it was better to shut everyone up than to drag it out in the courts.

SECTION III
THE CONSPIRACIES

CHAPTER 11

THE WINTER OLYMPICS VOTE-TRADING SCANDAL

Who: French Skating Federation, Judges Marie-Reine Le Gougne and Didier Gailhaguet

Offense: Vote Trading

Result: Suspension from International Skating Union and Judging

Although many of us naively cling to the notion that the Olympics maintain the highest standards of ethical sports conduct, that illusion has been badly shattered in recent years. In fact, the Olympics have gone from purely amateur to a mix of professionals and amateurs. Still, bad ethics are bad ethics. Take, for example, the 2002 Salt Lake City Winter Olympics and the infamous vote-trading scandal.

The complex scoring system in Olympics pairs skating affected two skating pairs in particular in 2002: Elena Berezhnaya and Anton Sikharulidze of Russia, and Jamie Salé and David Pelletier of Canada.

The short version of the story is that, during competition, the Canadian pair had what many believed to be a near-perfect performance, while the performance of the Russian pair showed some very minor problems. However, when the results were tabulated, the Russians won the gold, and the Canadians were deemed second-best. Naturally, there were many who claimed the judging was fixed, but that's to be expected in close competition. We all feel our favorites should win.

Given the subjective nature of judging, the objections might have simply faded into sports history. In fact, this scandal might never have surfaced at all were it not for a confrontation in a hotel lobby following the competition. French skating judge Marie-Reine Le Gougne was approached by Sally Stapleford, the head of the judging committee. Stapleford did not mince her words, demanding to know why the French judge voted the way she did.

There and then, Le Gougne admitted to voting for the Russians under pressure from the French skating federation, pressure specifically applied by Didier Gailhaguet, then-president of the French Federation of Ice Sports. Le Gougne's was not a calm and quiet admission either but an emotional outburst.

Multiple reports, including an ESPN.com article dated February 18, 2002, described Le Gougne's admission: "American attorney Jon Jackson, an [International Skating Union] championship judge, witnessed Le Gougne's outburst, along with Stapleford and two other technical committee members, Walburga Grimm of Germany and Britta Lindgren of Sweden."

Interestingly, Le Gougne would later deny making that statement. However, Jon Jackson was quoted in the same article as saying, "The French judge's characterization of what happened [that she never admitted to being under pressure] is inaccurate. Her admission was unsolicited, unequivocal and clear. There's no question about it. It was witnessed by at least four parties."

THE SCANDAL BLEW UP.

Before the damage got out of control, the International Olympic Committee moved to award the Canadian pair a gold medal along with the Russian pair. Though perhaps a halfhearted solution, it may have been the best solution possible to avoid an international controversy.

In the same hotel where the confrontation initially took place, Olympics officials gathered to question both the French judge and her director. Le Gougne immediately denied she was pressured to vote the way she did. "I judged in my soul and conscience," Le Gougne later said in an interview for L'Equipe magazine. "I considered that the Russians were the best. I never made a deal with an official or a Russian judge."

Le Gougne also stated that she felt physically threatened when she was approached in the lobby, a charge universally denied. Gailhaguet denied he had influenced the judge to vote for the Russians, but his denials fell on deaf ears. Katsuichiro Hisanaga, then the head of the Japan Skating Federation, was quoted as saying, "As far I know, it is not the first time for Didier to make such pressure. There were other cases in the past."

Hisanaga's comment caused Gailhaguet to fire back at the Japanese official. "Very honestly," he is quoted as saying, "if there is someone at the table of the council who had better shut up, I think it is Mr. Hisanaga. Because Mr. Hisanaga, since he has been vice president of the ISU, has brought about no reform whatsoever, no single positive point for the ISU. Overall, the competence of Mr. Hisanaga is left wanting."

Interestingly, French National Olympic Committee President Henri Serandour did not back Gailhaguet as strongly as might be expected.

"For the moment, I have not taken a decision. I am looking at how things develop. What could make me change my mind is the news," he said.

The hearing initially involved Gailhaguet — and not Le Gougne — meeting with the International Skating Union committee. Ultimately, in a special session, Le Gougne did meet with the committee and now admitted she was pressured to vote for the Russians.

Ottavio Cinquanta, then president of the ISU, said, "We punished her because she admitted having done this. If Mr. Gailhaguet or another one would admit a mistake, we will also punish him."

But why would this pressure have existed in the first place?

The voting pressure likely involved the Russians swinging their votes to the ice dance couple from France in a sort of quid pro quo. It would have been a swap and, in the eyes of the French and Russians, a win/win. The chairman of the ice dance committee, Russia's Alexandr Gorshkov, said he knew of no such vote swap. Nevertheless, rumors of bribery continued long after the incident.

A New York Times article from August 1, 2002, titled "U.S. Alleges Olympic Skating Bribery," reported: "Alimzhan Tokhtakhounov, described as a major figure in the Russian mafia, was taken into custody near his resort home—the dramatic allegations unveiled by U.S. Atty. James Comey suggest that Tokhtakhounov offered bribes to French skating officials and conspired to have French and Russian skating judges award each other's teams gold medals in separate skating competitions. He did this, the complaint alleged, to curry favor with French Skating Federation officials in the hope of winning an extension for his expiring French visa."

In the aftermath of the scandal, both Marie-Reine Le Gougne and Didier Gailhaguet were suspended from the ISU and were barred from participation as judges in the 2006 Olympics. In addition, the figure skating point system and judging guidelines have been changed since that time.

Ironically, at the 2014 Olympics in Sochi, Russia, rumors of another scandal emerged. An ethical flaw may still have been in play.

CHUCK'S ETHICS REVIEW:

I'll Scratch Your Back, If You'll Scratch Mine!

The tagline to my scandal headline could be: "Not that back-scratching is wrong, but unethical backroom deals most certainly are!" In the case of the 2002 Winter Olympics vote-trading scandal, it was all about the backroom deals. The deals were dirty and had nothing to do with what we picture as the Olympic ideal.

Are all Olympic judges on the take? I would say that the majority are not, but these judges certainly were. Just as a side note, regarding the word "judge," when you are charged with a crime, you are judged by a jury of your peers. In a capital case, the defense attorneys understand that it takes only one juror who disagrees with the prosecution to win. So, the entire group of skating judges, in this case, did not have to agree to declare a winner. It took only one or two judges to swing points, and that is what happened here. They played a cheating game and won.

It is far too easy to say this scandal was just about the money. Yes, you can always appeal to a crooked judge with enough money, but in this case, it was much more than that. If a judge from one country can assure the judge from another country of winning one competition in exchange for a win in another competition, then both countries win. It's a quid pro quo agreement. It doesn't make it an ethical argument, just a justification for bad behavior where all of the athletes ultimately lose.

With national pride at stake, winning a gold medal is a pretty big deal. At the Olympic level, where every skater is excellent, we are talking about fractions of points separating one medalist from another. Unless a skater does a face-plant or is downright awful, the outcome might be contested. But the voting usually seems fair to most casual observers, or at least within the realm of the acceptable for something so subjective. The judges can make subtle changes to their voting, and, aside from raising the interest of a handful of experts, the outcome will go unnoticed and be quickly forgotten.

If judging becomes unethical, the competition becomes an insider's game, the result of bribe money with prearranged medals. The athletes, the governments, and the millions of fans who support the Olympic ideal are made into fools. This is a prime example of unethical behavior at its worst. It may not be violent, but it turns a centuries-old ideal into a joke.

TAKING THE FALL FOR FOOLS

Though hardly innocent, French judge Marie-Reine Le Gougne took the fall for others because she admitted her guilt outright. Didier Gailhaguet, then president of the French Federation of Ice Sports, was initially excused from questioning because he did not admit he had pressured Le Gougne to vote a certain way. Only later did his guilt become apparent.

Le Gougne's actions are a clear example of what happens when we admit guilt. The consequences become quickly clear and unquestionable. If we are unwilling to admit guilt, then dealing with the consequences becomes a much longer process. In this case, even though he did not admit his guilt, Gailhaguet was still associated with the scandal almost from the outset. He initially avoided the direct implications of guilt because of Le Gougne's honesty, but he would pay the price later on.

Ultimately Gailhaguet's behavior was the most despicable because he threw everyone under the Olympic bus. Does this make Le Gougne innocent? Of course not. Once we head down an unethical path, we all share in any consequences that may come our way. But the consequences can become more complex and long-lasting when we insist on denying responsibility for our actions.

Adding to this mess was a shadowy figure with links to organized crime who was apparently guilty of offering bribes. You may ask how a person like this can get close enough to an association to be able to bribe judges. The answer is much simpler than you might imagine. Money attracts money, and power attracts power. Money can create power. This is a broader issue in construct. If you come into contact with a certain amount of money, then you have more access to power.

In this case, the money was coupled with the fact that the mobster wanted to extend his French visa to enable him to freely travel back and forth between France and Russia. He used his money to buy influence. He really didn't care about the outcome of the Olympics or which country won or lost. He was more concerned with his visa. He cared about the fact that, if he could arrange to give the French what they wanted, he could get his needs met.

FOLDING TO INFLUENCE

If we go back and dissect the bad ethics in play here, and how this scandal occurred, we find that the French judge had succumbed to pressure in the past. Why hadn't anyone noticed this pattern before? Quite possibly, no one wanted to know this was going on — a collective burying of heads in the sand. We want to believe there are no backroom deals taking place because we like to think of sports as being pure. We trust that officials' decisions, especially judging, are functions of that purity.

Discovering patterns of unethical behavior in an organized sport requires either someone who is totally impartial or someone who believes sports aren't pure and that there are people who voluntarily do improper things to influence competition. This is pretty strong stuff. It's human nature to want to believe in the Olympic ideal.

I am not at all surprised that a similar skating controversy occurred at the 2014 Sochi Winter Olympics in Russia. What is happening? The unfortunate thing is that the Olympics are all about national pride. For an athlete, you think you are going to be judged on your skill, prowess, and ability to perform. While that's certainly a part of the Olympic experience in a great many events, when it comes to competitions that are more subjective where judging is involved, such as figure skating or diving, there's a greater possibility of irregularities occurring that affect the outcomes.

Maybe we need to face some facts and admit that, as hard as we may try, we will never be able to totally eliminate undue influence. We will never be able to keep certain people from trying to peddle that influence. I hate to be the bearer of bad news, but I think there's a fairly high probability that, as these vote-swapping scandals have happened in the past, they'll happen again and again unless there is a radical overhaul of the judging systems. It's sad the Olympics have descended to this level.

Even though the IOC has had many years to fix the problem of judging in ice skating, it appears certain judges, were they so inclined, could still find ways to work around it. Maybe in the future human judges will be left completely out of sports like diving or skating. Maybe some type of objective computer program can be employed that watches athletic performances and judges them using standardized algorithms.

For now, we need to be vigilant in judging irregularities, bringing to light those patterns when they occur. We also need to trust that most judges are purists and are not looking to produce unfair outcomes. It ultimately comes down to promoting good ethics that encourage athletes to resist outside influences. Unless ethical training is enforced, and consequences are immediate and harsh, the playing field — or rink — will never be quite level.

Ultimately, What Is This IOC Scandal About?

This case is shallow on one level and yet very complex on another. On the surface, the Russians were saying to the French, "You vote for us, we'll vote for you." The two countries simply swapped votes and influence. Also in play was the basic greed of a Russian mafioso, who bribed officials to get what he wanted. In terms of deeper complexity, with all the accusations and cross-accusations, it would appear that just about everyone was, or had been, on the take. At root, this scandal is about an opportunity caused by the absence of ethics and a failure of the system to install controls. It's a long-term, ingrained breakdown in processes.

What do we say to an aspiring figure skater or to his or her parents who now feel that all their hard work and sacrifice won't make a difference? How can they justify working so hard to compete if the fix will always be in? Well, we need to reassure them that what happened in Salt Lake City in 2002 isn't necessarily the norm. We need to tell them not to worry about the bad ethics and ill intentions of a few others. "Try as hard as you can," we need to say. "If you're a good person with a good heart, no matter what happens to you, you can get back up. There will be second chances." We should not let our cynicism ever erase what is noble.

When judges act with bad intentions and are found out, they will always damage their reputations. In the overall scheme of things, does a damaged reputation mean anything?

It means everything.

CHAPTER 12

THE SALT LAKE CITY IOC SCANDAL

Who: International Olympic Committee

Offense: Olympic Bribery, Slush Funds, Payoffs

Result: Numerous Expulsions Due to Corruption

Sports ethics scandals sometimes bubble up at levels much higher than individual athletes, coaches or even athletic programs. They can exist between agencies, governments, and even international sports organizations. Yet, the lessons to be learned from studying bad choices on the part of huge organizations can be translated to our own communities, businesses, teams, and personal lives.

In 1991, Salt Lake City lost its bid to host the 1998 Winter Olympics. Nagano, Japan, won the bid by just four votes. The loss of the Olympics cut deeply into the consciousness of the entire U.S. Mountain States region. The Olympics, of course, produce major economic benefits, not only in terms of lodging and tourism during the competition but also in bringing government funding for roadways, transportation, and infrastructure.

Early in January 1992, officials of the Salt Lake City Olympic bid committee decided on a different kind of strategy to get the 2002 event to their home state. They created what they would label the "scholarship fund" to help favorably influence the thinking of the International Olympic Committee as they made their site selections.

The Salt Lake City bid committee was seemingly quiet until August 1993; its officials began contributing to a "scholarship" for the daughter of an IOC member, paying money toward her college tuition, rent, and expenses. The young woman's name was Sonia Essomba, who was then attending American University in Washington, D.C.

In 1995, Salt Lake City finally won the bid to host the 2002 Winter Olympics. This was after four previous attempts at trying to win the bid for this Utah venue. It was later learned that, in their effort to secure the bid, Salt Lake Olympic officials gave IOC members free credit cards when they visited the city and spent nearly $20,000 to take three IOC couples to the 1995 Super Bowl.

In addition to many other bribes, the officials provided a so-called loan of $30,000 to an IOC member to help a friend of that member who had a financial need and also paid for the plastic surgery of another IOC colleague.

In 1996, David Johnson, a top official of the Salt Lake Organizing Committee, drafted a letter on committee stationery. Johnson was second in command on the committee. He said to Essomba, "It will be difficult to continue the scholarship program with you. There is a check enclosed for $10,114.99, and it will have to be our last payment for tuition." When all was said and done, Essomba had received a total of $108,350 from the SLOC scholarship fund.

The entire arrangement with Essomba was kept quiet until November 25, 1998, when the Salt Lake City media reported that Olympic boosters had paid thousands of dollars in scholarships for family members of IOC officials, including Essomba. This was all done, they reported, during the proposal process for the 2002 bid.

Chris Vanocur, who worked at Salt Lake City's KTVX-TV, an ABC affiliate, broke the story after he received a copy of the 1996 letter to Essomba. As a result of media investigative reporting, on December 8, 1998, Salt Lake City Olympic bid committee officials admitted that six relatives of IOC members benefited from a $500,000 fund for "humanitarian assistance," but the committee denied any bribery charges.

The findings immediately triggered an investigation by IOC President Juan Antonio Samaranch. Allegations included payments and scholarships to IOC members and their families by the Salt Lake City group.

In one sense, the investigation had the opposite effect of what many anticipated. In addition to drilling down into Salt Lake City's transgressions, the investigation also expanded. On December 12, 1998, a senior IOC official widened the scandal, alleging IOC members had demanded bribes of up to $1 million from cities bidding to host the Olympic Games. Top IOC official Marc Hodler supported this statement, stating that corruption and vote buying were widespread, but he denied it had happened in Salt Lake City.

On December 14, 1998, the IOC investigation revealed that China may have been the latest casualty in the bidding and bribery war, as sports officials said Beijing may have lost the right to host the 2000 Olympics because of the unfair treatment it received during the bidding process. Shortly after, Samaranch announced he wanted an overhaul of bidding procedures. This would include taking votes away from all 115 members and banning candidate city visits.

On December 22, 1998, the U.S. Olympic Committee appointed a special commission to investigate alleged improprieties in the selection of Salt Lake City for the 2002 Olympics. A week later, U.S. authorities, the Salt Lake City ethics commission, and the IOC Commission each opened their own investigations.

Almost at once, the investigations began to turn up startling facts. For example, on January 7, 1999, it was revealed that Jean-Claude Ganga, a Congo IOC member, earned a $60,000 profit from a Utah-based land deal arranged through a member of the Salt Lake City bid committee. This information prompted the resignation of Salt Lake City Organizing Committee President Frank Joklik and his second-in-command, David Johnson.

On January 14, 1999, a very contrite Samaranch told the Associated Press that thirteen IOC members had been implicated and charged with corruption allegations. Nine risked expulsions. This revelation pushed Japan back into the spotlight. The Japanese media determined that a Nagano bid committee spent an average of $22,000 per member on each of sixty-two visiting IOC members, violating IOC spending limits. Conveniently, the accounting records had been secretly destroyed.

The Nagano allegations were followed on January 19, 1999, by the resignation of Finland's Pirjo Haeggman, the first IOC member to resign. Haeggman's resignation came on the heels of accusations that her husband had briefly worked for the Salt Lake City bid committee as well as a company associated with the Toronto Olympic bid. Then, on January 21, IOC chief investigator Richard Pound disclosed that Salt Lake City bidders had paid out fixed-figure cash gifts to some of the IOC members, although he reported no evidence of actual criminal behavior.

Libya's IOC member, Bashir Mohamed Attarabulsi, resigned two days later after investigators discovered that Salt Lake City Olympic boosters had given his son college scholarships to Utah schools.

Amazingly, the scandal then spread to Sydney, where an Australian official admitted he had offered $70,000 in inducements to IOC members on the night before the 2000 Olympic Games had been awarded. These inducements included bribes to representatives from Kenya and Uganda, made in an effort to help Sydney win the 2000 Games.

On January 23, 1999, senior IOC officials questioned 13 members allegedly involved in the corruption scandal. By the next day, the IOC executive committee was considering a large overhaul of bidding procedures and dismissing IOC members following the release of its investigative report. Two days later, on January 25, six IOC members faced expulsion after a review of corruption allegations for Salt Lake City's bid.

Here's where the case took an unexpected twist. On January 30, 1999, allegations surfaced that the IOC had ignored corruption claims made by Canadian officials eight years earlier. Predictably, this revelation caused the spotlight to shine on IOC President Samaranch, who faced criticism from European ministers and the U.S. over the bribery allegations for the 2002 Games.

The scandal soon became a runaway train. Nagano returned to the news once again when a possible new scandal materialized. A Japanese newspaper reported that more than $6 million had been spent entertaining Olympic officials during the bid to host Nagano's Winter Games. Following more investigation, on February 10, 1999, the IOC warned it was considering the removal of more members after releasing an ethics panel report looking into the Salt Lake City scandal. Meanwhile, the IOC continued to investigate the Salt Lake City 2002 and Sydney 2000 scandals.

On February 11, 1999, a new chief executive of the Salt Lake City Olympic Committee, Mitt Romney, was assigned to oversee the city's preparations for the 2002 Winter Olympics. Organizers set out new policy for openness and accountability.

On March 1, 1999, a U.S. Olympic Committee report asserted that, in the wake of the Salt Lake City corruption scandal, the IOC should undergo a thorough reform "at all levels." Continued investigation into Sydney's Olympic bid showed that there was no pattern of corruption but that several rules had been broken.

On July 20, 2000, after rejecting plea deals, the two chief organizers of Salt Lake City's bid to win the 2002 Winter Olympics, Thomas K. Welch, the former president of the Salt Lake City bid committee, and David Johnson, were indicted.

Since the Salt Lake City corruption case came to light, it has been revealed that similar bidding practices occurred for

Atlanta's 1996 Summer Olympics, Nagano's 1998 Winter Games and Sydney's 2000 Summer Olympics. In all, about 30 IOC delegates were linked to bidding improprieties.

With Romney at the helm as CEO, the Salt Lake City Olympic Committee brought in tens of millions in profits, thanks in large part to $342 million in federal funding, and despite a $379 million shortage at the start of Romney's leadership. Some have said the profits came from Romney's efforts; others have disagreed. The monies did allow the city to follow through on an earlier promise to create a $40 million endowment fund to be used for maintaining facilities built for the Salt Lake City Games going forward.

When delving into the Salt Lake City Olympic scandal, it's easy to allow discussion of Romney's participation to spiral into partisan politics. This case, however, isn't about Romney. It's about a sports ethics scandal that should never have been allowed to fester in amateur sports.

CHUCK'S ETHICS REVIEW:

Pay to Play! What's Done in the Dark Always Comes to Light!

If there was ever a doubt as to the power of unethical behavior to infiltrate any organization, it was erased with the 2002 Winter Olympics. The deeper this scandal went, the more it seemed as though virtually everyone at the IOC who was connected with the 2002 Winter Olympics was on the take. It is important to understand how something like this can happen to an organization because, if we're not careful, it can happen to our own athletic association or conference or business as well. Whether it is the IOC, SEC, FIFA, or NCAA, the culture of an organization dictates the systems they put in place. Let me explain what that means by talking about a parallel example: traffic safety.

If the culture of a U.S. state, for example, is to keep the interstate highway system as safe as possible, the state might put guide wires or a barrier across the center median to safeguard drivers who may fall asleep while driving. There's a system in place. Different states have different safety systems, but they're all designed to protect drivers.

Suppose a state had no highway safety systems in place. No guide wires, no warning strips on the shoulders, and no reflectors. Without safety systems, there could be mayhem on the roads.

The same can hold true in sports or the compliance of a publicly-traded company. The culture of an organization creates systems for safety or fair competition. If an organization fosters a culture where it is OK to say, "Is that the best you can do? How about upping your offer?" it is not likely to put many systems in place to encourage people to bid in an ethical manner.

In this case, the organization we're talking about is the IOC! There is a great deal of prestige associated with hosting events. But if the culture dictates that bribes are to be expected, even if everyone knows it should be illegal, then clearly systems of fairness are not in place. And don't be deceived into believing that a sophisticated, international governing sports body is necessarily ethical and aboveboard, while a local, smaller divisional conference may be unsophisticated and prone to bad ethics. When it comes to ethics controls and unethical behavior, it's case by case.

It is now impossible not to be suspicious of how the cities for every Winter and Summer Olympics in recent history have been awarded. There has just been too much money involved and not enough barriers to prevent cheating. I would go as far as to say that there have been business opportunities and connections larger than the award itself that we have never even heard about.

The acts of bribery IOC officials engaged in can have broader implications, even if the bribes didn't result in a winning bid. For example, if I offered someone a bribe to influence their vote and still lost to another city, the connections I made through the bribe may yet reap benefits far down the road. It's fairly safe to say that when a city is awarded an Olympic Games, the IOC and other officials reveal very little to the public about the actual selection process, facts lost amidst all of the celebrations. I'm interested in how Olympic bribes can be used to influence business relations that have little to do with the Olympics, behind-the-scenes deals seen as the cost of doing business in order to gain a lot of business. Who knows the ultimate rewards to those who bribed officials at multiple Olympics?

THE HYPOCRISY OF BAD ETHICS

Here is the challenge we have as a country: the hypocrisy of bad ethics. Were we doing anything differently than what other countries were likely doing all along? Olympic officials in Salt Lake City may have been doing a little bit less in terms of doling out bribe money from the half-million-dollar slush fund, but so what? Whether a bribe is $100 or $10,000, it's still a bribe. As a country that values truth and integrity, should we really be saying that, since everyone else is cheating, why shouldn't we? Should we not be standing up for higher principles and refusing to play the game?

Bribery is not measured on a sliding scale. Either you refuse to play the game or you play it. If officials in the U.S. had flat out refused to play the bribery game with respect to Olympic bidding, and the IOC was constantly awarding other countries the winning bids, sooner or later people would begin asking why the U.S. was being excluded. Public pressure would have come to bear on the IOC.

SO, WHO CARES? YOU SHOULD.

I know some will argue, "Who cares? Salt Lake City received a huge infusion of federal funds and rebuilt roadways, bridges, and other infrastructure." I would venture to say most cities that have had major international exposure received benefits long after the event was gone. Many would argue it was worth the outcome in spite of the black eye.

The black eye, however, never really goes away. Long after it occurred, the Salt Lake City IOC scandal continues to be discussed and analyzed, casting doubt on the fairness of

Olympic bidding even now. I doubt many people are driving over those roads today worrying about where they came from. Nevertheless, our own citizens paid out bribes that should never have been paid to people who never should have been placed in positions of authority.

THE OLYMPIC IDEAL

No matter the event or organization, the challenge is to allow competition to be fair. In the United States we seem to be a bit hypocritical. Some thought it okay to offer bribes and scholarships in Salt Lake City, but when a U.S. city didn't win the bid, they stood on an ethical Mt. Rushmore and yelled, "This is wrong! This is corrupt!"

Regardless of the outcome, participating in corruption is only going to exacerbate the existing problem. Personally, I think it's wrong for us to criticize the world for not acting ethically when we have turned a blind eye toward sports ethics here at home.

CHAPTER 13

ALAN EAGLESON AND THE NHL PLAYERS SCANDAL

Who: Hockey Sports Agent Robert Alan Eagleson

Offense: Fraud

Result: Imprisonment, Fines

Robert Alan Eagleson occupies a unique place in our sports scandals review, being the only person to have faced the prospect of potential imprisonment in two countries: Canada and the United States.

In the beginning months of 1998, Eagleson elected to be jailed in Canada and would be fined $1 million in Canadian dollars. He served only six months in a medium-security prison.

Born in Ontario, Canada, on April 24, 1933, Eagleson loved both hockey and the law. He studied law at the University of Toronto and began to see where there might be opportunities for him to direct his efforts as a promoter and agent. He did what many sports promoters might do and started networking in sports, specifically in the world of professional hockey. He soon cultivated some influential friends.

Eagleson came to realize that, although the 1959 version of the National Hockey League Players Association had failed, there might be a better chance in 1967. For one thing, in 1959, there were only the six original teams. By the 1966-1967 season, the league had undergone a major expansion to twelve franchises. With that many teams, the NHL could no longer be a good ole boys' club. Much more was at stake. Importantly for Eagleson, the league expansion also opened up possibilities for sports agents.

At the beginning of his career as an agent, Eagleson fought on behalf of a player against the owner of another hockey team, and he helped another player get his amateur status reinstated. He had higher aspirations, however, than just doing good deeds. He wanted power and status — and the money that went along with it.

Before we get into the many scandals that surrounded Eagleson, it should be noted that he did make contributions to the sport of hockey. The "Summit Series" he created in 1972, pitting the Soviet Union against Canada, still stands as perhaps the greatest hockey tournament ever held. Despite organizing the Summit Series, Eagleson's behavior doesn't come close to balancing the scales, especially once he got his hands on the league.

As an agent, the very first player Eagleson was able to get under contract was none other than the great Bobby Orr of the Boston Bruins. In 1975, when Orr's contract was up for renewal, Eagleson played Orr against both the Bruins and the Chicago Blackhawks. Boston made Orr a fantastic offer, which included a significant ownership stake in the team. But Eagleson hid the offer from Orr, who signed with the Blackhawks, though bad knees restricted his playing time in Chicago.

The bitter feud between the Bruins and Eagleson helped cut Orr's career short, though the facts would not come out until many years later. If all that were not bad enough, Eagleson mismanaged Orr's finances so badly that Orr was bankrupt by 1980.

Before those kinds of stories surfaced, however, Eagleson's popularity as an agent was sky-high. He turned his attention to the resurrection of the NHLPA. To make his plan work, he solicited the help of former NHL player Bob Pulford, along with executives he knew from the Toronto Maple Leafs and some prominent business people. Eagleson became the first executive director of the NHLPA.

The NHLPA, and by proxy Eagleson, promised to give the players what they had long sought: pensions and insurance plans to cover injuries. By the end of the 1970s, Eagleson was arguably the most powerful man in hockey. He represented nearly twenty players and was president of the Players association.

But Eagleson's rise to power was also causing concerns. There were more than a few suspicions that the tournaments he had been promoting were lining his pockets and not benefiting the NHLPA.

In 1989, two of a newer generation of player agents, Ritch Winter and Ron Salcer, tried to crack Eagleson's grip on the league, writing a bitter critique against him. They claimed that, as president of the players association, he was not giving other agents access to the players, the league, or even to basic support. They also claimed he was not reporting his expenses, such as travel, and that he was skimming money from the pension funds and advertising income.

In a 1998 interview in the Los Angeles Times, Salcer said of Eagleson: "This was a man who was more powerful than the prime minister in Canada. He dealt by intimidation and fear … I was hearing horror story after horror story. I watched players' salaries go up maybe 5% every year and we never knew who was making what … Alan Eagleson said to players, 'You're making more money than your parents. Don't rock the boat.'"

Helene Elliott, the writer who interviewed Salcer for the article, observed:

"Salcer made the rounds of NHL teams to alert players about Eagleson's double-dealing ... Slowly, Salcer [and] Winter ... gathered support and built a case they planned to present to players at an NHLPA meeting in West Palm Beach, Fla., in 1989."

Eagleson refused to let Salcer speak, but players, led by Marty McSorley, insisted Salcer be allowed to address the group. Evidence of Eagleson's wrongdoing was overwhelming. It included diverting money from dasher-board advertising and improperly lending NHLPA pension money to friends. Players voted to oust Eagleson, but the NHLPA executive committee — stacked with Eagleson cronies — overturned the vote. Still, it was the turning point.

What really led to Eagleson's downfall, however, was the power of the press. Starting in 1990, Russ Conway, a brilliant sportswriter for the Eagle-Tribune, a small-town publication in North Andover, Massachusetts, began an in-depth series of features on the NHLPA and its president. The results of Conway's investigations were shocking.

For example, Ed Kea, a minor league hockey player under contract to the St. Louis Blues, suffered a career-ending brain injury and had to go on disability. The NHLPA was supposed to award Kea $100,000 to help him through his recovery. But Eagleson hadn't paid the insurance premiums for minor league players. He never informed Kea that the insurance had lapsed. Eventually, Kea received about $20,000 of the award.

Conway would write a book about Eagleson titled "Game Misconduct: Alan Eagleson and the Corruption of Hockey." Among the conclusions Conway offered, summarized by Shawn Reznik of The Hockey Writers, was this: "From the five Canada Cup tournaments Eagleson ran, for instance, expenses consumed 70% of the receipts, and the players received just eleven cents on the dollar. In comparison, a 1997 audit of the 1996 World Cup of Hockey showed it made a profit of $14.7 million on receipts of $26 million which exceeded the net profits of all five Canada Cup [tournaments] run by Eagleson ..."

The drum beat against Eagleson grew louder until 1994, when the FBI charged Eagleson with thirty-four counts of fraud in two countries. The charges led to his imprisonment in Canada. His cronies and supporters drifted away. Many in professional hockey felt that Eagleson was never fully contrite. For that reason, among many others, when the Summit Players met for their 40th reunion in 2012, Eagleson was first invited and then uninvited. Veteran players profess that they revile him to this day.

CHUCK'S ETHICS REVIEW:

The Addiction of Power: How Power Can Consume Ethical Choices

Power can become such an addiction that it can cloud any original intention or accomplishment, no matter how good. As the quest for absolute power takes over, some people want more and more of it until they become just a shadow of their former, ethical selves. That is, of course, if they were ever ethical in the first place.

The initial problem here is that a man who was an active agent was also able to become president of a sports association. Even back then, I'm sure many people looking at it would have said it is a clear conflict of interest. Granted, the concept of hockey agents was in its infancy, but someone should have spoken up right away. It takes a special person to work on both sides of the fence and to do it fairly. An air of impropriety will always linger.

Eagleson saw an opportunity for great power, but he did not realize the tremendous responsibilities that came with that opportunity. The power quickly consumed him. For evidence, consider this: Eagleson didn't pay insurance premiums for players, but he loaned money to his friends.

How could such improprieties have happened? You might say that Eagleson was simply an out-and-out crook. He was more concerned about image, status, and wealth than the welfare of the players he was purportedly representing.

Eagleson's actions all seem very unsympathetic and callous. Why didn't he pay the premiums? Bluntly put, he would have had less money to do the things he wanted to do. Sure, he ran the risk that a player would get injured, but he either didn't think about that or he just didn't care whether or not it happened. It doesn't get much more unethical than that. His actions show exactly why, in any association — whether it's the NHLPA, LPGA, or the USSF — you can't function effectively if there's a conflict of interest. Do one job, and do it really well.

NOT IN A VACUUM

Hockey, while not as big as professional football or baseball, and while still in its infancy in terms of potential during Eagleson's day, was still a major business. In 1990, the average salary in the NHL was about $270,000. The total valuation of all twnt-one teams in the league was about $500 million, a figure that quickly shot up to $2.2 billion by 2005. By 2022, the value of just the New York Rangers exceeded $1.65 billion, with Toronto's value a shade less. Surely, Eagleson must have seen the NHL's potential.

We must ask: How does a person become so powerful within an organization within which all dissent or criticism is barred? In truth, it is through the oldest set of influences of all: fear and intimidation.

Take politics, for example. U.S. and Canadian politics aside, look at some political leaders and dictators who have been in power for decades. How is it that people don't rise up against them? Somehow, these leaders have so much power and influence that people are afraid to speak out for fear they will be put down and tortured. You can see examples of such quashing of dissent in the news every day, whether it's in North Korea or Iran, or many other countries.

That is pretty much what happened in the case of the NHL. Eagleson and his cronies became very powerful. The players were the ones who really got body checked. Hockey players coming into the league are not much older than teens. They didn't want to rock the boat, and the guys in power knew it.

The NHL players scandal underscores the need to continually train agents and associations on ethics issues. If we train those in positions of power to understand the natural tendencies of human behavior, we can create a conscientiousness about acceptable choices today, no matter how it was done in the past.

Today, hockey is a major business. The agreements and contracts made between owners and players are under increasing scrutiny. Diverting insurance premiums to personal accounts or cheating athletes out of insurance benefits would be considered reprehensible crimes: not legally or morally acceptable.

Going forward, the more training we devote to good ethics, choices, and consequences, the more we can create an ethical field of play. It is a conscientiousness that immediately calls into action a set of ethical standards, one that, in the face of ethical choices, says, "I cannot do that. I cannot cross that line."

CROSSED PURPOSES

From the beginning, Eagleson had an agenda that didn't include acting for the betterment of hockey. Eagleson recognized an opportunity for self-aggrandizement. He wanted to be the man, so to speak. He recognized the opportunity and thought that if he positioned himself properly, he could become the guru of hockey. Similar abuses of power have occurred in other sports. Look at some of the antics that have gone on in boxing promotion, in horse racing or even in the early days of NASCAR. Eagleson saw an opportunity to fulfill a need he had, and he took it.

As I look at this case, I see how it clearly demonstrates Eagleson's intentional disregard for the people he was supposed to be serving. It's a human behavior issue, one that reveals Eagleson's narcissism. It shows just how egomaniacal someone can be, and how far they will go to gain advantage, no matter how many people they have to step on to get there. This madness is hardly the sole domain of sports.

In the end, Eagleson hurt many good people because other good people stood by and did nothing. There were no ethical checks and balances. This scandal is what happens when ethics are left out of a sport at its highest levels. The pain trickles always trickles down.

CHAPTER 14

THE DANNY ALMONTE STORY

Who: Danny Almonte and Felipe Almonte

Offense: Fraud

Result: Loss of Reputation

Danny Almonte was "officially" born on April 7, 1987, in the town of Moca in the Dominican Republic. However, Danny Almonte was fictitiously born on April 7, 1989, in the town of Jamao al Norte, also in the Dominican Republic. This piece of fiction sparked the first of several inconsistencies in a Little League Baseball scandal that made news worldwide.

The story begins in 1995 when Almonte's father arrives in the United States to carve out a new life for himself. He took a job at a bodega, a small grocery store, in the Bronx.

As would later come to light, on March 21, 2000, Almonte's father inexplicably filed a second birth certificate in the Dominican Republic indicating April 7, 1989, as his son's date of birth. Perhaps the father hoped the first birth certificate would remain hidden. Felipe had apparently hatched a plan to skyrocket his son into stardom.

In April 2000, Danny Almonte moved to the U.S. to join his father. Felipe pushed his son into Little League Baseball. Granted, it did not take much of a push, as Danny loved baseball and wanted to play. He soon became a member of the Rolando Paulino Little League All-Stars.

Danny was a phenom — a super phenom. In Little League, the mound is just forty-six feet away from home plate, as opposed to sixty feet, six inches, like the older players use. Danny threw his fastball seventy miles per hour, mixing in curveballs and changeups, and he blew pitches past virtually every batter he faced. His heat, his fastball, translated into the Major League equivalent of a pitcher throwing at ninety to ninety-five miles per hour.

The young star began to gain national recognition. The Dominican Republic has produced some incredible baseball players, and baseball is often seen as a way out of poverty, but Danny, supposedly around twelve years old at the time, seemed head and shoulders above all of them. He was tall, lanky, and very strong.

The Rolando Paulino Little League All-Stars began to win and win big. They moved to the top of their league and qualified for the regional finals. On August 14, 2001, Danny threw a no-hitter against a team from State College, Pennsylvania. This was big stuff for a team from the sandlots of the Bronx. The team qualified for a berth at the Little League World Series.

The Little League World Series is held in a round-robin format. In his team's first matchup, Danny pitched a perfect game, striking out sixteen of the eighteen batters he faced and winning 5-0 against the team from Apopka, Florida. He then had a similar performance against another of the round-robin teams, this time giving up just one hit.

The Rolando Paulino Little League All-Stars would eventually lose the World Series principally because Danny was put on a rest day, as mandated by the league. Nevertheless, it was such a feel-good story — inner city kids making it to the World Series against all odds — that New York Mayor Rudy

Giuliani gave Almonte's team the key to the city. When all was said and done, Danny had struck out sixty-two of the seventy-two batters he'd faced and had won all the games he pitched. Unbeknownst to the public, however, trouble was brewing.

Danny Almonte was too good to be true, and quality baseball coaches are not stupid. No one this young star faced could believe he was only twelve years old. Even before the case fully exploded, two teams Danny had faced in the New York metropolitan area hired private investigators to secretly probe Danny's date of birth. The investigations turned up nothing, but things still didn't feel right.

Then, right after the Little League World Series, Sports Illustrated magazine writers Ian Thomsen and Luis Fernando Llosa decided to conduct an investigation of their own. Their article appeared on August 27, 2001, and it pulled no punches.

In part, they determined that the investigators for the other teams:

"... did not inquire at the oficialнa civil, the civil records building, in either Moca or Santo Domingo [the capitol of the Dominican Republic], where they could have found further reason to question Danny's age. According to birth ledgers in Moca examined by [Sports Illustrated magazine], Danny's [first] birth date was registered with the Dominican government in December 1994 by his father, Felipe, as April 7, 1987.... That means that when Danny Almonte was blowing away batters in Williamsport last week, he was officially fourteen years old."

The Sports Illustrated magazine investigation was quite complex and made for fascinating reading. In brief, the birth certificate Danny's team used to validate his date of birth was a copy of the second birth certificate filed in 2000. Those who came to Danny's defense in this scandal, starting with his parents and his coach, wanted everyone to overlook the truth. According to the Sports Illustrated article:

"... the Paulino team manager, Alberto Gonzalez, said that Danny was accused of being overage because he is so smart on the mound. 'He's just a little more mature than other kids right now ... The biggest plus is his mental approach. His mind is very focused. You tell him something once, and he will never forget.'"

As the investigation widened, it became evident that fraud had been committed. Danny's team was stripped of its wins, and the team fell into disgrace. Paulino, the founder of the team, and Felipe Almonte were banned from Little League for life. Little League disqualified the team for life as well. Interestingly, no one really blamed Danny.

In a follow-up USA Today article (August 17, 2011) titled "Almonte, Little League feel impact of scandal ten years later," in 2011, Stephen Keener, the president of Little League, was quoted as saying: "I hope he's doing OK. I really do. I always felt he was as much victimized as anybody.... He's the one that's going to have to deal with, 'Oh, you're Danny Almonte.' It's a bit unfair to him, too."

Despite the wishes of his father, Danny Almonte would never pitch in the Major Leagues. He did pitch in the Frontier League, an independent minor-league circuit, in 2007, but he fared poorly in only six appearances, mainly due to being out of shape, and was cut. Later that year, he joined the Western Oklahoma State College team, where he played impressively for two years. But by then, he had become an old prospect of twenty-two years and was not signed by any Major League teams.

In college, Almonte begged his coach to keep the media away from him. Nevertheless, in the New York Daily News (May 22, 2009), journalist Julian Garcia reported the comments of a Major League Baseball scout: "Certain teams may just as soon rather not bother with him, especially since he's a kid who, talent-wise, is kind of fringy ... Sometimes the baggage that may come with that is a detriment."

Little League Baseball has since tightened its rules on documentation, but as I write this, I can't help but wonder if some parent or coach somewhere isn't looking for another angle to try to live their life through that of their kid.

CHUCK'S ETHICS REVIEW:

Daddy Really Doesn't Know Best: Trickery Brings Tragedy

Before talking about Danny Almonte specifically, it might be worthwhile to explore the whole topic of parents behaving badly at athletic events and in and around athletics in general. We are seeing a steady increase in parents who are trying their best to bend or break the rules. It has become an ethical and, in some cases, legal problem ranging in severity from cheating to assaults on players, referees, and coaches.

The parents and grandparents who preceded the current generation of athletes might have been a little more like purists when it comes to sports, but I think there has always been an incredible push on kids by certain types of parents. Type A to the extreme, these parents want the vicarious thrill of living their lives, especially their childhoods, through their children. The big challenge today is that sports are so lucrative compared to what they were fifty or sixty years ago when our parents or even grandparents were playing.

Why are some parents pushing their kids so hard now? Simple. It can cost $50,000 or more for a year of college. So, if I have a kid who shows any kind of promise in a sport, and if that saves me the money of having to deal with a college education, I want to go for it. Unfortunately, some parents tend to forget the negative consequences of pushing too hard and expecting too much. Such behavior, if the parents aren't careful, takes a toll on kids down the road, especially if all they teach their kids are bad ethics.

In case after case, parents behaving badly on the sidelines or bleachers have been shown to cause their children tremendous embarrassment. This is especially true when parents fight with officials or with each other. I do agree that any parent or coach who so much as touches an official should be banned from the league and prosecuted. It has absolutely no place in sports.

YOUR KID ISN'T THAT GOOD

Parents often forget the odds game, which bears repeating. The odds of any child going through high school into the collegiate ranks and then on to become a professional athlete are ridiculously small. With baseball, before the pandemic, it was about 5% after college to make it to any MiLB team. Now it is less. In terms of MLB baseball, perhaps 1% make it. Sure, it's important to celebrate your child and embrace their accomplishments, but a perceived bad call by an official will have absolutely nothing to do with your kid becoming an NFL or WNBA player.

It's also a good idea to check in frequently with your child. Make sure that your hope for their success is also their dream. Notice I didn't say your dream, but their dream. Your dreams for athletic success are yours, and they often reflect your past. If you couldn't get a collegiate scholarship for basketball, your child isn't to blame for that. In any case, if your child's true wish is to become a mathematician or an actor, don't blame them for not meeting your expectations as an athlete.

Now, neither Danny Almonte's father nor his coaches stopped to consider the consequences of their actions or their motivations. I'm sure his father thought he could get away with the scam. The requirements for documentation in the Dominican Republic were far different then than they are today, and he took a big chance to make big bucks. The father thought he could propel his son into superstardom and riches, fame and glory. It was to be not just Danny's path to success but also the father's meal ticket.

Again, let's not view this case as a cultural anomaly endemic to the Dominican Republic. I have seen similar behavior by parents in Colorado or South Carolina. Danny had been a superstar, at least for a little while, and it brought local fame and recognition to the family for a brief time. As for the

MLB, to expect a kid to climb to that height is a completely different proposition.

As for the coach, I don't really think he knew Danny's real age in the beginning. The coach thought he had a young phenom on his hands, and by all appearances, he did, at least before the scam blew up. Danny was the pawn. He was a kid who just wanted to play baseball.

KEEP THEM AWAY!

After the scandal broke and Danny started to fade into the sunset of mediocrity, why would a college-aged Almonte beg his coach to keep the media away from him?

Let's give Danny Almonte credit. He was good for a fourteen-year-old, but when you're playing against kids far younger, you can appear to be a prodigy. It's like sneaking an NBA player into playing for your Division II basketball team. Everything might be good for a while until you're found out, and the axe comes down on the program.

When Danny Almonte was trying to make it as a college pitcher, of course, the media was going to hang around and ask questions. The media loves to do follow-up stories, and it's understandable. The first question was undoubtedly, "Why did you do it?" As if he, alone, did it.

The second question is a little more complicated. By the time you are college-age, you are no longer playing against twelve-year-olds, and in Danny's case, he was a so-so player against kids his own age. He was no longer special, and he had become old for an MLB prospect. The media will naturally start to ask questions about why the skill set dropped off so badly. They might also ask, "Do you think you have any shot at all of making it to Double-A ball? How about to the big leagues?" These are tough questions for anyone to answer, let alone a kid in his freshman or sophomore year.

Danny was so dominant in Little League that, unless he blew everyone away in college, he would always be perceived as a cheater and a fraud. In college, he wanted to be just another ballplayer and go to school. The media presence kept reminding him that he was just a mediocre talent, and that the adults who had once surrounded him had been cheaters. It was an embarrassment and a cause for shame.

ETHICAL TRAINING

League officials and coaches, even at the Little League level, should be required to participate in ethics training. In a perfect world, so should their parents. I think everyone should be required to participate in some kind of ethics training, but you would expect that answer from me!

Seriously, parents and coaches are willing to train their athletes to be excellent at what they do, but they are often unwilling to give them the proper motivation and the tools to play ethically. They don't often want to instill the awareness and knowledge that every choice has a consequence.

As Danny Almonte proved, the odds for making it into "The Bigs" are poor at best. Assuming a child gets to college on a baseball scholarship, there's still only about a one percent chance of that child making it to the Major Leagues. I don't care how good a parent might think their child is at seven or even seventeen, to not teach choices, consequences, and ethical behavior — on and off the field — is a waste of a huge opportunity.

Parents must be made aware of how any negative activity they might encourage in their children will have terrible, long-term effects on their young athletes. I'm purposely repeating this because so many parents and authority figures are having a real problem embracing this concept.

The Danny Almonte case was ultimately about fraud and deception for personal gain. Danny's father knew what he was doing. He knew that, if he changed the birth certificate by two years, his child likely would be dominant. Knowing how young kids develop, he knew his son was entering a more mature phase of life and would be competing against kids less mature, and he took advantage of it. The assumption seemed to be, if he could do so without being detected, then everyone would think his child was a prodigy, and he would gain the rewards that come with success.

For a while, the Almonte strategy appeared to be working. The interesting thing to me is how this case proves the adage that you can't hide everything forever. The cover-ups are ultimately discovered. I've seen this over and over again, whether in sports, sales, accounting or life in general. Danny was a victim. But, even sadder still, I'm sure some of the people close to him blamed him for not reaching fame and fortune.

I often wonder what would have happened to Danny if, rather than being rushed into the circus of his father's creation and exposed to ridicule, he had been able to mature slowly and been carefully coached into the role of a solid pitcher. What might his success have been then?

SECTION IV
THE SPORTS LEADERS?

CHAPTER 15

Spygate: It Was All about The Win

Who: Bill Belichick, Matt Walsh

Offense: Unauthorized Videotaping of Team Fined

Result: Fines, Terminations, Loss of Reputation

No matter how skilled you think you are at sports trivia, you've probably never heard of unsung sports media hero Tony Verna, the man indirectly responsible for starting the sports innovation known as instant replay.

On December 7, 1963, working as the broadcast director for CBS and using crude videotape equipment weighing more than a ton, Verna captured some of the action at the Army-Navy football game in Philadelphia and then immediately replayed it to the national television audience. The innovation was so unexpected that the play-by-play announcer exclaimed to viewers: "This is not live! Ladies and gentlemen, Army did not score again!"

While instant replay would soon become a staple of every game-viewing experience, it wouldn't be until 1986 that the NFL would use video for official replay review, thus making it possible to overturn officials' decisions on the field. Official replay review was itself overturned by the team owners in 1992. However, in 1999, they changed their minds and overwhelmingly voted to reinstate it. Instant video replay review has since become an integral part of the game.

While the NFL will forever be tied to instant replay and to technology, the opportunity for the abuse of technology has always been there, too. Technology can be used to enhance the game within the rules or, as we're about to see, it can be used flagrantly outside the rules as well.

SPYGATE

The NFL has created rules in order to maintain the most level playing field possible. One way in which it has done so is to establish strict guidelines protecting teams from being spied upon. Such restrictions are fundamental, especially in a thirty-two-team league where billions of dollars are at stake on any given Sunday.

Gaining any inside advantage is a huge factor for both defensive and offensive schemes. Spygate, the scandal involving the use of videotape to capture inside information, stands out as a major football scandal.

The beginnings of the New England Patriots Spygate scandal can be traced to sometime during the 2000-2001 season when Patriots video operator Matt Walsh began to secretly tape NFL opponents for the Patriots coaching staff.

Now, teams exchange videos of opponents. This happens all of the time. Coaching staffs and players note offensive or defensive formations or a player's tendencies or situational plays on the field. However, at the core of Spygate are allegations that Bill Belichick, head coach of the Patriots, expressly wanted Walsh to tape signals between offensive and defensive coaches and players. Belichick denied this, played it all down, and called Walsh a third-rate assistant who essentially undertook the taping on his own.

In a website article titled "Exclusive: Belichick Talks On Spy-Gate" (May 16, 2008), CBS News reported: "It was Walsh who shot video during Belichick's first two seasons in New England in 2000 and 2001. He [Walsh] went public this week, calling the coach 'arrogant.' Walsh claims Belichick's contention that he just 'misinterpreted' the rules was false and that the taping was actually a deliberate, illicit scheme by the Patriots to cheat their way to victory."

Let's examine some of the events as they unfolded.

On January 27, 2002, Walsh, the video operator, secretly taped the AFC Championship game between the Patriots and the Pittsburgh Steelers in an effort to steal signals. In a May 19, 2008, blog post, Bill Chuang of The Football Expert website wrote: "During the AFC Championship Game against the Steelers on Jan. 27, 2002, at Heinz Field, Walsh was instructed not to wear anything displaying a Patriots logo. Walsh said he turned the Patriots sweatshirt he was wearing inside out. Walsh also was given a generic credential instead of one that identified him as team personnel."

In other words, Walsh went undercover. The video he shot allegedly helped the Patriots coaching staff figure out the opposing team's signals. The Patriots beat the Steelers 24-17 and won the AFC championship.

Then, on February 2, 2002, the Patriots allegedly videotaped a walkthrough practice held by the St. Louis Rams before Super Bowl XXXVI. An article in the Chicago Tribune (February 3, 2008) reported that, after the New England Patriots team picture was taken at the Superdome in New Orleans the day before Super Bowl, one of the Patriots team personnel stayed behind and reportedly videotaped the Rams practice.

On February 3, 2002, New England beat the heavily favored Rams 20-17. The team kept the videotaping of the Rams practice quiet.

In the early months of 2003, Walsh was fired by the Patriots.

Then, on August 31, 2006, the Patriots allegedly recorded a training session of the New York Giants as it prepared for the teams' preseason game. Whether one event influenced the other is hard to say, but on September 6, 2006, the NFL specifically reminded coaches not to videotape signs and signals from other teams.

In November 2006, Patriots video assistant Matt Estrella was caught taping a Green Bay Packers game. Security members on the field ordered him to stop. Almost a year passed when, on September 9, 2007, a camera was confiscated from Estrella during a game. According to an article on ESPN.com from May 2008, "NFL security officials confiscate a camera and videotape from 26-year-old Patriots' video assistant Matt Estrella on the New England sidelines when it was suspected he was recording the Jets' defensive signals during New England's 38-14 victory in the season-opening game at Giants Stadium."

The next day, Eric Mangini, the head coach of the Jets, turned in the Patriots to the league office. On September 11, 2007, NFL Commissioner Roger Goodell found the Patriots had violated NFL rules.

The day after that, Belichick called a news conference in which he apologized to everyone involved. He made it clear that, other than his brief apology, he would have no further comment for the media. When pressed for more details, he walked out of the press conference.

On September 13, 2007, Goodell tore into the Patriots. Aside from confiscating all of the Patriots tapes and recording equipment, Belichick was fined $500,000, and the Patriots were fined $250,000. On September 14, 2007, ESPN on-air sports personality Chris Mortensen was not shy about expressing his feelings. Mortensen claimed that Belichick had been taping signals since 2000.

On September 16, 2007, Patriots team owner Robert Kraft was interviewed during a game and said he had no knowledge that any sideline videotaping had taken place. Then on September 22, 2007, the NFL destroyed all of the tapes and papers the Patriots had turned in to them.

From November of 2007 to February 2008, there was back-and-forth talk between politicians, such as then-Pennsylvania

Senator Arlen Specter, and the NFL as to the final disposition of the tapes. The NFL gave assurances that all materials had been destroyed. But no one could understand why such evidence had been destroyed in the first place.

The scandal turned out to be far from over. On February 2, 2008, the accusations about the Patriots taping the Rams before the Super Bowl in 2002 finally came to light.

On February 13, 2008, Goodell and Sen. Specter met to talk about the taping. Two days later, Specter stated that he was not happy that the destruction of the materials had taken place at New England Patriots headquarters and not at the NFL offices.

Belichick denied seeing any practice footage but said he thought taping the signals was permissible. Toward the end of February, Specter again weighed in, stating he felt like the NFL was thwarting his investigation. Nevertheless, the NFL approved of the way Goodell had handled the destruction of the tapes.

As a result of another communication innovation, in April 2008, the NFL approved the use of a communication system to have signals radioed to the helmets of the players. For better or worse, this technology would certainly change football signal calling.

Shortly after that, Walsh turned over eight tapes to Goodell, but the Rams Super Bowl walkthrough tape was not in the collection. Nevertheless, the tapes were all from 2000 to 2002, confirming that something had transpired during that period.

In the aftermath of the scandal, some coaches, such as Baltimore Ravens head coach John Harbaugh, claimed that Spygate forever stained the Patriots' titles. Other coaches, including Mangini, said they regretted turning in the Patriots in the first place.

After turning in Belichick and the Patriots, Mangini failed to secure another coaching job in the NFL for many years. He finally landed an assistant coaching job with San Francisco in 2013, saying at the time that he just wanted to move on. But the 49ers released him along with most of the rest of the coaching staff after firing Jim Tomsula following the 2015 season. In January 2017, Tomsula was hired as defensive line coach for the then-Washington Redskins, proving yet again that the NFL coaching fraternity is a small and closed club.

CHUCK'S ETHICS REVIEW:

Ethics Be Damned: It Was All About the Win

Over time, many sports fans have expressed belief that the leadership of the New England Patriots is more concerned with winning than it is with sportsmanship and ethical behavior. Certainly, when it came to using technology to gain the upper hand, such as taping signals from opposing teams, it was apparent the Patriots were pushing the ethical envelope.

It's quite possible that the Patriots thought at the time, "Why shouldn't we engage in this behavior if we can get away with it?" When you're in an environment where technology evolves quickly, sometimes that technology can afford you an advantage for a short time before the rules are changed to stop you.

The handheld video camera was available as a bulky-but-portable technology in the late 1980s. By the early 2000s, the camcorder was within everyone's reach. It was small enough to be concealed and a no-brainer to use. It became incredibly difficult for those trying to maintain a competitive advantage to put the video camera genie back in the bottle once it was released.

Allegedly, New England took advantage of that technology. The NFL and other teams felt New England knew the rules, while the Patriots said the rules were ill-defined and they had simply misinterpreted them. In reality, the rules were not so ill-defined. Although maybe not as explicit as it should have been, memoranda in regard to videotaping had been circulated throughout the upper echelons of the league well before the taping activity took place.

It goes without saying, perhaps, that the concept of sports is to win. It doesn't necessarily mean, however, to win at all costs. Before the advent of sophisticated technology, spies used binoculars. One could ask whether the technology used by Belichick and others was substantially different. The answer is no, it wasn't substantially different, but it was still outside the rules.

The NFL should have anticipated the misuse of the portable video technology early on and clearly spelled out its illegality, but that's 20/20 hindsight kind of stuff. There was an opportunity for the Patriots to operate in a gray area, and they took advantage of it. They pushed it. I think they knew they were pushing it, and the NFL did as well.

No doubt, technology will be abused in the future. Rules are set up regarding known technology. League officials try to anticipate the future, but technology always seems to be several steps ahead of the rules.

I'll give you an example from a recent seminar where I made a presentation on sports ethics and technology. In the state of Montana, you can't record a conversation with someone on your cell phone unless they agree to it. If they do not, the conversation is not admissible in a court of law. That is what the law says, but technology can still be used to bring about expected outcomes. If I've got a cell phone that lets me record any conversation I want, then stop me if you can. The reality is, if one records a conversation — illegally or not — and releases it to the media, the damage is often already done.

Imagine there's a high school coach or PE teacher who loves to shame and bully her overweight students. Let's say a student secretly records one of her angry rants. Now, the law states that such a recording is technically inadmissible in a court of law. But we know that if the student brought the recording home and played it for her parents and then later for the principal, chances are the teacher would be looking for a new job. Even if the student posted the recording on social media and said, "This is how my teacher treated me," it may still be enough to pressure the teacher to resign. The person on the other end of the technology, in this case, the coach, could say nothing to refute the charge of bullying.

The point is that technology is transformative. It changes us. It has changed sports. It changes business organizations and associations, and it will continue to do so. Nevertheless, to ensure a level playing field, the rules pertaining to the use of technology must be current, clearly defined, and shared with all involved, on or off the field.

If the NFL is aware of a new technology and sees a risk of its abuse, it must anticipate potential abuses and not react to them after the fact. Just imagine tiny spy drones zipping around a stadium. Security must keep pace with technology if not stay ahead of it. I don't know if there is someone at NFL headquarters whose job it is to study emerging technologies, but it might be an idea worthy of consideration.

TALENT LEVEL VERSUS MESSAGE

I have to appreciate the talent and the coaching ability of Bill Belichick. It would be crazy not to. However, the scandals in which his team has been embroiled demonstrate that, at some level, the outcome of games is far more important to Belichick than following the rules. The message it sends is: Ethics be damned.

Belichick said he was sorry the spying happened but admitted no guilt. He refused to answer questions and walked out of a press conference. I suppose that was his way of saying, "Well, you caught us." Suppose he had admitted guilt. Would that have changed anything? Maybe a little. But remember that the fine the NFL levied on the franchise at the time was fairly substantial, about a half million dollars.

Maybe that seems small next to the tens of millions of dollars a team might earn from winning a playoff game, but at least it was a significant amount. It set a bit of a precedent and was certainly a strong incentive to follow the rules. Let me add that, a short time later, the NFL strengthened its rules governing this kind of cheating. In fact, Spygate was responsible for moving football communications technology toward helmet communications. It also became clear that the NFL needed stronger security rules.

As for Eric Mangini, the whistleblower who ultimately suffered after coming forward, we sometimes have to remind ourselves that we live in a culture that renounces squealing. In our society, we do not perceive the propensity to snitch as a positive trait. While whistleblowers bring many of the wrongs in our society to light, in reality, we don't trust people who are willing to rat on someone else. It is an ironic twist that we sometimes think more highly of the perpetrator of a crime than of the person who uncovers it.

Did the Patriots break the rules? Yes, they did, and while Bill Cowher has said that other teams did as well, New England really capitalized on it. Beyond the technology and its unfair use, you have to wonder what message the Patriots are sending to their fan base. How many gray-area violations does it take before some of the fans say, "You know, maybe this isn't right."?

If winning at all costs is the message coming from the top, what's the message being sent down to the college level, and what's the message being sent down to the high school level and lower? The impact of the Patriots' actions can be felt not just by student-athletes in New England but by those all across the country.

Is there a point at which fans stand up for what is right in terms of sportsmanship? Or, is it about Belichick doing nothing more than reflecting the attitude of the fan base and the ownership? It's an interesting ethical question.

Remember, too, that the NFL commissioner works for the owners and not the other way around. In addition to Spygate and Deflategate — not to mention wildly creative, now-determined-to-be-illegal formations — New England may be the master of pushing its luck.

Is there a culture in place in the NFL that says, "As long as you break the rules and aren't caught, then there's no problem."? If you are caught, is that just the cost of doing business? There are thirty-one other NFL owners and ownership groups. How will they react if there's another Patriots scandal? It remains to be seen.

CHAPTER 16

DESHAUN WATSON – SO MUCH PROMISE, SO LITTLE TIME

Who: Deshaun Watson

Offense: Alleged Sexual Assaults of More than Sixty Women

Results: Major Fines, Loss of Sponsorships, Four Cases Still Pending

In August 2022, the NFL and embattled former Houston Texans quarterback Deshaun Watson agreed he would serve an eleven-game suspension and pay a $5 million fine after dozens of women accused him of sexual assault.

Watson's legal saga has derailed a career that seemed like a sure thing only a few years prior. But when the allegations against him surfaced in March 2021, it appeared that yet another promising playing career was being snuffed out too soon.

The average NFL career is only 3.3 years, though quarterbacks average a bit more — 4.44 years, according to statista.com. Watson is far from the average player, though. Barring injury, a player of Watson's ilk can have a career that is counted in decades. So, what went wrong?

In 2014, Watson stood poised to conquer the football world. After a highly successful high school career in Gainesville, Florida, Watson was heading into college at Clemson University. Watson's six-foot-three-inch, 215-pound frame is prototypical for a modern quarterback. His combination of size, mobility, and accuracy is assuredly not typical, however.

AMAZING COLLEGE CAREER

In his freshman campaign under head coach Dabo Swinney, Watson made the most out of his limited time on the field. He went 93 for 137 passing in five starts for 1,466 yards and 14 touchdowns. Watson also rushed for 200 yards and five touchdowns, with Clemson going 4-1 in games he started.

However, injuries upended Watson's freshman year. A broken bone in his hand caused him to miss several midseason starts. A torn ACL in his knee ended his year with only Clemson's bowl game remaining.

Watson had successful surgery to repair his knee and was back and healthy in 2015. The Tigers would finish the year at 14-1 with their sophomore phenom at the helm. Only a 45-40 loss to Alabama in the 2016 College Football National Championship game marred an otherwise storybook season.

While he put up gaudy numbers in 2015 — 4,109 passing yards, thirty-five touchdown passes, and twelve rushing touchdowns — Watson's 2016 effort with Clemson turned out to be one for the ages. His rushing output was reduced, but his 4,593 passing yards with 41 TDs helped Clemson return to the National Championship.

Clemson faced Alabama for a rematch in the 2017 National Championship. For much of the game, it appeared as if history would repeat itself, though the momentum ebbed and flowed. Finally, Watson capped a two-minute fourth-quarter drive with a short touchdown pass to clinch a 35-31 victory.

For the second year in a row, Watson was a Heisman Trophy finalist. With a championship under his belt, he decided to forgo his senior year and enter the 2017 NFL Draft. He would not have to wait long to find out which team he would be joining. He was a natural leader and everyone wanted him.

THE NFL AND OUT?

In the first round, the Houston Texans selected Watson with the 12th overall pick. His selection marked only the second time the Texans had ever selected a quarterback in the first round.

Houston tried to ease Watson into his new role, choosing to start Tom Savage in its first game of 2017, but changed course at halftime and inserted Watson. He did well enough to earn the starting assignment, but another torn ACL spoiled Watson's rookie season. The surgery to repair the tendon was successful, though, and Watson was ready for his return in 2018.

With Watson under center, the Texans finished the 2018 regular season with an 11-5 record, good enough to win the AFC South division. Though Houston lost its Wildcard game 21-7 to the Indianapolis Colts, Watson appeared to be the Texans' QB of the future.

Watson and the Texans went 10-6 in 2019, winning the AFC South again and defeating the Buffalo Bills 22-19 to advance to the Divisional Round of the playoffs. The Kansas City Chiefs ended that run, but the Houston brass had seen enough to become believers in Watson.

In the offseason, Watson and the Texans agreed to a *four-year contract extension worth $160 million, with $111 million guaranteed.* The contract made Watson the second-highest-paid player ever at the time, following only the Chiefs' Patrick Mahomes.

"I'm lost for words," Watson told the NFL's Kevin Patra. "The money is great. It's life-changing. It's great. But the biggest thing is for the (organization) to just trust in me and believe that I'm their guy."

He was their guy, but, like many similar situations in sports history, the honeymoon was not to last. Houston's 2020 season was not what Watson or the Texans would have hoped, ending in frustration with a 4-12 record. Watson struggled to gel with new personnel, and he requested a trade at the end of the season.

Unfortunately for Watson, that offseason would be rocky more for his dealings off the field than on it. In March 2021, Houston attorney Tony Buzbee filed the first several of what would eventually become more than 30 sexual assault lawsuits against Watson and the Texans.

Watson's trade value plummeted, and his future in the league was suddenly in doubt. How could he lead any team to victory, given his choices?

The following July, ten women filed police reports with the Houston Police Department alleging that Watson had sexually assaulted them. Though the veracity of the reports had not yet been determined, the media circus caused Watson to lose several endorsement deals, including a lucrative deal with Nike.

Though he was eligible to play and was still making his $10.5 million salary for the year regardless of playing time, the Texans benched Watson for the entirety of the 2021 season.

In March 2022, the Texans and the Cleveland Browns finalized a trade for Watson. Houston got the Browns' first-round picks in 2022, 2023, and 2024, plus its third-round pick in 2022 and a fourth-round pick in 2024, all in exchange for Watson and a sixth-round selection in 2022.

His five-year deal with Cleveland gives Watson a fully guaranteed $230 million and a $45 million signing bonus.

Also, in March 2022, Watson settled all but four of his accusers' lawsuits out of court. He has always maintained his innocence. That same month, grand juries in Houston and Brazoria County declined to file sexual assault charges against Watson, ending his legal jeopardy in the matter.

In June 2022, The New York Times published a report alleging Watson had made sixty-six appointments with massage therapists between 2019 and 2021. According to the report, Watson and the Texans arranged for the therapists to meet with Watson at The Houstonian, a spa and hotel in Houston's posh River Oaks area. That same month, Watson finally spoke about the allegations publicly.

"I never assaulted, disrespected or harassed anyone," a defiant Watson said at the Browns' practice facility. "I just want to clear my name."

The following July, the Texans settled some thirty lawsuits with women who had filed or intended to file charges against Watson, who undoubtedly owes his second chance to his otherworldly skillset. Players with less to offer and less name recognition can and do have their careers end over similar allegations, even less serious ones.

The extent to which $5 million will affect Watson's bottom line is debatable, but the effect on his legacy is undeniable. He lost one full season and will lose most of another one, and his reputation has suffered a hit that will remain with him for a long time, possibly for life.

CHUCK'S ETHICS REVIEW:

Deshaun Watson: Some Things Money Can't Buy

I believe in second chances and in the redemption of trying to fix our poor choices. Heck, I wrote an autobiographical book entitled "Second Chances." I know what the basement of despair looks like. Hopefully, my daily striving for redemption over several decades, my speaking to audiences throughout this country and in many foreign countries about choices, consequences, and ethical behavior has been my greatest accomplishment. I have been most happy to know that I have dissuaded many people from ethical missteps.

So, what do I see when it comes to Deshaun Watson? Frankly, I could weep at seeing some of his alleged unethical and alleged abusive choices because he is throwing away an all-too-brief career with bad choices.

HITTING IT BIG

First, it is hard to be a nanve young man or woman with incredible talent playing collegiate sports, hitting the draft lottery, and then being catapulted to incredible wealth. The rocket ship of fame carries young athletes beyond hometowns, roommates, friends, spouses, teachers, coaches, sports agents, and often — common sense.

Yes, I am annoyed at professional sports for hurling these kids from relative obscurity into the universe of multi-millionaires and incredible monetary privilege without so much as one session of honest, true-life ethical training. It is a disconnect.

Imagine, then, that you are young and rich. You are showered with adoration and endorsements. You have gained an entourage of hangers-on, and you are pampered by your team and the ever-present media. If that was not enough, factor in biology. The frontal cortex, where rational thought takes place, is not yet fully developed, and the hormones are raging.

By all accounts, you should have everything you think you want, much like a king in medieval times or the glutton at an all-you-can-eat Las Vegas gourmet feast. Everything should be yours for the taking! Ah, but these are not medieval times. Vegas does not have such feasts, and not everyone is available for a young person's dalliances.

Without the filter of ethics, you make your move or, in Deshaun's case, many moves on the women who throw themselves at celebrity just to bask in its glow and — surprise! — they are less than enthused when there are consequences.

You mean I'm not the one?

After the glamour, the glitter, the wining and dining, and the many alleged affairs, at least some of the women awakened to a harsh reality, and it wasn't pleasant. Deshaun was there and gone; goodbye, have a good life and all of that.

I am not making fun. The human heart is as delicate and vulnerable as it is strong. He seemingly saw them as available for the taking, and he physically took what he could.

In the light of day, many of these women were more than willing to file complaints of sexual assault against Deshaun Watson. Apparently, the feudal idea of conquering women without consequence is out of style, but no one conveyed that ethical fact to Watson. The women who now allege they all said no went after any pocketbook they could find. And those pocketbooks emptied undisclosed dollars from Watson to his victims.

"I never assaulted, disrespected or harassed anyone," a defiant Watson said.

Who am I to say if he is being completely truthful? What I can say with certainty is that far too many young women strongly disagree with him. Every choice has a consequence. If we look at his statement above, we can also focus on the words he left out; on the distinctions he omitted. These cases have mostly been settled out of court under the cover of lawyers, agents, concerned sponsors, and big money. My question is, is he defiant enough to stand before a judge and swear to tell the truth?

THE PLAYERS

Some athletes think of themselves as "players," but not in the sports sense. They believe their money, clothes, penthouses, cars, and other trappings place them above societal expectations, and they try to live that lie. They invariably fail. Ethically, they are adrift in a sea of opportunists. Unless ethical behavior is taught and imprinted, there is no compass.

On the other hand, please don't believe that all professional athletes are bad people. From an NFL perspective, I can quickly rattle off names such as Russell Wilson, Thomas Davis, J.J. Watt and Von Miller, all of whom have solid reputations borne of ethical and down-to-earth upbringing and the reinforcement of core values. True, they may have occasional scrapes, like the rest of us, but nothing remotely connected to having thirty-plus sexual assault accusations in rapid succession.

Many sports stars are also made to understand that they can be "marks." For that reason, they are vigilant about with whom they associate. They realize they are celebrities, so they keep a watchful distance from people and try to make good choices. Again, understand they must focus on surrounding themselves with ethical people who can keep them on the right path.

I would like to think Deshaun Watson can recover from this set of incredibly poor choices. However, my doubt stems from the fear that, unless he is taught to walk in the light of an ethical lifestyle, he will keep self-destructing until an extremely promising career is finally ruined.

CHAPTER 17

George O'Leary, Almost the Mountain-Top

Who: George O'Leary and the University of Notre Dame

Offense: Resume Padding

Results: Termination after five days, loss of reputation

By all accounts, George O'Leary was off and running to a highly successful football coaching career. After earning his bachelor's degree in physical education from the University of New Hampshire in 1968, he started the same way many coaches do, by coaching in high school. Between 1968 and 1974, O'Leary compiled a 37-8-1 record while coaching at two different high schools in Long Island, New York. His talent was unmistakable, and he was quickly recognized as a potential Division I college coach.

O'Leary left high school coaching for a position at Syracuse University, where he remained from 1980 to 1986. While at Syracuse, he rose in rank to become the defensive line coach and then an assistant head coach, helping to build the defense during the Orange's 11-0 championship year in 1988.

O'Leary's huge break came when Georgia Tech hired him away from Syracuse. He first became Tech's defensive coordinator and then its defensive line coach from 1987 to 1991. In 1990, Georgia Tech amassed an 11-0-1 record and split the national championship with the University of Colorado. O'Leary's work as a coach was now creating a lot of attention in both the collegiate and professional ranks.

George O'Leary had a secret or two

When he was hired by Syracuse in 1980, much like anyone who fills out an application prior to starting a new job, O'Leary had to fill out information on his schooling and his career. He asserted that, while at the University of New Hampshire, he had earned three varsity letters in football, from 1966 to 1968.

In reality, O'Leary never played football for UNH. As a matter of fact, he was a transfer to New Hampshire from the University of Dubuque in Iowa, a small Division II school of about 1,500 students. It would have been impossible for him to earn three letters in football and graduate in just two years.

O'Leary stayed with Georgia Tech until the end of 1991, when he decided to take a shot at the NFL professional ranks. The San Diego Chargers hired him as an assistant coach in 1992 and retained him in 1993. By then another curious milestone had suddenly appeared in his biography.

According to the San Diego Chargers media guide, O'Leary "earned a master's degree in education at New York University in 1972 while coaching on the high school level."

O'Leary left the Chargers and professional football in 1993 and returned to coach at Georgia Tech in 1994. In the updated biography that appeared in Georgia Tech's media guide, O'Leary falsified his football exploits at UNH and invented the fact that he had earned a master's degree from "NYU-Stony Brook University." It was a doubly compounded fabrication, as O'Leary never earned a master's degree, and there is no school named NYU–Stony Brook University.

Despite the resume padding, all seemed to be going reasonably well. In fact, as O'Leary rose from interim head coach to tenured head coach, the destiny of Georgia Tech rose as well. In 1998, he coached the university to a 10–2 record and defeated Notre Dame in the Gator Bowl. This fact probably caused, or at least encouraged, Notre Dame to knock on his door when they were looking for a new head coach in 2001.

In all of college sports, there are few mountaintops as coveted as the Notre Dame head coach position. Notre Dame attracts international attention and has tremendous media coverage.

When Notre Dame offered the position to O'Leary, for a salary bordering on $2 million a year, it naturally created widespread attention. The media, hunting for news with local connections, is always pleased to get an interview with a local boy who makes good. No one was out to do him harm; it was simply a feel-good story on a slow sports day.

George O'Leary's biography immediately caught the eye of The Union Leader newspaper in Manchester, New Hampshire. Through calls made to UNH, the paper's research staff quickly determined that O'Leary had not lettered in football. In fact, no one in the football program could ever remember him even playing for the team. The lie about his playing days at New Hampshire had stood for twenty years, until it didn't.

When the lie was uncovered, a humiliated O'Leary offered his resignation to Notre Dame, but the university refused it, giving him its support. Notre Dame officials were willing to let a youthful miscue stay in the past. However, in triggering a deeper level of investigation, they asked if any other facts had been fabricated. O'Leary then admitted he had lied about the master's degree as well.

Notre Dame fired O'Leary five days after it had hired him. In an article appearing in Sports Illustrated magazine (December 14, 2001), O'Leary was quoted as saying, "Many years ago, as a young married father, I sought to pursue my dream as a football coach. In seeking employment, I prepared a resume that contained inaccuracies regarding my completion of coursework for a master's degree and also my level of participation in football at my alma mater. These misstatements were never stricken from my resume or biographical sketch in later years."

O'Leary returned as a defensive coach in the NFL for one season with the Minnesota Vikings in 2002, and in 2004 the University of Central Florida named him as its head coach. He came to achieve a respectable level of recognition at UCF, helping to turn the program around. His name, however, will always be associated with his five-day tenure at Notre Dame.

CHUCK'S ETHICS REVIEW:

Fake It 'til You Make It: The Downfall to Deceit

There's no doubt that George O'Leary was having an outstanding career before this scandal became public. There was no good reason for him to pad his resume this late in the game. Yet, from time to time, life throws temptations our way. Sometimes, though we know better, we are willing to let things go because it is the expedient thing to do.

In terms of O'Leary's mindset, there were probably two different levels of thinking in play here. On the very surface level, O'Leary was willing to do whatever was necessary to win and to advance in his career in order to ensure he got what he needed. He was ambitious, and it's easy to understand that. He had a young family, and he wanted to improve his odds for bigger jobs. By adding those extra fibs, he made sure he was pushed over the top.

On a deeper level, O'Leary may have been intentionally sabotaging himself for purposes he may not even have realized. Perhaps, for some strange reason, he needed to experience the consequences that were bound to come from this bad choice. Perhaps he didn't think he deserved good things in life. There could be hundreds of reasons for doing something so obviously self-destructive.

There are hundreds of collegiate coaches who never lettered in football. Often a guy who sits on the bench and analyzes every aspect of the game sees more and knows more than the elite athlete who simply does what comes naturally. O'Leary had no reason to feel inferior just because he hadn't lettered in football.

NON-EXISTENT SCHOOL

At some point, O'Leary compounded his fib about his collegiate athletic record by making up a nonexistent university. It would have been so easy to correct, but this is a far more complex psychological issue than it is a simple ethical one. At some point, when you lie, you have to do more to maintain that lie — so you make up another and another. It's like resume quicksand. Why O'Leary would create a fake school and a fake degree is illogical. Why would he do it unless he had some deeper reason that made him unwittingly want to derail his career?

As you may know, I speak in front of many business groups and am sometimes asked about resume padding. My advice is simple: Fix that resume! Especially with the internet connectivity we have today, it's far too easy for others to verify your information. It is especially easy in an industry such as sports.

Considering the billions of dollars at stake in the sports industry, it should not be surprising that the athletes are a relatively small pool of people. Someone will know you — or know of you!

I was recently at a large sports seminar that focused on the topic of internet marketing and ticket sales, which is simple enough. The speaker mentioned a statistic in her presentation that just didn't feel right. In days of old, everyone might have just sat there nodding. The guy next to me, though, did a quick search on his smartphone and, in only a few seconds, discovered that her numbers were way off. Out of courtesy, he didn't say anything, but he immediately knew she was mistaken in her presentation. It damaged her authority. If she was lying about that statistic, what else was she presenting that wasn't true? She was supposed to be a high-powered consultant. In fact, she was a sloppy and ill-prepared consultant, which is to say, no consultant at all.

So, if, for instance, a woman lies when stating that she was an assistant coach for a Division II school whose name just doesn't ring a bell, or if a guy fibs that he was the founding partner of an apparel company that did annual running short sales of $50 million, and either thinks they can pad their resume with those accomplishments, you had better believe they can be found out — and fast.

Be honest — always! Far too many people have been outed for padded resumes and questionable job applications! Jobs are hard to come by. One small lie can knock you out of the competition.

If you're hiring someone, whether within athletics or not, and you want to get at the truth of their resume, the best questions to ask are the ones a candidate would not expect. If I were going to interview someone for a job, I would probably want to do some preliminary investigative work, which is not as complicated as it might sound. You can then use the information you uncover to ask specific and pointed questions. For example, if a coach says he attended a certain school as a student in the communications department, I might find some interesting facts and ask him a question like: "Name your three favorite instructors in the communications department and what you liked about them." If they truly did attend, they could easily answer .that question. If they did not attend, the question might be met with silence and a blank stare. They just cannot prepare for what they do not know.

COME CLEAN, PLEASE

Suppose, when considering a head coaching job, a potential candidate had come to me as a friend and said, "Chuck, I need your help. I want this job, but...."

If someone tells me the truth, I'm open to a discussion. To illustrate, let me draw on my own past. Close to thirty years ago, I was convicted of a felony. This is a well-known fact, and I've written about it and spoken about it on numerous occasions. I'm not proud of that fact, but it's the truth.

Many times, I've gone on interviews where, after a couple of minutes, I've said, "Before we get too deep in conversation, I want to know if your organization has any policies against hiring employees or consultants who had a prior felony?" The question shocks the interviewer, of course. Most people don't come out with something like this upfront. I feel that if I practice being more transparent, it opens up the dialogue better than if I had tried to cover something up in a dishonest manner.

I think O'Leary wrestled with transparency. In the quote above, he said, "These misstatements were never stricken from my resume or biographical sketch in later years." He's using passive voice to remove his own agency, making it sound as though it was somebody else's responsibility to strike the inaccuracies. The obvious truth is that it was up to him and him alone to do it.

If asked, I would have advised George O'Leary to stand on his credentials and his successes and not on his lies. He was and is a very good coach. That is good enough. During his interview at Notre Dame, if the athletic director had said, "George, we like you but we can't budge on the qualification that you must have a master's degree," then at least the dialogue would have taken place. Sometimes, no matter how much you want something, you just can't overcome certain roadblocks.

The University of Central Florida is not as academically prominent or as rich in history as Notre Dame, but George O'Leary realized great achievements as a coach there, both on the field and with regard to improving the academic records of the student-athletes he coached. Maybe it is a small consolation, but he should be at peace with himself, knowing he had to overcome a huge mistake to bring UCF to national prominence.

He retired from UCF in 2015.

SECTION IV

Every choice, good or bad, leads to a consequence. O'Leary falsified his resume, and, ultimately, it caused him to be fired only five days into a coaching job that is the stuff of dreams. Is it possible that he used his firing at Notre Dame and the embarrassment it caused him as a platform for helping others at UCF? I believe it is more than possible.

CHAPTER 18

DONALD STERLING – "I OWN A TEAM, YOU DON'T"

Who: Donald Sterling, Shelly Sterling

Offense: Blatant Racism, Law Suits filed by the NBA for Disregarding League Rules

Result: Forced to Sell Team

In November 2016, former Los Angeles Clippers owner Donald Sterling settled his lawsuit with the NBA, ending a saga that had become a public spectacle and one of the ugliest chapters in the league's history.

Sterling's tenure with the Clippers had already reached its ignominious end when he filed the $1 billion lawsuit two years earlier. In the suit, Sterling accused the NBA of antitrust violations and of conspiring with his wife, Shelly, to take the Clippers franchise from him.

In the end, Sterling, who was the longest-tenured NBA owner ever at the time of his ouster, reaped a record profit from the sale of the Clippers. It was the end of a winding road of missteps and self-destruction that would epitomize the franchise and infamize its owner.

Sterling was originally named Donald Samuel Tokowitz when he was born in Chicago on April 26, 1934. When he was an infant, his family moved to LA's Boyle Heights area, then a bustling immigrant enclave in a racially divided city.

Sterling did well in school, working his way through college and graduating from Southwestern University Law School in 1960. Citing his belief that an anglicized name would benefit him financially, he changed his name to Sterling in 1959.

After graduating from law school, Sterling started his own practice in LA, specializing in divorce and personal injury law. He soon got into real estate, however, purchasing several apartment buildings beginning in the 1960s.

Buying a team because he could

By the 1980s, Sterling had amassed a fortune. In May 1981, he bought the struggling San Diego Clippers NBA franchise from businessman and film producer Irv Levin for $12.5 million. With Sterling entrenched in business just up the coast in LA, rumors of a move flared.

The fledgling team owner *assured* reporters that he had no designs on moving the Clippers elsewhere. He would lead his team to victory.

"The best is yet ahead," he is quoted in the San Diego Union newspaper as stating, saying he would do everything in his power to "make this one of the best franchises in basketball."

"I am prepared to do whatever is necessary to get the players we want."

History proves that statement was misleading. That same paper, now the San Diego Union-Tribune, cites former employees describing Sterling as miserly. He and his wife are said to have chided staff over long-distance phone calls and counted the sheets of paper in copy machines. There was even a purported lawsuit alleging unpaid hotel bills for road games. The so-called leader (because he could) could care less about supporting his people.

The Clippers had struggled under Levin, with several consecutive fifty-loss seasons to show for their efforts. Under Sterling, the struggle continued. The Clippers notched a 17-65 record for the 1981-82 season. Consequently, the team had a hard time filling seats with spectators.

With money flowing in the wrong direction, and despite his promises, Sterling began eyeing a move to LA.

He attempted to move the Clippers after his inaugural season, but *the NBA blocked him.* Sterling then hired LA Lakers executive Alan Rothenberg in an effort to assuage the league's concerns about the franchise's operations. Rothenberg did help improve the Clippers' top-down organization, but those improvements did not really translate into more victories.

After several more losing seasons, Sterling finally decided to move the team in 1984, *NBA refusals be damned.* The Union-Tribune describes a pitiful scene as the Clippers left town, with a proud Sterling informing sullen San Diego sportswriters of the move and a lone Mayflower moving van trundling off toward LA.

The NBA attempted to stop Sterling once again. The league filed suit and fined the rogue team owner $25 million. Sterling countersued, and the parties eventually settled on a fine of $6 million. More importantly, Sterling got to keep the Clippers in Los Angeles.

The move was not a cure-all by any definition. The 1984-85 team's 31-51 record was a fair representation of the decades of futility in store for the Clippers in LA. The team managed only one winning season over the next twenty years, with only three playoff appearances in that time span.

The Clippers' fortunes finally began to change in 2010 with the addition of power forward Blake Griffin to the roster. Star point guard Chris Paul then joined the team in 2011, and, as of this writing, the Clippers still have not posted a losing record since then. However, Sterling would not be able to share in "his team's" success, and with good reason.

RECORDED CONVERSATIONS

In April 2014, gossip magazine **TMZ** published excerpts from a phone call between the octogenarian Sterling and his mistress, V. Stiviano, aged five decades his junior. Apparently, things had by then soured, as Stiviano had recorded Sterling admonishing her for bringing Black men to Clippers games, among other things.

The language he used in the phone call was overtly racist and obscene. There was no gray area in terms of what Sterling thought of people of color.

"It bothers me a lot that you want to broadcast that you're associating with Black people," Sterling tells Stiviano in *one of the least offensive portions* of the recording. "Do you have to?"

It only gets worse from there. Sterling tells Stiviano that it is okay for her to sleep with Black men, but not for her to bring them to games. He then excoriates her for associating with Magic Johnson.

"Don't put him on an Instagram for the world to have to see," he said. "And don't bring him to any of my games."

The backlash was instant, and it was intense. Social media was alight with angered fans and **NBA** players, current and former.

"I couldn't play for him," said Lakers star Kobe Bryant on Twitter. Other players agreed.

The Clippers led the Golden State Warriors two games to one in the first round of the 2014 playoffs at the time the story broke. The Warriors defeated LA 118-97 in Game 4 on April 27.

On April 29, NBA Commissioner Adam Silver announced that Sterling would be *banned from the NBA for life and would be fined $2.5 million*. The league would also try to *force Sterling to sell the Clippers franchise.*

"This league is far bigger than any one owner, any one coach, and any one player," Silver said at the time.

The Clippers rebounded in the playoffs, defeating Golden State in seven games but eventually losing in the next round to the Oklahoma City Thunder.

Within a month, Sterling had multiple offers for the team, but the standout bid was from former Microsoft CEO Steve Ballmer. It totaled $2 billion, but Sterling balked.

Experts working for the Sterling Family Trust had Sterling, who was suffering from early-stage Alzheimer's disease, *declared mentally incapacitated*, giving Shelly the power to sell the team.

Sterling then entered into a years-long lawsuit to fight the sale. That suit was thrown out of court with prejudice in November 2016, leaving Sterling with only state courts still available. Rather than drag out the process any longer, Sterling settled with the league out of court.

Though the terms of the settlement were never released, it is safe to assume Sterling had quite the payday from the Clippers. He and Shelly had initiated divorce proceedings but reconciled and remained together.

The league's fine notwithstanding, the price Sterling paid was not monetary. He had long faced accusations of racism and of having a "plantation mentality" about owning a team, but this time *his words were on tape.* Sterling's name is now synonymous with the word racist, and in the current zeitgeist, that is just about the worst thing a person can be.

CHUCK'S ETHICS REVIEW:

Old Dogs and Old Tricks?

Like Donald Sterling, my stepfather was an unrepentant racist. He was so unrepentant that he could not fathom his flaws. No matter what you said to my stepfather or how many times you corrected him, it seemed that you could never remove the racist streak from the man.

I'm quite confident that I'll be skewered for saying this, but in his generation, especially in the South, they were programmed from birth. Does it excuse his racism? Heavens, no.

However, it is possible to understand his behavior when his upbringing and mindset are put in the proper context. I cannot bring myself to make excuses for the man, but I at least learned to know him a bit more.

Donald Sterling, as with many people of his generation who were in positions of power and wealth, wielded his authority without regard for whom his actions would impact or offend. Privilege was a club he used to bash everyone around him. His sense of ethics was twisted and warped.

There are different facets of Sterling's poor choices. While lying is not right, it is no surprise that he would tell the city of San Diego one thing and then decide later to abandon that commitment, uproot the team, and go to Los Angeles under cover of night.

Donald Sterling believed that the rules did not apply to Donald Sterling. He was rich and ruthless, and he would do what he damn well pleased, and that he did. The NBA's governing bodies tried to stop him with the threat of monetary loss but to no avail. League fines are to men such as Sterling what parking tickets are to the common man, less really. They perhaps feel a sting of inconvenience — and a little miffed — when they pay them, but they play the odds and continue to break the rules.

The feeling of power and the arrogance that went with Sterling's mindset created a false sense of security. He got fined, but he had his way. Sterling had no filter. He spouted racism and mocked people whom he deemed were beneath him, abusing the privilege that came from his position as a team owner.

HELL HATH NO FURY — ENTER THE MISTRESS

Ah, but there is a consequence to every choice, and most of the time those consequences come in unexpected ways. Enter an estranged mistress, and the reality as to the true soul of Donald Sterling came out, as he shared his true feelings about Black people with her. It was ugly.

Sterling, and we don't need to recap it again here, obviously felt there was a difference in people based on race. While less likely to express that opinion in public, he was more than happy to share it with his mistress.

Here's what's important: You can't hide the truth. It will always come out. Truth is much like water. It has the uncanny ability to penetrate places that people think are protected. Regardless of what one might try to hide, eventually, it comes out.

Sterling is a racist. It is never acceptable, but in a league where more than 80% of the players are Black, and about 54% of the fans are people of color, to be a privileged racist is what you might call a bad look. No one in his organization was strong enough to stand up to him. On the other hand, no one wanted to work for him. The team kept sinking. The NBA made it clear it was going to force him to give up the Clippers, and that is what it did.

We can't change Sterling. He is irredeemable. What can be changed is to allow new management to come in, composed of people who understand that hate has no place in any aspect of professional sports or in our larger society. Do I believe racism in ownership groups ended with the unceremonious removal of Donald Sterling? I would be a complete fool to think so.

In 2022, Sterling, now suffering from dementia, was still worth an estimated $4 billion, which could explain why his wife never left him. Though, as a caveat, the conjecture is strictly stated as my opinion. In any case, losing the lackluster LA Clippers has probably not affected his net worth one iota.

Nevertheless, I am pleased that, with a new ownership group, better athletes, and a competent head coach in place, the team has slowly improved.

We can be smug if we'd like and say that Donald Sterling is a racist loser of massive proportions, and companies across America have successfully thrown out the vestiges of racism, having made a commitment to equity and inclusion. It is nice to consider but patently false. As a business ethics and sports ethics speaker and consultant, I am not so quick to join the Kumbaya bandwagon.

In recent years, General Electric, Southern California Edison, Walmart, Johnson & Johnson, Abercrombie, Google, Amazon, McDonald's, Pinterest, state governmental agencies, promotional boards, medical facilities, and charities have all faced allegations of racism.

Donald Sterling may have been illustrative of a fossilized old dog with the same old Jim Crow tricks, but he was not unique. We still have a lot of work to do.

SECTION V
DRUGS OF ALL KINDS

CHAPTER 19

ALEX RODRIGUEZ AND THE BIOGENESIS OF AMERICA SCANDAL

Who: Alex Rodriguez, Biogenesis of America

Offense: Illegal Use, Sales, and Distribution of Performance-Enhancing Drugs

Result: Suspensions, Fines, Imprisonment, Loss of Reputation

Alex Rodriguez made his debut with the Seattle Mariners on July 8, 1994, and by the 1996 season, he had become the Mariner's full-time shortstop. That first full year, he would be selected as Major League Baseball's Player of the Year. He continued with Seattle through the 2000 season.

On December 11, 2000, he signed a ten-year, $252 million contract with the Texas Rangers. Rodriguez proved his worth in Texas, and in 2003 he won his first Most Valuable Player award with the Rangers. However, there were already stirrings within league circles that "A-Rod" wanted to play on a much larger stage. On February 6, 2004, Rodriguez was traded from Texas to the New York Yankees in a blockbuster deal.

Though his 2006 season in New York would have been good by most professional standards, his overall production declined, and Yankee fans grew critical. At the start of the 2007 season, there was something different about Rodriguez. He had reduced his body fat and looked ripped, more like a linebacker than an outfielder. He had also grown distant from some of his teammates. Nevertheless, at the end of 2007, after another stellar season, he was awarded his third MVP.

On December 13, 2007, things started to unravel. The Mitchell Report on steroid abuse was released. Though Rodriguez was not named in the report, former MLB player and admitted steroid abuser Jose Canseco told the Fox Business Channel he "could not believe Rodriguez was not in the report," implying that the perception that Rodriguez was clean was inaccurate.

The rumors of Rodriguez using performance-enhancing drugs led to a television interview on December 16, 2007, during which he told "60 Minutes" he never used PEDs. The interview only fanned the flames of suspicion.

On February 7, 2009, a bombshell exploded. Sports Illustrated magazine reported that, back in 2003, A-Rod had tested positive for the banned steroid Primobolan and a synthetic testosterone. Then on February 9, 2009, Rodriguez admitted to ESPN he had used banned substances from 2001 to 2003. He said he felt a great deal of pressure to play well, recalling that back then, guys were kind of playing it "loosey-goosey."

On February 17, Rodriguez identified his cousin, Yuri Sucart, as the person who had supplied him with PEDs in the early 2000s. A few days later, the New York Daily News linked Rodriguez to a trainer from the Dominican Republic named Angel Presinal, who was alleged to have steroid associations.

Many sports fans, being partial, viewed all that had happened as maybe just the indiscretions of youth. But, on March 1, 2010, the New York Daily News uncovered a connection between Rodriguez and Toronto doctor Anthony Galea. Galea had supposedly helped Rodriguez recover from hip surgery, but Galea was under investigation for something else: providing other high-profile athletes with PEDs.

Fast forward to Rodriguez's involvement with Anthony Bosch, the founder of Biogenesis of America, a company now infamous for its association with PEDs. Bosch claimed he met Rodriguez on July 31, 2010, stating Rodriguez asked him why some other players in the league were performing so well. The two apparently developed an association after that point.

On January 26, 2013, news reports surfaced linking Rodriguez to Bosch, who was by then under investigation by MLB. This was confirmed a few days later when Biogenesis turned over documents to MLB that included Rodriguez's name along with the names of several other major league stars. Rodriguez denied any association, but on April 12, 2013, The New York Times reported that A-Rod had arranged to buy documents (records) from Biogenesis of America that MLB now intended to use against him.

Finally, on July 12, 2013, Rodriguez met with MLB investigators about his connection to Biogenesis. The MLB investigation was damning. On August 5, MLB suspended this once-untouchable baseball player for 211 games for violating drug policies. Rodriguez appealed, but it was an uphill battle at best. What does seem curious is that it took so long for MLB to react.

On August 11, Victor Conte, the founder of BALCO Labs, another company that made PEDs, said Rodriguez had approached him in 2012 asking about "supplements."

AVOIDING SCRUTINY

In trying to avoid the 211-game suspension, Rodriguez began arbitration with MLB, mounting a high-profile defense. On October 3, 2013, Rodriguez filed a lawsuit against MLB and its commissioner, followed by malpractice suits against the Yankees team doctor and the surgical hospital that had treated him. Soon after, he went on a New York radio show and denied having used PEDs. Though his suspension was slightly reduced, he vowed to take the fight to federal court, but his bluster was short-lived.

On January 12, 2014, the former president of the now-shuttered Biogenesis lab said he personally injected Rodriguez, who soon withdrew his lawsuit against MLB. On February 18, 2014, MLB dropped its lawsuit against Bosch. The former president of Biogenesis of America agreed to tell all he knew about Rodriguez.

Rodriguez returned to the field in 2015 with the Yankees and had an impressive year for a thirty-nine-year-old slugger, hitting thirty-three home runs and driving in eighty-six runs. He was booed relentlessly during the Yankees' road games and fell into a slump near the end of the season. The slump continued in the 2016 season until he was finally reduced to a pinch-hitting role.

In August of 2016, Rodriguez held a press conference with Yankees management to announce his imminent retirement. He finished fourth on the all-time home run list with a total of 696. The 211-game suspension denied Rodriguez of any hope he might have had of catching Barry Bonds, another suspected PED abuser, for the all-time home run record.

CHUCK'S ETHICS REVIEW:

A-Rod: Drugs Determined the Ethical Downfall of a Super Player

Was Alex Rodriguez the victim of his own ethical shortcomings? It is difficult to say, as this case is very enigmatic. While we can't say Rodriguez got away with anything, at least not in the end, we don't know how history will regard him in the future. What we do know is that Alex Rodriguez could have retired with an even greater fortune and more awards than he did.

Why did it matter if A-Rod abused PEDs at all? In reality, I don't know that he cared. He probably thought it was unfortunate that he was caught, but I don't think he lost too much sleep over it. Should we care? Well, ask yourself if it bothers you if a co-worker or a competitor cheats?

If the rules of competition state that PEDs are not acceptable because those substances allow people who use them to gain an unfair advantage, most of us would probably take issue with one athlete or team using them while opposing players or teams do not use them.

One's success in virtually any sport is based on performance, whether it is a batting average in baseball or a 100-meter dash time in track. Because every sport is a competition, and because we measure athletes against each other in fair competitions, when one athlete gains an unfair competitive advantage, it undermines the foundation of that sport.

For example, we know that a baseball bat must conform to a certain set of regulations. "Corking" the bat (hollowing out the insides and filling it with cork) is illegal for good reason. Suppose some brilliant scientist could treat the wood used in making bats with a magical, rubbery substance that couldn't be detected and that allowed the bat to weigh and look the same but yet produced hits of 500 feet or more. Unless everyone had them, it would completely change the competitive nature of the game. How would you judge one hitter against another? You couldn't.

The use of PEDs works much the same way. It produces an unfair competitive advantage for certain athletes, thus calling into question the fairness of competitions and rendering the outcomes of those competitions suspicious at best. How many more games would the Texas Rangers or the New York Yankees have lost had Rodriguez not been using PEDs?

Now that A-Rod's career is over, his career statistics — fourth in career home runs (696), third in runs batted in (2,086), and eighth in runs scored (2,021) — should have made him a surefire Hall of Famer. And he would be if not for the cloudy circumstances under which these statistics were achieved. Whether those statistics will be marked with an "asterisk" is anyone's guess at this point.

AN ETHICAL OBLIGATION?

I've been asked if Rodriguez had any kind of ethical obligation to admit to using PEDs. Or was it all about the money, and ethics be damned? I think there's an ethical obligation to admit to doing something that's wrong, but I don't think it's a natural reaction with unethical people. I don't think they are very likely to admit their transgressions, because they are willing to make an unethical choice in the first place. I have known of top-notch pharmaceutical sales reps who later admitted to the bribery of purchasing agents, and their response was something to the effect of, "It was expected of me to perform." In "performing," they cost their organizations huge fines and terminations.

In Rodriguez's case, it could have been about the money or it could have simply been that he wanted the praise and glory that comes with success. I don't know the foundation for his motivation, but it is clear that he and others were certainly willing to give themselves what they should have perceived to be an unfair advantage.

I should state that physicians assigned to Major League Baseball could have probably examined Rodriguez's blood chemistry at any time. Although they may not have found PEDs, other indicators might have raised a red flag. But MLB never tested him. Perhaps MLB officials in those days assumed most athletes were willing to tell the truth, so why go to the trouble of testing them? Or maybe no one wanted to rock the A-Rod boat!

My guess is that the type of substance athletes such as Rodriguez was using was difficult to detect with the available technology. Also, it may have been difficult to detect the drug in just one person. If you were looking for substance "X," it would have meant a blood chemistry analysis on everyone in baseball, which would have created a huge uproar at that time. The player's union would have gone nuts.

CREATING SPACE

The scandal, as we've presented it, is highly condensed and, in its full length, is quite complex. Yet, we can note with certainty that players around Alex Rodriguez began to distance themselves from him more and more as rumors of his drug use surfaced. My sense is that these other players might have done so because they knew the truth, or at least thought they did, even as Rodriguez continued to profess his innocence.

When players cheat, other people can get caught up in the circumstances. You can imagine some MLB players starting to go down the path with Rodriguez, contemplating PED use for themselves. But soon, they realize its dangers. Seeing they might be sucked into the vortex of suspicion and recrimination; they don't want to be considered guilty by association. It is like watching a whirlpool in a rip tide. At some point, you realize it's a catastrophe waiting to happen, and you know it won't be good for you, so you back off and keep your distance.

Let's be honest about all of this. Say you work out or play with the same set of athletes every day. You watch them, or you "spot" them, or you run the steps with them, and you know their routine. You go on vacation for a few months, and when you come back the person you normally work out with has gained twenty pounds of muscle, and his or her body fat is down to almost nothing.

Your teammate does not have to tell you anything, and you don't even have to ask, but you just know something has changed — something unusual. The pharma sales rep who made huge sales through bribes was suddenly seen driving a luxury car. You might not say anything besides, "Good for you," or "Nice ride!" but something seemed amiss.

What is interesting in Rodriguez's case is that not only were laboratories developing these substances, but the physicians treating A-Rod for his hip were giving him PEDs. There's a whole cottage industry of companies making money off this gray area of performance.

I don't care what the sport or business is, in a competitive environment, every athlete or organization is always going to seek the best possible competitive advantage. If you've given an athlete or even an organization an advantage, the financial rewards can be tremendous. These rewards can extend to certain members of the medical and pharmaceutical professions who entice athletes with career-extending or strengthening treatments and drugs. We shouldn't be surprised. Also — let's be honest — some physicians are fans. They want to get close to these guys because it's glamorous. It's like rubbing elbows with stardom. They figure that, if they can help these stars, then maybe there will be huge rewards for them down the line.

Technology is always changing and improving, and this fact applies to almost anything in sports. Look at the use of digital technology, new fabrics, new training tools, and new techniques. From an ethical perspective, the question becomes this: When does a certain technology cross the line from what's permissible and legal to something that's outside the rules completely?

Are we heading to a whole new class of super athletes using PEDs who might compete in their own leagues? It's an interesting debate.

One additional point I want to make concerns the question of long-term health effects: The negative effects of PEDs are now better understood than they were a couple of decades ago. What do we know about the effects of PEDs in use five or 10 years ago, or about drugs in use under the table at this very moment? What about the scientists or physicians who administer and develop these medications? This is a whole new, and separate, ethical area for discussion.

A-ROD'S RETURN TO BASEBALL

Does it bother me that Rodriguez made a comeback in baseball? No, not really. Does it bother me that he used PEDs while he was building those records? Yes, it's bothersome. Considering the incredible attention he would be getting from the media today, you've got to wonder whether he even needed PEDs in the first place. Wouldn't that be ironic? At the end of his career, he may have been demonstrating what he has always had — his natural ability.

I'd like to think so. I'd like to believe that in the end, he was as clean as he claimed to be all along, though I have read columnists who remained dubious. Back to business for a second: If a sales rep was fired for giving out bribes, would you ever trust that rep again if he or she became a superstar at another company?

One thing is clear: Unlike in the past, if Rodriguez had been caught cheating again, MLB would have banned him from baseball, and he would have lost huge amounts of money.

You don't need to look any further than Lance Armstrong to get an example of what happens when you push the limits. I wonder how it would have turned out for Armstrong had he just played it clean. Though not covered in this book, the Armstrong case bears review for unethical drug use.

I think this scandal demonstrates two things. First is the willingness of some athletes to violate the rules of the game in order to win. Second is the whole cottage industry of chemists and physicians who are more than willing to help athletes achieve their performance goals by any means necessary.

Then there is the willingness to tell the truth and be honest. Like many of us who have made unethical choices, Rodriguez found it was easy to opt out of integrity. For him, it came down to trying to protect the choices he'd made. He knew what he was doing was wrong, and yet he did not pause to consider what he needed to do to protect the sport.

What's fascinating is that ultimately it wasn't Alex Rodriguez who broke this scandal open; it was his suppliers. It is a good lesson. Those motivated by the money fled like rats off a sinking ship. Their penalties were fines and jail time.

SECTION V

Rodriguez will always have a core of passionate fans, mostly Yankees fans probably, but I would expect that. Fans do what fans do. Baseball fans at large, though, don't have the same level of admiration for A-Rod. They are not likely to forget his transgressions, and his legacy will absolutely reflect that.

The one thing millions of dollars cannot buy is a good reputation.

CHAPTER 20

THE PITTSBURGH PIRATES COCAINE TRIAL OF 1985

Who: Pittsburgh Pirates, Dale Schiffman, Kevin Koch

Offense: Cocaine use and distribution

Result: Imprisonment

Before the scandals involving performance-enhancing drugs, Major League Baseball was rocked by a recreational cocaine drug scandal. The scandal shattered baseball's all-American image, and, in a way, it mars baseball to this day. Though cocaine use would be discovered across the league at that time, no team was more affected than the Pittsburgh Pirates.

On May 30, 1985, a grand jury convened in Pittsburgh, naming seven drug dealers and distributors, along with several baseball players, as part of a powerful cocaine network. The next morning, the FBI banged on Dale Shiffman's door and arrested him for dealing drugs.

Shiffman was a freelance photographer who had spent a great deal of time around the Pirates. He got to know many of the players on a personal level. Apparently, Shiffman had connections, as players often approached him asking to buy cocaine.

In an episode of the scandal that now seems ridiculous, Shiffman was eventually turned in, by the "Pirate Parrot," no less. More specifically, Kevin Koch, the man in the mascot suit, reported Shiffman. A third dealer, Curtis Strong, was associated with the Philadelphia Phillies as their catering manager.

At one time, Koch had been Shiffman's closest friend and ally. Early on, they saw a goldmine of an opportunity to deal drugs to MLB players. Shiffman and Koch worked out a system: Shiffman scored the coke, and Koch delivered it to the players. The Pirate Parrot mascot was a drug pusher.

According to the FBI, this cocaine distribution scheme had been in place since the late 1970s. Reporting for SB Nation on April 26, 2012, Jim McLennan wrote:

"'At the conclusion of that interview [with Koch], we had a list of drug dealers, and a list of the professional baseball players to whom they were selling cocaine,' said FBI investigator Wells Morrison. 'Every ball player that we spoke with identified additional ball players who were also using cocaine.'"

The result of the widening investigation at that time was that thirteen MLB players from a number of different teams were hauled in front of a Pittsburgh grand jury. A total of twenty-one players would eventually be implicated in the scheme.

On February 28, 1986, MLB Commissioner Peter Ueberroth threatened to suspend eleven players, seven of them, for a full season with a loss of pay. However, he offered to lift those suspensions if the players would meet certain conditions. These were big-name guys, not just guys collecting splinters on the bench. They included former National League MVPs Keith Hernandez and Dave Parker, along with Dale Berra, son of the famous Yogi Berra, and Lonnie Smith. Other players were threatened with suspensions of just sixty days, as they had lesser infractions.

Of the players threatened with one-year suspensions, the commissioner said they would be allowed back into baseball after giving up 10% of their salaries to fund drug treatment programs, agreeing to participate in drug-related community service, and, naturally, submitting to random drug testing.

The position of law enforcement at that time was that the dealers should be criminally punished, but that the players were just victims. Of the drug dealers who were punished, the largest sentences came down on Strong and Shiffman. Both were given twelve-year sentences, though they each served only a few years.

After his release, in an interview with HBO's Bryant Gumbel, Shiffman expressed bitterness that he had gone to jail and the players hadn't so much as missed a single game. He maintained that he'd had only four or five clients and was not so much a dealer as he was someone who was just helping out a handful of players who had befriended him.

Of the big names that had been threatened with suspension, Parker and Hernandez would continue on to have successful careers. In fact, one day after his grand jury appearance in Pittsburgh, Hernandez was given a standing ovation his first time up at bat.

While it may be inaccurate to say that the drug dealers caused some of the players to descend into addiction, their presence certainly did not help. Pittsburgh pitcher Rod Scurry had been the first baseball player the FBI approached. Scurry started to buy cocaine from Shiffman in 1982. He would battle a cocaine addiction for years and would ultimately die of a cocaine-related heart attack in 1992.

Willie Mays Aikens, who was playing for the Toronto Blue Jays at the time of the scandal, had scored drugs from Strong. He admitted to being high whenever he played. He would continue using cocaine, and in 1994 he was convicted of selling crack cocaine and saw jail time.

When the dealers and players were caught, Shiffman estimated to authorities that seventeen of the twenty-five players on the

Pittsburgh Pirates team — about 70% — were using cocaine. Though New York Met Keith Hernandez would later retract his words, at the time of his threatened suspension, he said that about 40% of all Major League Baseball players were using drugs.

At the conclusion of the grand jury investigation, MLB Commissioner Peter Ueberroth was quoted as saying: "Enough is enough. Baseball's going to accomplish this. We're going to remove drugs and be an example."

MLB's commitment to removing recreational drugs was largely seen as a joke. Lonnie Smith, one of the players caught in the drug scandal, was to have been randomly tested for drugs several times, as per the terms of MLB's agreement with the players. But the Kansas City Star reported on July 29, 1987, that "Smith labeled Ueberroth's claim that baseball is 'free of drugs,' as a farce."

Predictably, MLB fired back that it wasn't a matter of how many times Smith had been randomly tested that was important but rather that he stays off drugs. It was a weak response, to be sure. Peter Ueberroth asked every MLB player to submit to testing on a voluntary basis, but the Major League Players Association rejected the idea. Not one player was punished as a result of the 1985 scandal, nor was any player tested for drugs.

CHUCK'S ETHICS REVIEW:

Pirates: Sniffing Out So Many Ethical Issues!

Baseball, the American pastime, seemed to have been more concerned about its image than it was with suspending players involved in the 1985 cocaine scandal. It was more of a logical position than we might expect. Major league games were, and remain, family-oriented events, complete with fireworks, sing-alongs, the seventh-inning stretch, and so forth. All of a sudden, MLB finds a number of players from many different teams involved in illegal drugs — distributed by a mascot. It is a huge image issue.

In baseball, you obviously have to have the players to be successful. The thinking of MLB may have been, "We can't go after the players because that would hurt the image of the entire league, so we have to go after other targets." They had to do something to bring the pulse back to baseball.

In terms of sports ethics, we see situations like this over and over again. When an issue such as drugs becomes public, it typically follows the same pattern. The league or team says they'll take a "hard stance," then they say they'll go after the player or players involved. There is invariably a lot of saber rattling at first, but then they start to backtrack a little, saying they are not going to do anything that will create a lot of problems for the sport.

What does that mean for sports ethics, especially at the professional level? It usually means that those in leadership roles are willing to talk the talk but not willing to walk the walk. It seems more important to play games with the media and the fans than to create harsh consequences that have a true impact.

I'm aware that the players involved in this scandal gave up a percentage of their salaries, but how was that percentage measured and where was it spent? We don't know. Why not levy harsh suspensions and require public service announcements at MLB games? To do so might have taken the matter to the fans, who might have stayed away from ballparks if it bothered them enough. Major League Baseball chose a much easier way out.

We Don't Care; We Love You Anyway!

Mets star Keith Hernandez was hauled before a grand jury for his illegal drug use. The next day, fans were giving him a standing ovation. Fans are fanatical by definition, and from the perspective of some fans, winning at all costs often trumps doing whatever is necessary to maintain the integrity of the sport. So, what does the standing ovation say? It says, "We don't care what he does, or if he did drugs; we just want him to do well on the field."

Contrast the public reaction to guys like Hernandez with that of Dale Shiffman. Shiffman was bitter, and at first, we might actually side with him. After all, he served jail time for dealing, while the players were let off the hook and continued to play.

But there are two levels on which we can look at this. On the surface, Shiffman's resentment over serving jail time was the victim's game. "Yes, I was doing some small-time dealing," he might have been saying, "but I'm just the photographer, and, after all, they were the ones using." Instead of owning up to the fact that he was dealing illegal drugs, Shiffman tried to redirect the blame. What the players would or would not pay in terms of jail time wasn't his concern. He must be accountable for his own actions. Instead, he played the victim.

On a deeper level, Major League Baseball tried to convince us that they took care of everything because they brought the sources of the drugs — Shiffman and other dealers — to justice. But they certainly didn't take care of everything. Yes, Shiffman was dealing drugs, but he was a small-time nobody who was only the team photographer. He needed to take ownership of his problems and he should have been punished, but he was also expendable — and MLB knew it. What MLB really failed to do was to follow through on its commitment to do random drug testing, at least for the players involved in this scandal. By doing so, they could have set an example for other players and for the fans, especially kids who were most certainly paying attention. They might have also discouraged other potential drug dealers from trying to get into the game. They didn't, and it was soon business as usual.

The MLB officials played with the deck chairs on the Titanic, but they did little else. MLB wanted to create the illusion that it was cleaning it all up and that the game still had integrity, so what did it do? It punished only the expendable people.

REJECTION OF TESTING

One logical question that arises from this scandal is: Why would the Major League Players Association reject random drug testing of players? Secondarily, while people in all sorts of professions must undergo testing for substance abuse, what did MLB have to fear?

Simply put, MLB's fear was that, if it was going to make everyone undergo random drug testing, it might just find what it was looking for. Suppose several players had tested positive? Or maybe as many as one hundred? That's significant, especially if they are well-known players. If there is a policy or program in place to detect illegal drugs, then the question becomes: If players test positive, what are you going to do about it? What will the corrective action be? Deciding on appropriate recourse could hamper the whole process.

Let me give you a related example. Suppose there could be a chip that could be implanted in every car that would relay its speed back to the local police departments in real-time. Every time someone went over the speed limit, they would automatically be caught. What would we say to that? Society would be outraged. It would be like Big Brother was looking over our shoulders. That is what it would be like in MLB if every player was continually subject to drug testing. It would create a huge fear.

As with any group, members of the players association know that some players are abusing illegal substances, yet rarely are they willing to expose the problem because they don't want the entire membership put under the microscope. Many members assume that if some players are implicated, it will implicate the whole group. Similarly, if you are a great driver and rarely go over the speed limit, you would not want to pay a higher insurance premium next year because the insurance company determined that most people were speeding.

FAST FORWARD

We might compare the Pittsburgh Cocaine Trial of 1985 and the Major League Players Association's subsequent rejection of testing to more recent situations, such as Alex Rodriguez, Mark McGwire, and Sammy Sosa using PEDs. I think the two are much more connected than we might imagine.

Everything builds on something else. For example, let's say that, back in the 1985 case, MLB had mandated random drug testing. Perhaps their rationale was that it would make sure the sport was clean.

Let's further say that the MLPA agreed to go along with it for the good of the game. In fact, they agreed with MLB that extremely severe consequences among their members should be instituted and enforced. If that had happened, then, yes, things would have certainly changed. Its leadership would have placed the sport of baseball in a very strong position. In fact, because MLB and the players would have taken a strong position earlier, the later use of PEDs may have been lessened or minimized.

On the other hand, if in 1985, MLB had taken an extremely weak position — perhaps because of the "Big Brother" fear — and said they weren't going to test anybody within certain time periods, or that they were going to give everyone in baseball six weeks warning prior to testing, there would be almost no consequences. As it was, MLB's position was pretty weak. So much so that, when the use of PEDs came along, MLB wasn't prepared to deal with the issue and had no foundation on which to build a credible drug monitoring program.

CLOSE TO POWER

Time and time again, in these scandals, we see relatively minor characters finding their way to people of power. You might ask, what do people such as a photographer or a catering managers hope to gain from a relationship with big-league players?

Minor influences find their way to people in power because, quite simply, power can offer prestige, wealth, and a feeling of self-importance. Outsiders seek power because they have little power themselves. This doesn't happen only in sports; it can happen in business, politics, entertainment, or almost anything else. Anyplace there's power, people of influence — great or small — will find their way into an athlete's life. By the way, sometimes a person of influence may appear minor at first but may become significant as time goes on and the stakes change. It is the classic case of a relative or friend with absolutely no financial power convincing the athlete that he or she will handle the athlete's financial affairs. Maybe it doesn't mean so much or make much of a difference when the athlete is playing single-A ball, but with a multimillion-dollar deal at the MLB level, poor financial advice or untrustworthy dealings can cause major damage.

What some athletes gain by allowing these influencers into their lives, especially athletes who have come from humble backgrounds is a sense of familiarity and community. As humans, we bring all kinds of fears along with us through life. It's often hard to trust others and make allies. When athletes confuse spouses, friends, or friends of friends with professionals, though, it can create big-time problems.

Despite having grown up together or sharing common interests, a friend or parent with no financial or public relations background has no business controlling an athlete's wealth, contracts, appearances, or reputation. Just because someone comes from your neighborhood or family doesn't mean they have the credentials to control your finances.

I would also say there's a lot of ego in play here. Athletes will sometimes let friends into their inner circle as drivers or gofers because they want to help them out. They feel they owe these friends something. At the same time, having their friends now serve them fuels their egos. In reality, they're playing each other. It is no different than if I knew an attorney for the Rolling Stones, and the attorney got me backstage for one of the Stones' concerts. All of a sudden, I make it into that circle. I feel important, and, of course, it feeds the rock stars' egos as well.

With respect to the Pittsburgh Cocaine Trial, the photographer was only that — a photographer. Because he had access to the players through the mascot, it gave him the illusion of being connected to power. In counseling athletes at any level, I remind them that their success is based on their abilities on the field, not on the ego rush that wannabes give them off the field.

At base, anything that causes you to lose focus or puts you at risk needs to be removed. Most outside influences don't do anything for your career. They aren't on the field with you. They sure as heck won't be there if things go wrong. The best thing you can do is to say goodbye to them.

In Pittsburgh in 1985, someone, perhaps a team manager, needed to kick the photographer out of the locker room and off the field — permanently. It would have been a start. By the way, I have little doubt that lots of people, including the managers, had an idea of what was truly going on.

CHAPTER 21

KAMILA VALIYEVA DOPING SCANDAL, 2022 WINTER OLYMPICS

Who: Kamila Valiyeva, Russian Olympic Committee

Offense: Failed blood test

Result: Major turmoil, loss of reputation, loss of medals

Months after her positive drug test sullied the 2022 Winter Olympics, the case of Russian figure skater Kamila Valiyeva continues to frustrate international anti-doping organizations and her competitors alike, and resolution for all parties remains elusive.

The entire ordeal has come to symbolize the struggles that international sports competitions such as the Olympics have faced ensuring Russian Olympic Committee compliance with anti-doping rules.

Since 2008, scores of Russian athletes have had their Olympic medals stripped from them. Some of the punishments were the result of failed drug tests administered during the Games. Others resulted years later after International Olympic Committee investigations and with the use of enhanced testing techniques.

During the 2014 Sochi Olympics, allegations surfaced that Russia had *instituted a vast, state-sponsored doping scheme.* In 2018, the ROC handed over a computer database to IOC investigators, who then determined that *parts of it had been erased or manipulated.*

Two years later, the Court of Arbitration for Sport handed the ROC a severe set of penalties. There was an order to reimburse $1.24 million in investigation costs. There was also a $100,000 fine and $452,000 in court costs. Crucially, Russia would be barred from competing under its own name, flag or anthem at any international competition for the following two years.

Then-president of the World Anti-Doping Agency (WADA), Witold Bańka, said in a statement at the time that WADA was vindicated by the ruling.

"The (CAS) panel has clearly upheld our findings that the Russian authorities brazenly and illegally manipulated the Moscow Laboratory data in an effort to cover up an institutionalized doping scheme," said Bańka.

Exception?

Luckily for Valiyeva and her compatriots, the IOC made an exception, allowing *Russians who could prove they were clean to compete under the ROC banner.*

Valiyeva was born in 2006 in Kazan, the largest city in the semi-autonomous Russian Republic of Tatarstan. She began participating in sports at an early age, settling on figure skating by age five.

She made her first appearance on the world stage in 2019 at the International Skating Union's Junior Grand Prix in France, winning the gold medal. There, Valiyeva became just the second female ever to land a quadruple toe loop in competition.

Valiyeva continued her meteoric rise in junior competitions over the next two years. Her ability to incorporate quadruple jumps, sometimes in combination with other jumps, helped her notch some of the highest scores ever for a junior skater, including a couple of world records for points.

In 2021, Valiyeva competed at the senior level of Grand Prix figure skating for the first time at the Skate Canada International. There, she beat her own world record for free skating points (180.89) and total score (265.08) to take the gold medal.

Valiyeva next placed first in the 2021 Rostelecom Cup, a Grand Prix event held at the Iceberg Skating Palace in Sochi, Russia, the site of the 2014 Winter Olympics.

FALL OFF THE PLATFORM

Her next competition was on December 24, 2021, at the 2022 Russian Figure Skating Championships. She won gold again, qualifying her for a spot on the ROC Olympic team.

The very next day, on December 25, 2021, Valiyeva submitted a sample for drug testing analysis. The chain of events that followed that sample would be a source of contention between the ROC, the IOC, and the Olympic committees of several other nations.

As the 2022 Winter Olympics approached, prognosticators pegged the fifteen-year-old Valiyeva as the favorite to win gold in Beijing. Her main competition consisted of her fellow Russians, Anna Shcherbakova and Alexandra Trusova, both seventeen years old at the time.

The trio even had a catchy nickname. Coming into the Games, reporters and fans had taken to calling them the Quad Squad, obviously because each was able to land some version of the coveted quadruple spinning jumps.

Predictably, the ROC won gold in the team event. The U.S. team, led by eventual men's singles gold medalist Nathan Chen, took its first-ever silver in the event, and Japan got bronze.

Two days later, news broke that Valiyeva's drug test, the one she had taken back on December 25, *had come back positive for the presence of trimetazidine*, a medication that allows the heart to function properly even with lowered oxygen levels in the blood. This drug is on the WADA list of *banned substances*, grouped as a hormone and metabolic blocker.

In practice, trimetazidine *enables athletes to recover faster*, an obvious advantage in days-long figure skating competitions.

STRANGE MANEUVERS

The Russian Anti-Doping Agency immediately suspended Valiyeva from competing, but it rescinded the suspension after she appealed. In response, the IOC then announced that there would be no medal presentation ceremonies for any event in which Valiyeva earned a medal.

That decision meant that *none* of the 18 members of the three medaling teams (including the U.S.) would get a ceremony in Beijing, and none of them would head home with a medal in hand.

The US Olympic Committee leadership expressed frustration with the news.

"Not only did they achieve a best-ever finish, most-ever points scored, and firsts in three different disciplines," said USOPC spokeswoman Kate Hartman via Twitter, "but they also continue to embody the spirit and principles of Team USA."

With Valiyeva all set to compete in the singles competition, a ROC podium lockout seemed in the offing. What happened next shocked and saddened most spectators and participants, yet likely seemed a fitting end to many fans.

Valiyeva was shaky to start her free skate routine, opening up the competition for the gold medal right from the start. But, once she collapsed both literally and figuratively on the ice, her infamy was assured. She had already earned enough points to finish fourth, but there would be no singles medal for her, even if she never would have held it.

A stunned Japanese Kaori Sakamoto was practically gifted bronze by Valiyeva's collapse. Shcherbakova climbed the top step, accepting the gold medal in a ceremony that might otherwise not have happened. A petulant Trusova took the silver medal, though her displeasure was picked up in an ugly hot-mic incident.

"I hate this sport!" she yelled in Russian. "Everyone has a gold medal. Everyone! But I don't!"

A visibly shaken Valiyeva got an earful from her coach, Eteri Tutberidze.

"Why did you let it go?" asked the exasperated coach. "Explain it to me. Why? Why did you stop fighting?"

The image of Valiyeva sliding on the ice will be the indelible image of those Olympic Games. As a protected person, the only likely penalty she will pay is losing her team gold medal. The other teams will surely be promoted a spot each, assuming the appeals process ever reaches a conclusion.

In the end, none of the controversy makes much sense. A girl who is perhaps the most talented competitor that figure skating has ever known will carry an asterisk next to her name for the rest of her career.

Valiyeva likely would have won gold in Beijing *had she remained clean.* Yet, no one in a position of power is accusing her of doing anything wrong.

A failed drug test in someone so young, especially within an organization with systemic doping violations such as the ROC, is a failure of leadership. There were ample adults around the young lady all through her brief career.

What were they doing?

CHUCK'S ETHICS REVIEW:

Kamila Caught in a Country's Greed

On the rink, the spotlight is always on the athlete, but the blame in the Kamila Valiyeva fraud is on the support mechanism that propels them to potential greatness. I contend that no kid at five years of age thinks to themselves, "I will be the best someday by using performance enhancing drugs!"

It's silly to even think such a thing, yet why does this stuff keep happening to the Russian Skating Federation?

First, there is the win-at-all-costs attitude. Is this philosophy limited to the Russians? Heavens no, and to think so is nanve. This book is riddled with stories from all sports and all nationalities that show that "winning at all costs" is, in some minds at least, worth the risk. However, there is almost always a boomerang effect. Unethical behavior comes back to haunt and the Russians are often the prime offenders.

Do I blame this young woman, who yelled "I hate this sport,"? It is impossible for me to make that leap. I believe Valiyeva was directed (make that ordered) by her handlers, managers, and coaches to take a performance-enhancing medication. In their way of thinking, apparently, the drugs would not be detected.

Over time, drugs have certainly become more sophisticated and difficult to spot. The Russians believed they had "a winner" in finding an undetectable PED. However, the mechanisms to catch doping have become better as well.

The most important consequence in this unfortunate event — an event that could have been prevented — is the psychological damage done to a gifted athlete. She is now tainted and embittered. The unethical leadership, if you want to call it that, has only experienced a minor political setback. They lost their bragging rights. As long as the consequences of their actions aren't severe, they will continue to abuse the system in this manner.

Another talented person, taking another drug, will probably come along and not fall at a critical juncture. It takes severe life altering consequences for most people to have permanent behavior change. The Russian Olympic skating team has come close to permanent Olympic altering consequences, but they are generally clueless and uncaring in pushing the envelope.

I might add that the idea that this behavior of putting something over on everyone else in a sport or industry is solely endemic to the Russians is erroneous. Recent major scandals in industries as diverse as healthcare (Purdue Pharma), automotive manufacturing (Volkswagen) and banking (Wells Fargo) all involved leadership unethically using underlings as pawns.

Unless the Olympics develops an ethical sense, young athletes will continue to be tossed aside as disposable chessboard pieces.

SECTION VI
VIOLENCE MOST FOUL

CHAPTER 22

THE NEW ORLEANS SAINTS BOUNTY SCANDAL

Who: Greg Williams, Sean Payton, Mike Cerullo

Offense: Alleged Bounty on Opposing Players

Result: Suspensions, Terminations

It's no secret that professional football is tough and violent. That said, there are unwritten codes for violence among players that they, for the most part, observe. There have been secret "awards" for big game-day hits in the past. For example, a defensive squad might hold a pool for the biggest hit against the other team. But *bounties are different.* The NFL in no way forgives a player for intentionally trying to hurt another player so badly it ends his career — nor do most of the other players.

Discussions about taking players out occur often in locker rooms. It would be nanve to say this never happens. But the New Orleans Saints bounty scandal, or Bountygate, was something else, because it was formalized and approved by the coaching staff.

A much larger issue serves as a backdrop to Bountygate: concussions and permanent brain damage. Concerns about traumatic brain injuries have dramatically increased in football as physicians have learned more about the injury. Many are questioning the long-term viability of the game, and no one is more aware of this fact than the NFL brass.

During the period the Bountygate scandal unfolded, Junior Seau, a Pro Football Hall of Fame linebacker for the San Diego Chargers and Miami Dolphins, went from having a highly successful career to retirement to depression and dementia and then, tragically, suicide. His story, it turns out, wasn't as unique as it seemed.

The protocols regarding hits have changed. Medical screenings have become standard and, certainly, public attitudes toward brain injuries have been transformed. The NFL front office is hypersensitive to any further erosion of the image of the game, even as it is increasingly seen as being needlessly violent. But before that change could happen, the New Orleans Saints Bountygate scandal would play its role in bringing violence to light.

The origins of Bountygate can be traced to January 15, 2009. On that date, the New Orleans Saints named Gregg Williams as its new defensive coordinator.

A year later, on January 16, 2010, Saints linebacker Jonathan Vilma allegedly offered $10,000 to any teammate who could knock out opposing quarterback Kurt Warner in the second round of the 2009 playoffs.

The next week, Vilma allegedly made a similar offer to any teammate who knocked Minnesota Vikings quarterback Brett Favre out of the NFC Championship Game. In that game, Favre received a number of questionable hits, and, after review, on January 29, the NFL fined the Saints $30,000 for various hits against the Vikings.

A few days later, the NFL began an investigation of the New Orleans Saints' so-called bounty program. Specifically, the NFL was looking into claims that certain people in the Saints organization had offered bounties for various intentional hits and injuries against opposing teams. On that date as well, Gregg Williams forced Saints assistant coach Mike Cerullo to destroy any incriminating evidence against both Williams and assistant head coach Joe Vitt. Cerullo would eventually become a whistleblower and a key witness against the Saints. On February 7, 2010, the Saints won the Super Bowl, the first for the team and its long-suffering fanbase.

On February 24, 2010, former Saints player Anthony Hargrove met with the NFL. Hargrove described a meeting he had with Williams regarding bounties. He would eventually receive an eight-game suspension from NFL Commissioner Roger Goodell.

On August 5, 2011, the NFL made major changes to the Collective Bargaining Agreement that gave Goodell much more power in the realm of disciplining players.

The following season, on January 15, 2012, reports emerged that Gregg Williams was reportedly changing defensive coordinator jobs from the Saints to the St. Louis Rams. A mutual split between the Saints and Williams was in the works.

On February 9, 2012, Saints quarterback Drew Brees released a statement denying he had any knowledge of a bounty system. It was probably a good idea to do so. For all we know, opposing teams might have taken aim at Brees.

Then on March 2, the NFL released its report linking Gregg Williams and multiple Saints personnel to a bounty program that had lasted from 2009 to 2011. Williams issued an apologetic statement regarding the bounty program, saying he had shamed the organization. The bounty program was not only well-organized but also widespread. According to an NFL investigation, twenty-two to twenty-seven defensive players were involved with special prizes awarded to "cart-offs" and knockouts. The Saints had specifically targeted quarterbacks Favre, Warner, Aaron Rogers, and Cam Newton. The scheme obviously was not limited in scope to only a couple of players and a few isolated incidents.

Four days later, head coach Sean Payton released a statement taking full responsibility for not overseeing the coaching staff, allowing the bounty program to take shape. The apology did little good. On March 21, 2012, the NFL announced a number of severe penalties against both the Saints organization and multiple players and coaches. Shortly afterward, three coaches, including Payton, appealed their suspensions with the league office. The NFL reviewed the request but ultimately denied it, upholding the suspensions and determining that Payton had covered it up.

In early May 2012, the NFL suspended four Saints players, including Vilma, for the entire upcoming 2012 season. Vilma filed a defamation suit against Goodell, and, in May, he would take his case to federal court. In early September 2012, the National Football League Players Association filed a motion with the NFL to stop the suspensions, and a few days later, Vilma met with Goodell to discuss the bounty allegations. Again, it did little good. In October, Goodell reinstated the suspension. Predictably, the players predictably.

On November 19, 2012, the players' hearings began. Paul Tagliabue, the chief arbitrator in the investigation and a former NFL commissioner, vacated the suspensions of the players. Yet, it would not be until January 22, 2013, that Payton was allowed to return to the Saints organization.

Williams was initially suspended from coaching indefinitely but was reinstated the next year. He became defensive coordinator first for the Tennessee Titans in 2013 and then for the St. Louis Rams in 2014. In January 2017, Williams was hired as the defensive coordinator of the Cleveland Browns, but the stigma of Bountygate follows him.

CHUCK'S ETHICS REVIEW:

Beat 'Em Up Boys! Dollars for Destruction!

It is just plain wrong. That is my answer whenever I am asked about the New Orleans Saints bounty scandal. But before we get into specifics, let me say that this case should serve notice to every high school or collegiate head coach and athletic director: Make sure you carefully monitor every aspect of your program, because its integrity depends upon it.

Now, what could have been done to halt Bountygate from happening in the first place? The no-brainer answer is that the people who were offered the bounty could have said, "No, I'm not going to do that." However, for a player to take that kind of a stand, he would have had to be ethically aware and courageous.

Let's be honest. The guys who were offered extra inducements were already paid well to play the game. The amount of money they were being offered for a career-ending hit on an opponent was, as the expression used to be, chump change. Sure, the playing career of an NFL player lasts, on average, only three and a half years. Maybe a little extra cash seemed enticing. And, yes, there might have been those who would have taken the money, while others would have said it just wasn't right. Ultimately, it was less about the money than it was a matter of ethical conscience.

So, if some players knew it was wrong, why didn't they stop it? It's completely possible that someone in the Saints organization who'd been offered a bounty might have stepped up but was afraid to. Maybe he was thinking he didn't want to be the one to say anything. The bonds inside the confines of a football team can be very tight. It is a strong fraternal organization, much like the police or fire departments. Players may have decided they didn't want to intentionally take down another player, so they didn't participate. They may have not wanted to squeal, either.

If you are in the business world, it might be interesting for me to ask if any of you ever observed workplace bullying or sexual harassment? Was it dismissed or ignored? What was the outcome of reporting it?

This scandal came down to accountability on the part of the head coach and his coordinators. They had the power to stop the unethical targeting and didn't, and it came back to haunt them big time. Sometimes, a coach, even at the high school level, needs to step back from X's and O's and focus on playing the game hard but also on making sure that ethical controls are in place. It's a tough balance, I know, but it is achievable.

Now, Vilma and the other players who were initially suspended were ultimately allowed to play. The NFL found it easier to punish the team management and coaching staff and to leave the players alone, which is not surprising. It sounds simplistic, but you have to have players to play the game. In this case, the players might have done something inappropriate and unethical, but management should have known what was going on. They decided to bury their heads in the sand, and as a result, the NFL fined the owner and punished the coaches. It was easier and safer that way.

Was this enough? There's much less tolerance nowadays for intentionally trying to injure another player, but even in 2009, I feel the NFL should have come down harder on the team and its players. Encouraging players to injure their opponents has no place in any sport.

Head coach Sean Payton ultimately suffered most of the consequences of this scandal for not properly overseeing his team's actions, though he may not have known all the details. Was this fair? Yes, it was. As I said above, team members and assistant coaches probably should have been more heavily penalized, but the harshest penalties needed to start with the head coach. Without proper standards of conduct set forth by the head coach, teams can spin out of control.

WHISTLE-BLOWERS OFTEN SUFFER

Mike Cerullo, the man who was the whistleblower in this scandal, has said he was vilified and subjected to slander for his part in revealing Bountygate. So, is it worth it to stand up and do the right thing? That could very well be the hardest question to answer in any sports ethics case because, historically, across any sports organization, the whistleblower is almost always maligned and belittled. The cost to the whistleblower is often significant. That said, whistleblowing is the number-one way unethical activity is uncovered.

Standing up for what's right often causes a dramatic change in the life of the person brave enough and tough enough to do so. In blowing the whistle on another coach, Cerullo earned self-respect he otherwise would not have had he allowed the scandal to continue. He possibly also saved the playing careers of many players.

I do know that Cerullo was made the head of football operations at Princeton. He was able to land on his feet and has proven that there is life after getting out of a lousy situation. I realize that some fans and media continue to attack Cerullo's credibility to this day. It takes big shoulders to be a whistleblower.

OTHER SETTINGS

Before we leave this important topic, I want to revisit high school and college programs. If I were directing the coaching staff of any program and I were to find out about anything resembling a bounty, I would ask the players whether it was worth it. I would want to know how they would feel if there was a bounty placed on their heads.

High school players don't often think through the consequences. Really, can I explain to a sixteen-year-old what it is like to get a knee replacement at age fifty? It's hard for them to understand, but we have to make them try.

Obviously, a bounty program in high school or college would point to a breakdown in coaching and supervision. Yes, I know the platitudes — "Football is war," etc. But it is not war; it's a game. You can play the game as hard as you want, as long as it is within the rules. An inadvertent hit is one thing; a hard hit is within the rules. But an intentional tackle to take out a kid's kneecaps or to cause a concussion runs contrary to every sensibility an athletic program should cultivate and display.

The athletic department and coaching hierarchy must be aware of any unethical activity occurring in their programs. If I were an athletic director or principal, I'd be extremely harsh with any high school or collegiate coach who would suggest a bounty program. Suspension would be the least of it. The coach would not see the inside of my school's locker room again.

There was a case in 2015 where an assistant high school coach told his players to knock an official out of the game — and they almost did. In that case, the reward wasn't money. It was the approval of the coach. But it still demonstrated the same motivation: to win at all costs, no matter how unethical. The coach who ordered the hit was suspended from coaching. He should not be allowed to coach young athletes again.

CHAPTER 23

TODD BERTUZZI, STEVE MOORE, AND ON-ICE VIOLENCE

Who: Todd Bertuzzi, Steve Moore, Marc Crawford

Offense: So-called "Code-Red" Hit on Steve Moore by Todd Bertuzzi

Result: Fines, Suspensions, Permanent Injury

"Canucks coach Marc Crawford was incensed. Threats were made. "There's definitely a bounty on his head," Canucks winger Brad May said, as quoted by The Vancouver Sun. "It's going to be fun when we get him." — Sean Fitz-Gerald, National Post, March 7, 2014, "Steve Moore-Todd Bertuzzi case reaches its ten-year anniversary without final resolution"

NHL players fight. They get injured. Hockey is one of the few sports played in North America where intense cross-border rivalries exist. The Todd Bertuzzi blindside hit on Steve Moore triggered emotions in both Canada and the U.S., sentiments that had not been seen in hockey for years. The hit and the circumstances surrounding it still raise arguments today. The question remains: Who ordered it?

On February 16, 2004, a rookie forward named Steve Moore took to the ice for the Colorado Avalanche for a game in Vancouver, British Columbia. Moore had played for Harvard, and though a native of Toronto, Ontario, Moore had earned his reputation playing in the U.S.

On the night the scandal was set in motion, the Vancouver Canucks team captain was Markus Naslund, who was then the league's leading scorer. During the game, Moore took a run at Naslund and floored him with a vicious elbow to the face. Naslund flew to the ice and sustained a concussion and two lacerations that each required several stitches. Naslund was the team's biggest star, and the Vancouver crowd went crazy. There was no doubt they wanted blood.

The shot Moore put on Naslund was cheap, but the officials did not call it on the ice. The league office likewise failed to act when it reviewed the hit later on.

On March 3, 2004, the teams met again, this time in Denver. Not much happened in the way of retribution, maybe because the NHL commissioner was in the audience or because the playoffs were coming up and each team needed to focus on winning. Either way, the game went by without incident. Meanwhile, there were rumblings from the Canucks, especially from the veteran Bertuzzi, that there would be payback, but not much else happened.

By that time, Bertuzzi, a winger, had spent close to ten years in the league. He was a proven veteran. He had no great love for the Colorado Avalanche, going back to the 2001-2002 season when he was penalized ten games for leaving the bench during a fight. Bertuzzi was not only a scrapper but also a goal scorer, and he often played with Naslund. They had a bond, and Bertuzzi likely felt a need to settle the score. Years later, in a Vancouver Postmedia News interview on September 26, 2008, Naslund said he felt sorry for Bertuzzi because Bertuzzi had stood up for him.

On March 8, 2004, just five days after the previous game, the Canucks would indeed get another chance at the Avalanche on their home ice. From the beginning of the game, the

Canucks were taking every opportunity to take chip shots at Moore and challenge him to fight.

Moore skated away from a few challenges, but, well into the first period, he finally got into it with Canucks enforcer Matt Cooke.

Moore and Cooke went at it and fought to a draw. Maybe it should have ended there, but as the game went on there was already blood in the water. Every time Moore made it onto the ice, the crowd wanted his head.

The taunts increased as the third period began. Bertuzzi came up behind Moore, grabbed his jersey, and sucker-punched him. It could have ended there as well, but Bertuzzi drove Moore face-first onto the ice and piled on him.

Moore didn't move. A pool of blood grew on the ice and collected around his face. The cheering of the crowd turned to stunned silence. Moore was taken off the ice unconscious. He had three cracked vertebrae and a concussion, and the incident ended his professional hockey career.

Bertuzzi held a press conference soon after the incident. He was tearful and seemed genuinely remorseful. At the same time, the media maligned the violence in hockey. A March 10, 2004, article in USA Today, for example, quoted a witness to the event. "Who among us," said the witness, "would notice if, this autumn, we found ourselves surveying a sports landscape without major league hockey? And how many of us would complain?"

For his part in the incident, Bertuzzi was given a suspension. Bertuzzi missed 17 months of hockey, but since the 2005-2006 season was a lockout year, the number of games he actually missed was fewer than 20. The fine for the incident cost Betruzzi nearly $502,000. He did plead guilty to assault, but a Canadian court of law dismissed the case.

In July 2006, Moore turned down a $1 million settlement and proceeded with a lawsuit against Bertuzzi and the Canucks ownership group. He said he was after the truth. The hearing was scheduled for September 8, 2014, but by August 19, the case was settled out of court. The terms were never disclosed.

Why would a scandal of this nature continue for 10 years? The answer to that question might be best expressed by Yahoo Sports' Greg Wyshynski, who wrote, "One thing missing from [this] demonization of hockey: The name 'Marc Crawford.'"

This statement is, perhaps, the greatest reframing of the incident in the last decade. That Crawford, then the Canucks head coach, allegedly ordered the "code red" on Moore, telling his players to make him "pay the price." Did that mean to hit him? Did that mean doing what Bertuzzi did?

"...Crawford [claimed] he 'gave no direction to the players in general and to Bertuzzi in particular, to retaliate for the injury to Naslund, or to engage in any conduct outside the rules against Moore.'" Whatever the truth is, Crawford's role in this incident has only deepened over the years.

As the head coach, what should Crawford's role have been? In his March 7, 2014, National Post article, Sean Fitz-Gerald wrote: "Colorado defenseman Derek Morris made a strong allegation about Crawford, the Vancouver coach: 'The worst thing about it is their coach is over there laughing about it, and that just shows the class of that guy.'"

Bertuzzi admitted in 2007 that, during the second intermission, Crawford made it clear to his team that he wanted Moore to "pay the price." Crawford denied ever having made this statement. There were even back-and-forth lawsuits between Bertuzzi, Crawford, and the Canucks management. Bertuzzi retired from hockey in 2015. Crawford currently works as an associate coach for the Ottawa Senators. Moore has not been medically cleared to play hockey and will probably never play hockey again.

CHUCK'S ETHICS REVIEW:

An Eye for An Eye and No One Wins

Yes, of course, I know that hockey is a tough sport played by tough people, but that's not what this case is about. It is about something deeper. On the night Steve Moore's career came to an end, he had already gotten into one fight. I have always wondered why it was necessary for coach Crawford to allegedly tell his players to go out and get Moore again. I mean, really get him.

At issue here was a long-standing need for revenge. The anger spilled over from earlier games and grew beyond what's normal in hockey. The Canucks counted on the fact that hockey was already perceived as a rough, tough sport. They thought they could use that perception as cover to bring about their revenge. It backfired on them.

WHEN IS ENOUGH, ENOUGH?

What does it mean to get revenge in a sport? I think the coach should have drawn a line, and the Canucks never should have sought revenge in the first place. The ethical thing to do would have been for the Canucks, and especially coach Crawford, to recognize that what they were planning to do was more than just dropping the gloves, having a fight, and being done with it. It was pure and simple retribution.

Admittedly, Moore played unfairly when he delivered the cheap shot to Naslund two games earlier, but that didn't give the Canucks the right to radically modify their on-ice behavior so that their primary aim became not to win the hockey game but to punish Moore. I know all about hockey history and hockey traditions, and I know how mental and physical toughness are hallmarks of the game.

The role of "the enforcer," a physical player whose main role is to protect other players on his team, is a longstanding one in hockey. But I also know that younger players have grown increasingly concerned about brain damage. They are beginning to second-guess unnecessary violence in the sport, especially when it happens outside the rules.

In any case, Crawford should have said that enough was enough. I know this may not be what some hometown fans want to hear, but they weren't on the ice. Fans should not get to decide on-ice behavior any more than a hockey player has the right to tell a fan how to behave at work. No matter how hard the fans clamored for blood, the Canucks should have ignored them.

Just how far does revenge have to go before everyone is satisfied? Is revenge fulfilled when someone receives three cracked vertebrae and partial paralysis? How about complete paralysis? What would have been enough? After the first fight, the Canucks had already made their point.

THE JOKER

The reports seemed to agree that, when Moore got severely hurt, Crawford was joking about it. On one level, it is a reprehensible action, but, on another level, it is maybe not so much of a surprise. Because what you are really looking at here is typical human behavior. If Crawford's objective was to instill pain, damage ,or harm, then that was his mindset to begin with; that was what motivated him. As sick as it sounds, once the pain you hoped to dish out has been delivered, of course, you're going to be pleased and happy.

When the Canucks first entered the cesspool of unethical choices and got the consequence they had been looking for, it would appear they were initially pleased. But it is not much different from going to war.

In our daily lives, we would not be happy to see someone shot and killed. That would not be a normal reaction unless we were soldiers in a war zone, and then what do we do? We acknowledge and praise the outcome we were looking for, but we have to be extremely careful not to blur lines. You don't want to be happy that you killed somebody. It is not a joking matter. In the case of a hockey game, the same rules apply. A kid got badly hurt. He was unconscious and bleeding on the ice. That was no joke, and it was not funny.

As for the NHL, they were relatively silent on the case back then, even though a huge fine was levied and a suspension was handed out. But when this incident occurred, there was still an "old school" streak in play. At the time, there was a lot more tolerance for unethical and inappropriate behavior than there would be today. The concussion issue has finally raised its ugly head in the NHL. It will become even more prominent going forward.

Would I have liked to have seen the league take a tougher stance in response to this incident? Of course, and there were indeed calls for a jury trial and a possible lifetime ban, as well as a deeper investigation into the coach's possible role. Ultimately, we must compare this case to the NFL, which is just now taking a stance on issues such as domestic abuse. Going back ten or fifteen years, the NFL did not consider domestic abuse to be very important, at least not publicly. The behavior professional sports leagues focus on changes with time, and, in some cases, it takes certain individuals — who see violence or other issues for what they really are — to step forward and enact change.

Whether Bertuzzi was caught in the middle is hard to say. Naslund said he felt sorry for Bertuzzi because Bertuzzi had stood up for him. While the public saw Bertuzzi as the villain, part of Naslund's comment had to do with how the team left Bertuzzi twisting in the wind. He may well have taken the fall for the actions of others, including the coaching staff.

Let me give you an example. Let's say you're a CIA or MI6 operative. Your superior gives you an ambiguous direction: "We want X." The intent is clear, but the superior didn't tell you to assassinate another person, didn't tell you specifically how to "get X." Most intelligence agencies would say, "By the way, if you're caught, tough. We're going to disavow any knowledge of your actions."

In Bertuzzi's case, the coach didn't appear to say, "I want you to hurt the guy." But he did say something to the effect that he wanted the player on the other team to "pay the price." The intent was clear, even if the details of how to accomplish it were not.

Now, everyone in that locker room knew what was meant by the coach's words. Were they appropriate? Was it ethical?

Why did Bertuzzi feel it was his responsibility to take action? The coach gave an ambiguous direction, and one person saw an opportunity. "I'm going to be the hero," he seemed to say to himself. "I'm going to take on the banner and the mantra of what the coach wants us to do for the team." Meanwhile, the coach was implying: "But, oh, by the way, if you get caught or if there are any repercussions, we don't know anything about this. We don't know what caused you to go rogue."

I can understand Naslund feeling sorry for Bertuzzi. It was one guy standing up for another. After Bertuzzi made the hit and the crowd went from going crazy to complete silence, I think a lot of people said, "Whoa, this maybe went a little too far!" I don't believe Naslund would have wanted it to go that far, even if it was done in his honor.

Why was Bertuzzi the one who took out Moore? Did someone — a coach, the players — single him out for the job? We don't know the real answer to that question. We never will. When a team is given the responsibility of carrying out a bounty before the third period of a hockey game, who is going to pay the price for that? Is one person given that responsibility? Or, is the coach just creating the opportunity in the minds of all the players? Once the deed is done, is that player elevated in everyone's eyes, or is he ultimately playing the fool?

What I do know is that Todd Bertuzzi had a nearly 20-year career, and by all accounts, he achieved a great deal of success. Still, he's best remembered for the incident with Steve Moore. In fact, it has largely defined him.

CHAPTER 24

RAY RICE AND THE ELEVATOR

Who: Ray Rice, Janay Palmer, NFL, Baltimore Ravens

Offense: Assault on Fiancé in Elevator

Results: Suspension, Banishment from Football

The Ray Rice scandal quickly progressed into a dual sports ethics conversation because, in a sense, the NFL and its commissioner were also on trial. To this day, the ripples from this ugly incident are still being felt, and, unfortunately, this type of behavior continues to occur.

This case began on February 15, 2014, when Baltimore Ravens running back Rice hit his then fiancé, Janay Palmer, in an elevator of the Revel Casino in Atlantic City, New Jersey. The assault rendered her unconscious, and Rice had to literally drag her out of the elevator. People saw him drag her, and Rice told them not to notify the police. Nevertheless, the entire incident was caught on video, and Rice was arrested for simple assault by the Atlantic City Police.

The following day, Rice talked to people at the Ravens organization about the incident. While we do not know exactly what he said to team personnel, by February 17, 2014, he had hired a lawyer.

By February 19, the incident went public. Ravens coach John Harbaugh spoke at the NFL scouting combine about the assault, stating that there was a lot of information that had not yet emerged.

Then, a full month later, on March 18, a grand jury convened. Oddly, on that same day, Rice and Palmer got married.

On May 1, 2014, Rice pled not guilty to aggravated assault. He applied for what is known as the first-time offenders' program, and, by May 20, he was accepted into the program. The way the program works is that, upon successful completion of the course and the mandated counseling, the arrest is expunged from the public record.

Although the assault was public knowledge, on May 23, 2014, Rice and his new wife held a press conference. Rice said it was a private matter, and he was doing all he could to make things right. Then, on June 16, the couple privately met with NFL Commissioner Roger Goodell. The NFL made its decision on July 24, handing Rice a two-game suspension, to be served at the beginning of the regular season.

Ray Rice reported to the Ravens training camp on July 28, 2014, and despite the acknowledged assault and subsequent penalty, he received a standing ovation from the fans at his first practice. At a Ravens press conference, he told everyone that his actions were "inexcusable" and that the assault did not "represent who he was."

The next day, Goodell told the media that he stood by his decision. Nevertheless, on August 28, 2014, the commissioner sent a letter to all the team owners stating that there would be changes made to the NFL's personal conduct policy.

THE TAPE!

While we should not engage in conjecture, the lightning rod moment, in this case, came on September 6, 2014, when celebrity gossip and entertainment news website TMZ.com published a copy of the hotel's elevator tape. Aside from making the tape public, TMZ also sent the tape to the NFL for comment.

The NFL claimed it was the first time it had ever seen the tape. Meanwhile, the public exploded with outrage when they saw the tape. The Ravens terminated Rice's contract. In media interviews that same day, Rice said that all he could do was stay strong for his wife and child.

Here is the point in the scandal where the NFL and the media sharply disagree. On September 10, 2014, the Associated Press claimed the NFL had been in possession of the tape since April 2014. The NFL denied it. Many pundits loudly called for the resignation of the commissioner, but he refused. Some NFL owners began their own investigation. League officials said they planned to cooperate if, while conducting their own investigation, they determined that the tape had been purposely withheld. Following these actions, the NFL informed the NFL Players Association of Rice's suspension. The NFLPA then filed a legal appeal.

On November 5, 2014, Rice made his case in front of a judge, who served as a neutral arbitrator. The focus of the appeal was to determine if, at any time, Rice had lied to the NFL about what had happened. Rice said he was very specific in talking to the NFL, but Goodell and his legal team said he was quite vague. Goodell also said that, prior to seeing the actual tape, he did not think that Rice had struck his wife.

The next major milestone in the case came after the NFL and the NFLPA argued their cases in front of another judge. On December 1, 2014, Rice was fully reinstated to active status. He was theoretically allowed to sign with any team he chose.

On January 6, 2015, a ninety-six-page report on the incident proved inconclusive, but it was clear that the NFL had badly bungled their handling of the case. The report, along with his reinstatement, provided Rice the opportunity to sue the Baltimore Ravens for wrongful termination and for the money still on his contract — about $3.5 million. The lawsuit proceeded, and eventually, Rice was awarded nearly $1.6 million.

To this date, Rice is still out of football, though he is technically eligible to play. Domestic violence issues continue to plague the league and professional sports as a whole.

CHUCK'S ETHICS REVIEW:

In Life, Intention Creates Behavior

I'm confident that, five hours before knocking out his fiancé in the elevator, Ray Rice had no intention of changing his life forever. But Rice's intention to subdue his fiancé fostered behavior that resulted in consequences he never could have imagined. The Ray Rice scandal is, unfortunately, one of several domestic violence cases that have recently marred professional sports.

We have also seen domestic violence in baseball, basketball, hockey, and even women's professional soccer.

To begin this ethical discussion, let's start with Roger Goodell, the current head of the "nonprofit" organization called the NFL.

As the Rice investigation exploded, the public called for Goodell's resignation, yet he remains firmly in place as the league's commissioner, currently with a $63 million annual contract. Goodell is apparently smart enough to know how to play the political game of balancing the financial needs of the owners with his own need to create a firm financial base for himself. It isn't always the most qualified or the smartest person who gets a job; it's often the person who best understands the political nuances enough to both get the job and then keep it.

Nowadays, the NFL can seemingly do no wrong. My feeling is that, had the organization been on shaky ground, and had team owners expressed consternation at Goodell's handling of the case, the owners would likely have gotten rid of Goodell.

Indeed, the owners likely would have gotten rid of anyone in order to put themselves back on firm ground, which is, quite frankly, true of most businesses or associations. The NFL is a business. As long as everything is okay, there is no problem. When things begin to go south, somebody's head is going to roll. The people in this case who held most of the power — the owners — had enough confidence in Goodell to keep him in the job. Is he any different from any other CEO who survives a corporate scandal because he or she has made the organization and its shareholders money? No, and that is what fans don't always understand.

THE DOMESTIC VIOLENCE ISSUE

Acts of domestic violence in professional football are not new. They were well-documented in the 1960s and even earlier. We have to wonder why it took the league so long to address this issue. In the world in which we live, the tolerance for certain behaviors has changed, though the actions often do not.

We can cite lots of things from the past that are no longer tolerated as they once were. What happened in the 1960s often isn't acceptable today.

Here's an example from the television series "Mad Men." In the 1960s, everybody smoked. There was a virtual fog of cigarette smoke in every office. Modern audiences saw the show and scratched their heads at the smoke-filled rooms. We have mostly moved on from rampant public tobacco use. We just do not tolerate it anymore.

We know that domestic violence exists not just in the NFL but throughout society. There is now a level of intolerance that suggests we have finally had enough. Did this turnaround take too long to happen? Absolutely. We can make sure that domestic violence is no longer acceptable anywhere and at any level of society, including college campuses, as demonstrated by the Katie Hnida case discussed earlier.

Now, it's interesting — and very disturbing — to wonder what would have happened if the tape in the elevator never existed.

Would the case have simply gone away? Honestly, if the tape had not existed, and so had not gotten the public's attention, I think Rice would have received only a hand slap or a stern lecture. There is a dramatic difference between private behavior that is dealt with in private, and public behavior that is dealt with in public.

Again, is that wrong? Is that a double standard? Absolutely! No one deserves to be on the receiving end of domestic violence. But, in this case, it seems as though there was a fight between the old ways of handling domestic violence versus the newer pressure to deal with it decisively.

HOW SERIOUS IS THE NFL?

For many years, it has been asserted that the NFL is not serious about domestic violence but merely pays it lip service. I agree. I believe it is time to put ethics counseling in third-party hands. Remember that it is the senior people in any organization who create the culture. The culture creates the boundaries and the standards.

Let's consider a more innocuous behavior: using bad language in the workplace. The challenge comes when the owner of a company uses bad language and then says, "It's my company, and I'll do or say whatever I want." If that is the culture of the organization, it cannot say that it doesn't tolerate such behavior. If the head of the organization does it, why should others in the organization not do it, also?

To change that behavior, we have to change the bias. In terms of the NFL, leadership must change the league's level of tolerance for inappropriate behavior. Good ethics must be generated from the league office and strongly enforced by ownership. The media has become much more aware of player behavior, and the media is everywhere. But the NFL should be the arbiter of such behavior, not the media.

I firmly believe that NFL leadership is much more responsive to the media than to the fans. The fans bring them wealth, but the media has a greater potential to influence the fans than do league officials and team owners. So, the league has to look at the media and say, "Who is our greatest influencer and how do we play to that party?" I would say thousands of fans would have probably cheered Ray Rice's return to a football field. If not for media coverage, I could see that happening. The clock is ticking, however, and that window may have already closed. Rice still has a rough road ahead of him.

ABOUT RAY RICE

Will Ray Rice ever again get a job in football? My answer is that it is possible, but it may no longer be probable. He is too old. The train has left the station.

Let's compare and contrast Rice with Michael Vick. You know, Michael Vick never intended to be the poster child for animal cruelty. In his mind, he fought dogs, a sporting event that gave him an adrenaline rush. Well, we, as a country, as a people, just cannot tolerate that. He ended up spending time in Leavenworth prison. To the credit of his image handlers, he did help to sponsor an animal cruelty bill.

Did Vick return to football? Yes. Did he fully regain his status? No. He never reclaimed the reputation he had been building. He went deeply into debt — a result of other poor choices — and became embroiled in lawsuits. He officially announced his retirement on February 3, 2017.

Rice never intended to be the poster child for domestic abuse, but he is. Because of our choices, we end up being labeled. Sometimes you have to accept that label. It will never allow you to do or to be what you started out as. The question is this: Can you take what you have left and be the best at it, using it to your advantage?

We could ostensibly say that the NFLPA should have taken the position that Rice was wrong and should have been punished more severely, especially when the tape emerged. However, think of the NFLPA as playing the role of a defense attorney. The defense attorney is not worried about whether the client is innocent or guilty. The defense attorney asks the client if she or he is guilty, and if the client says innocent, that is good enough for the attorney to mount the best defense possible.

The NFLPA, while not an attorney per se, does have the responsibility of making sure the rights of the players it represents are upheld. The NFLPA wants to ensure that everyone is being treated fairly and equally. It does not make a judgment as to whether someone such as Rice did the right thing or the wrong thing. It wants to know if he was treated properly within the confines of the rules or whether his rights were violated. If they were violated once, they could be violated again.

AVERTING THE INCIDENT?

The Ray Rice case, as presented, is fundamentally about what happened with Rice and his fiancé during and after their encounter in the elevator. So, let's take it before that. Let's talk about the ability to be in control of yourself and your emotions. This is conjecture on my part, as I do not know either Rice or his wife. An argument pops up. It happens between most couples, of course. This argument may have been something minor to start with, but it got worse. It spilled out and spilled over. Now the argument may escalate into a metaphorical, verbal knock-down/drag-out kind of thing, and both parties say things they might not mean and may later regret.

However, they walk away, and, though they are both steaming mad, they follow a certain decorum. Most rational people don't make their arguments public. They hold themselves together

The assumption that day with Rice and Palmer was that the elevator was a private space where they were free to act privately. If you look at the extended footage, and by no means am I defending Rice, he is fussing at her, and she is fussing at him. They get into the elevator and she spits on him. They were both acting like immature kids, but he was a powerhouse of a man.

You can almost see it building up in Rice's head like a teapot, and all he wants is quiet. But it boils over. He hit her. Did he intend to knock her out? Was he a habitual domestic abuser? I don't know the answer to those questions. But what I do know is that Rice responded to an explosive situation because, in addition to failing to control his temper, he did not recognize that, in the world we live in today, images are almost always being recorded.

Had Rice known there was a video camera in the elevator, I believe he would have had the strength to avoid that confrontation. He would have held himself in check. Perhaps, when we hold ourselves in check and take a breather, we pull back from our emotions and calm ourselves. Unfortunately, such behavior didn't happen that night.

Rice should have assumed there was a reasonable chance that something was being recorded. Twenty-five years ago, this would not have happened, but today we are walking around with CIA-type tools on our smartphones. From an ethical perspective, we have to realize that, when emotions are high, we have the potential to lose control. We have to know that, if we're going to lose control, someone may be watching. It's a given. Are you willing to lose control with the knowledge that someone somewhere is watching?

I do believe that Ray Rice could have maintained control had he been aware of this.

Of course, there are much deeper issues in play here than just fears over surveillance cameras. A spouse spits on her husband, and the husband then knocks her out. That's not rational, mature behavior. It goes way beyond any ethical discussion and lands in the realm of anger management and, frankly, intensive psychological or marriage counseling. Had Rice and Palmer received such counseling long before this, the incident may not have escalated and the consequences could have been avoided.

And as the sunset fades on Rice's career, he might take heart in knowing that since "the elevator incident," several more

NFL players have been charged with domestic violence. He is hardly alone.

The league is possibly waiting for "girlfriend to become a murder victim before serious ethical counseling is made mandatory,

CHAPTER 25

AARON HERNANDEZ
DEALER, DUPE OR DEVIL?

Who: Aaron Hernandez

Offense: Murder, Drug Dealing

Result: Sentenced to Life in Prison, Suicide in Jail

In the history of cautionary sports tales, it would be difficult to top that of former NFL superstar Aaron Hernandez. When, as a New England Patriot, Hernandez caught a touchdown pass from Tom Brady in Super Bowl XLVI in 2012, he was on top of the sports world.

Eighteen months later, Hernandez's life was in tatters.

Aaron Josef Hernandez was born in Bristol, Connecticut, in 1989. His father, Dennis Hernandez, played football at Bristol Central High School and then at the University of Connecticut. Both of Dennis Hernandez's sons would also play at Bristol Central High and commit to UConn.

When Aaron Hernandez was sixteen years old, his father died during a routine hernia operation, leaving his youngest son without a father figure. Hernandez's mother, Terri Valentine-

Hernandez, soon began an affair with her cousin's husband. A disgusted Aaron moved into the home of the spurned cousin, Tanya Singleton.

Many of Hernandez's friends and teammates would later point to this time as the beginning of his downward spiral. In the documentary "Killer Inside: The Mind of Aaron Hernandez," they describe Singleton as a lifelong mentor for Hernandez. But they also say her home was a place where he was more exposed to criminal elements than his father would have allowed.

Hernandez's friends say his father had a violent streak. He was a man who had fully absorbed the machismo of the football world. A few of Aaron Hernandez's friends also discuss the now-accepted fact of his bisexuality. And so, the avenues for internal conflict build.

Still, the young tight end somehow managed to showcase his talent through high school sports. He lettered in basketball and in track and field, but he shined brightest in football. By the time he graduated, Hernandez was widely considered the No. 1 tight end in the nation.

Hernandez changed his mind about UConn, committing instead to the University of Florida. Under head coach Urban Meyer, Hernandez showed uncanny speed and unusually soft hands, fast becoming a trusted target for Florida QB Tim Tebow.

When the Florida 'Gators won the 2009 National Championship Game, the stock of many of the participating players improved. Both Tebow and competing Oklahoma Sooners QB Sam Bradford were Heisman Trophy winners and would be first-round draft picks in 2010. Hernandez also found himself in the 2010 NFL Draft. His physical maturity and natural ability were never in question. He was ready for the NFL, but he would be leaving the Gators with baggage.

There were persistent rumors that Hernandez had failed multiple drug tests for marijuana while playing for Florida. The school *admitted to just one failed test.* Hernandez had also been one of several Gators football players questioned regarding a *double shooting* there in 2007, but no charges were filed.

Hernandez was also involved in a fight in a Gainesville bar in 2007, where he punched the bar owner after refusing to pay his tab. Not for the first or last time, however, Hernandez's celebrity kept him out of trouble. Again, no charges were filed.

His off-field shenanigans surely contributed to Hernandez waiting more than three rounds to be drafted. He watched Tebow go in the first round, and several of his teammates would follow.

The New England Patriots finally picked him in the fourth round, 113th overall. Hernandez, who signed for base pay, was the second tight end that the Patriots drafted that year. The other one was Rob Gronkowski, in the second round.

The two tight-end sets that Patriots head coach Bill Belichick utilized to feature both his young phenoms became a headache for opposing teams. Gronkowski's size was the perfect complement to Hernandez's athleticism. The Patriots' 2012 Super Bowl loss to Eli Manning and the Giants seemed just a stepping stone to a championship.

The following summer, Hernandez signed a record contract for an NFL tight end – $40 million over seven years, with a $12.5 million signing bonus. He had achieved his dream.

When a double murder occurred in the streets of south Boston that same summer, no one considered Hernandez a suspect, even though he was spotted on security footage at the same nightclub as the victims on the evening of the crime.

Hernandez was injured for much of the 2012 season, but he made a late return to help the Patriots to an AFC Championship appearance. The loss would be his last football game.

GRISLY DISCOVERY

On June 17, 2012, a jogger in Bristol discovered a dead body in a secluded area. It did not take police long to deduce that the only person the victim, Odin Lloyd, knew in the area was Hernandez. In fact, Hernandez's fiancé, Shayanna Jenkins, was the sister of Lloyd's girlfriend.

The evidence against Hernandez was overwhelming. Surveillance footage placed him driving a rental car in the area with two accomplices. Hernandez had rented the car in his own name, and he returned it with a spent .45-caliber shell casing loose on the floorboard. Police matched the casing to the brand found at the crime scene.

Hernandez had also recently installed a surveillance system at his mansion, which police obtained. It showed him carrying a pistol immediately before and after the time of the murder.

Hernandez's time in jail during his trial was dotted with violent infractions and threats of violence against corrections officers. The jury found him guilty of first-degree murder, and he was sentenced to life in prison without parole.

After moving to his permanent home at Souza-Baranowski Correctional Center in May of 2014, Hernandez was charged with the 2012 double murder in Boston. Though the evidence against him was compelling, an excellent legal defense saw him acquitted of both counts.

SUICIDE

On April 19, 2017, five days after his acquittal, Hernandez hanged himself in his cell with a bedsheet. As would soon come to light, one of his motives for suicide was an archaic Massachusetts law that would vacate his murder conviction if he died in prison while his case was under appeal, forcing the Patriots to pay out much of his contract. The plan worked initially, and Hernandez's conviction was indeed overturned. However, the Massachusetts Supreme Judicial Court reinstated the conviction in 2019.

Thus ended a sordid tale, but "something positive" did result from it. Because he hanged himself, Hernandez's brain was undamaged and available for study.

In 2017, Ann McKee, director of Boston University's CTE center, which studies chronic traumatic encephalopathy, released her findings. The twenty-seven-year-old Hernandez suffered from Stage 3 CTE, the result of repeated concussions. He was the youngest such victim on record by nearly twenty years.

"We're seeing accelerated disease in young athletes," said McKee at a press conference. "Whether or not that's because they're playing more aggressively or if they're starting at younger ages, we don't know."

No one held Hernandez to account for his crimes until he committed one that could not be ignored. He is implicated in other shootings, fights and violence for which he never had to pay any price.

SECTION VII
ETHICAL FOOLS

CHAPTER 26

A Shot to the Knees: Nancy Kerrigan and Tonya Harding

Who: Nancy Kerrigan, Tonya Harding, Jeff Gillooly, Shawn Eckhardt

Offense: Assault with a Weapon

Results: Lifetime Ban for Harding, Fines and Imprisonment for Gillooly

An iconic sports scandal image from the mid-1990s shows American skater Nancy Kerrigan sitting on a bench and crying. "Why, oh why, oh why?" she exclaims. Her painful moans came right after her knee was smacked by a telescopic baton in an intentional assault as she was making her way from the ice rink. It was unlike any wacko sports scandal seen to that point — and possibly since then, too.

This case begins in 1990 when Olympic skater Tonya Harding married Jeff Gillooly. With everything that has passed since then, we tend to forget that Harding was a pretty amazing skater. In fact, in 1991, she was the first U.S. figure skater to land the triple axel in competition, a gutsy move. That year, Harding was the epitome of women's figure skating, finishing first at the U.S. Nationals. She was simply the best, and everyone gushed over her.

However, in the Winter Olympics held in Albertville, France, in 1992, Harding did not make the medal stand. American Kristi Yamaguchi won the gold, and Nancy Kerrigan took the bronze.

There was an intense rivalry between Harding and Kerrigan before the Olympics, and it only got worse in the aftermath of the 1992 competition. Kerrigan was tall, sleek, and elegant; Harding was strong, less refined but pugnacious in her approach to life. These two styles seemed to clash in the minds of judges and fans alike.

Forward to January 6, 1994, when Kerrigan was hit in the kneecap after a skating practice in Detroit. She was preparing for the U.S. Nationals competition that evening and, as a result of the injury, could not participate. Harding won the competition in her absence.

The circus that would define the scandal quickly exploded. A minister friend of Harding's bodyguard, Shawn Eckhardt, met with the FBI on January 11, 1994, to discuss Eckhardt's role in the attack. The minister was obviously motivated by a higher ethical purpose. Eckhardt claims he had Kerrigan assaulted as a publicity stunt for his bodyguard company.

BACKSTORY UPON BACKSTORY

Eckhardt contacted the man who actually perpetrated the assault around Christmas of 1993 to see if he would slice Kerrigan's Achilles tendon. Thankfully, the man refused, so they settled for the kneecap instead.

On January 12, 1994, the FBI arrested Gillooly, who is now Harding's ex-husband, and his co-conspirators, including Eckhardt. Two days later, Kerrigan was well enough to begin practicing, much to everyone's great relief.

On January 18, Harding separated from Gillooly and, about a week later, held an emotional, tearful press conference denying she had anything to do with the attack. The Nike corporation, Harding's sponsor, donated money to support Harding in her efforts to remain in Olympic competition.

However, on January 30, investigators found some interesting trash in Gillooly's dumpster: evidence to implicate Harding in the attack. Harding would later admit she knew the attack would occur.

On February 1, 1994, Jeff Gillooly pleaded guilty to being part of the assault.

Gillooly became a laughingstock, and popular televisions shows such as "Saturday Night Live" and "Late Night with David Letterman" routinely made fun of him. On February 10, Tonya Harding sued the U.S. Olympic Committee in an effort to force it to allow her to compete. It worked, but it did her little good. On February 25, 1994, Kerrigan earned a silver medal, while Harding stumbled to an eighth-place finish.

From then on, Harding's life began to spiral downward. On March 16, she pled guilty to conspiracy. Broke and desperate, Harding and Gillooly signed a contract on June 1, 1994, to allow Penthouse magazine to show stills from a sex tape they had made. Yes, they had sunk that low. Perhaps the pornography was the final straw, but on July 1, 1994, Harding was banned from ice skating for life. Less than two weeks later, Gillooly was sentenced to eighteen months in prison.

In the months to follow, Harding's life continued to spiral. The first U.S. woman to land the triple axel was reduced to skating as Mrs. Claus in a Christmas show. Gillooly was released from prison on March 14, 1995, and was so anxious to start a new life that he changed his last name to Stone.

On September 9, 1995, Kerrigan married her longtime manager, Jerry Solomon.

Harding didn't quietly fade away. In fact, her life started to become increasingly bizarre. In 1996 she claimed she was the victim of an armed robbery, but no one saw it. In 1997 she told the police her truck had been stolen from a mall. It was never proven.

On February 6, 1998, about four years after the attack, ESPN convinced Kerrigan and Harding to meet. It did not go well, and Kerrigan refused to accept Harding's apologies. Nevertheless, in 1999, Harding was cleared to skate in a non-Olympic event: the ESPN Skating Championship.

The story does not end with great redemption, however. Harding was arrested in 2000 for assaulting her boyfriend with a car hubcap, and she spent three days in jail. Whether she was pushed into it or desperate for money and a return to the limelight is unclear. Harding then decided to try her hand at boxing. She made a few celebrity appearances in the ring, but in a real bantamweight fight in 2003, she was soundly defeated.

Eckhardt would die of natural causes in 2007, and in 2008 Harding appeared on the "Today Show" to promote her book, "The Tonya Tapes." She claimed that her ex-husband Gillooly and his friends had raped her and that her mother had abused her. Her mother has denied the allegations. Gillooly, now Stone, has never commented on the scandal. Harding would again marry in 2010, and in 2011 she gave birth to a son.

CHUCK'S ETHICS REVIEW:

Only One Way to Win? A Low, Unethical Blow Creates Inescapable Consequences

Tonya Harding had a spectacular fall from grace. She fell so far that it is hard to remember that, at one time, she had it all. But instead of training harder or working with a new coach, her response to losing was to want to bust Nancy Kerrigan's knees.

When you read and analyze this case, it's hard not to come to the conclusion that Harding exhibited anti-social behavior. Now, when you combine that type of behavior with narcissistic tendencies, it all starts to make sense.

I need to emphasize that not everyone who commits unethical behaviors is deeply, psychologically damaged. But I cannot help but believe that when Harding said to herself, "She beat me," and responded by wanting to smash Kerrigan's kneecaps, it wasn't just unethical, it was unnatural. It just screams that Harding was dealing with significant psychological challenges.

HORRIFYING DISCUSSIONS

It's horrifying to know that the perpetrators of this act had actually discussed inflicting a career-ending injury, especially one as gruesome as cutting Kerrigan's Achilles tendon. Harding was out of control. Those around her were out of control. How could Harding and her entourage be attracted to such unethical behavior? An unrealistic sense of self-importance, a deep need for admiration, and a lack of empathy: That's pretty much the definition of a narcissist.

There are many people who have narcissistic personalities, and some can be quite charming. So, while Harding may not have been able to take a bat to someone's kneecaps or a razor to the Achilles, she could have been capable of convincing someone else to do it. She was influential enough to turn an idea into reality.

Most of us would say, "I don't believe a sane person would do this!" But we're not talking about a sane person here, and Harding didn't attract sane people either. Compare this case to, for example, a coach urging his players to intentionally hurt players on other teams. Is that not the same thing? It isn't quite as graphic as cutting someone's Achilles tendon, but in this case Harding was charming or charismatic enough that she was able to convince someone else to do her dirty work.

This case represents so much more than the motivation to win at all costs. In a larger sense, it reflects how we as a society perceive success and fame. We saw Harding at the top of her game, an American icon. She was an incredible skater in her own right. In that moment of potential competitive glory, though, she thought she deserved it all, even as a skater who was just a little bit better was beating her. She thought she should have been the one basking in the limelight. So, she took action that wasn't just unethical and illegal — It was crazy.

"HOW DARE KERRIGAN DO THAT TO ME?"

Harding's solution for dealing with the competition was not to be better; it was to take out her competitors — literally. It was not so much about her winning as it was a desire for praise, glory, and attention. It has played out that way time and time again over the rest of her life so far. That pattern of behavior has kept repeating itself.

Going forward from the Kerrigan incident, Harding kept making one lousy choice after another. Why did she think she had no other alternatives? I believe she was a very unstable individual. Unstable personalities tend to repeat unethical behavior over and over again. Harding's mental instability has certainly played itself out time after time. The challenge for the people around such personalities, however, is to avoid getting sucked into such crazy behavior, no matter how charismatic or charming, or forceful such a personality may be. I don't know if Harding has sought counseling or if she has changed at all since her last public misstep. Unless she has changed radically, I doubt she is able to make positive ethical choices even today. She is still a narcissist; it seems, making reality TV appearances on various shows.

A GENDER ISSUE?

The Tonya Harding scandal does make an argument that female athletes should be as equally trained on the topic of sports ethics as men are. Just the other day, I listened to Billie Jean King being interviewed on the radio. King was already an exceptional tennis champion when her match with Bobby Riggs propelled her into the national spotlight. A long-time advocate for gender equality, King made the important point that men and women have an equal capacity for making good and bad choices and for behaving in ethical ways. Sports ethics training can help both male and female athletes compete more honorably.

Tonya Harding's behavior demonstrates that both men and women have the capacity for mental instability that can work its way into the competition. Whether in skating or tennis, hockey, or football, an unstable person might be tempted to intentionally cause injury to another player. True competitors, however, don't set out to harm other competitors.

The Tonya Harding case reveals that it is not always about acting either ethically or unethically. Sometimes people's actions are driven by deeper issues. It is pretty clear that Harding was unstable and somehow convinced others to participate in all of the craziness.

CHAPTER 27

RYAN LOCHTE TRASHES BATHROOM, DANCES WITH STARS

Who: Ryan Lochte, James Feigen

Offense: Fabricating a Crime Event, False Accusations, Destruction of Property

Results: Swimming Ban, Loss of Reputation, Forfeiture of Prize Money

"It's heartbreaking and it stinks." – Ryan Lochte, on his ten-month U.S. Swimming ban.

There is no argument about the swimming ability of Ryan Lochte. Born August 3, 1984, in Rochester, New York, the graduate of the University of Florida is a twelve-time Olympic medalist. His most recent Olympic gold was as a member of the 4x200 Olympic freestyle relay at the 2016 Summer Games in Rio de Janeiro.

At thirty-two, Lochte was one of the older men on the team. The Olympics are hardly amateur in this day and age, and Lochte's good looks and media presence earned him several major endorsements and television appearances.

Prior to the start of the 2016 Rio Summer Olympics, the big story concerned the ability of the country to hold the event at all. Brazil was in the midst of financial turmoil and political scandal. Rio de Janeiro, Brazil's largest city, was harshly critiqued for its high crime rates, extreme poverty, pollution, and even the presence of mosquitoes carrying the Zika virus. Security in Rio was at an all-time high, as the city was understandably sensitive to world opinion.

There were a handful of documented criminal incidents prior to the start of the Games, but by and large, the days before the opening ceremony, the first week of competition, and all of the first week's award ceremonies were uneventful.

On August 14, 2016, headlines flashed throughout the world that Lochte and three other members of the U.S. Olympic swim team were robbed at gunpoint. The initial public reaction was a "see, I told you so" kind of response, one that screamed Rio was all the bad things people had expected.

Lochte, pastel-colored hair and all told the international media that he and the other swimmers were in a taxi when they were pulled over by what they thought were uniformed police in an unmarked police car. One of the "officers" got out, put a gun to Lochte's forehead, and demanded Lochte's money and wallet. The assailants did not take his cell phone or credentials. They allegedly robbed the other swimmers in the same manner.

James Feigen, one of the other swimmers, backed Lochte's police report. Surprisingly, Lochte was already back in the U.S. by August 16, way before the closing ceremonies.

The police stated that, in their preliminary search, they couldn't find the cab driver to corroborate the story, nor did they find any witnesses. Suspicions began to mount as the seemingly scary incident started to overshadow the Olympics themselves.

On August 17, a judge seized the passports of the other swimmers, as doubt was starting to turn into anger throughout Rio and all of Brazil. Meanwhile, back in the U.S., Lochte began admitting he might have exaggerated his story at the time because he'd been drinking.

Then on August 18, 2016, the Brazilian police held a press conference. They said they believed the crime Lochte had reported was a complete fabrication. Brazilian Police Inspector Alexandre Braga said that Ryan Lochte had lied.

Under questioning, swimmers Gunnar Bentz and Jack Conger confessed to lying about the robbery. They said the group had caused damage to a gas station restroom and that Lochte was allegedly "highly intoxicated" that evening and fought with the gas station's security guard. The security guard had pulled a gun on Lochte and demanded restitution from the group before they could leave.

An eyewitness to the scene said that the four U.S. swimmers initially refused to pay for trashing the restroom. They were told that if they did not pay, the police would be coming.

On August 19, swimmer James Feigen agreed to pay $10,800 to a charity for his role in fabricating the story and creating an international incident. Also, on that date, swimmer University of Georgia swimmer Gunnar Bentz apologized to the coaches, swim team members, and the UGA student body for his actions. The attorneys for Bentz and Conger distanced the two swimmers from Lochte, saying the pair had nothing to do with the fabrication.

On August 22, 2016, just a little more than a week after the initial story broke, all of Lochte's major sponsors withdrew their support, including Speedo, Ralph Lauren, and Airweave mattresses. On that same date, Lochte made the following statement:

"If the USOC says I can't swim anymore, I think that would be the most hurtful, just because I put so much time and effort into this sport. I mean, that would be heartbreaking. My true friends still support me, being behind me 100 percent, so that's what keeps me going."

Lochte would not have to wait too long for his answer from the U.S. Olympic Committee. He received a 10-month suspension from international competition, and he would have to forfeit $100,000 in bonus money that goes with winning the gold medal. Athletes at Lochte's level also receive monthly funding from the USOC and USA Swimming, which he now would not collect. To further add insult to injury, Lochte was banned from traveling to the White House to meet with the President.

On August 25, 2016, Brazilian police charged Lochte with filing a false report, though he will likely never pay a fine.

The irony in all of this is that a month before the Olympics, the reality TV competition "Dancing with the Stars" offered Lochte a contract to appear on the show. After the Olympic debacle, the show hyped Lochte getting a second chance. Unlike his major sponsors, the show pushed him. He was good press, but he finished in a lowly seventh place out of eight contestants.

His publicist then convinced a reality TV channel to do a series called "What Would Ryan Lochte Do?" It was canceled after one season. A cough drop company next offered Lochte a minor contract, with a slogan saying that the cough drop is "forgiving" on the throat.

His fifteen minutes of fame had ticked away.

CHUCK'S ETHICS REVIEW:

Forgive Me, I Guess, But It's Still a Joke

Ryan Lochte seemed to have everything to gain after winning the Olympic gold. The logical question anyone might ask is: Why would he get loaded, trash a bathroom, assault a security guard, and then lie about it?

As to why he would get loaded and behave badly, it's the one question Lochte might answer with the least honesty or integrity. It is difficult for me to speculate on an answer other than to say that he appears to have not yet learned how to make positive choices in his life.

In an almost absurd extension of the above question, we might then wonder why Lochte would go to the pains of trashing a bathroom. The answer to that one is easy: He was loaded. Lochte managed to erase years of success with an incredibly stupid set of choices. It has been clear since the dawn of alcohol that muddled; drunken minds do not think straight. To say that Lochte wasn't thinking straight is likely an understatement.

Lochte is the perfect example of someone who had not been properly trained to make ethical choices. As for lying, that one is easy, too. When life gets out of balance — and Lochte's was absolutely out of balance that night — the human mind seeks to find a quick solution.

Once Lochte had trashed the bathroom, the reasonable choice for him that night would have been, to tell the truth and accept responsibility. However, when faced with potential outcomes that might have been less than pleasant, such as worldwide media exposure, it is quite common for the mind to conjure up mostly false stories that might lessen the consequences. Kids do this all the time. In his state of mind, Lochte was nothing more than a big kid. The problem was that no one was in the mood to hear lies from a thirty-two-year-old kid with hair dyed a pastel color and a little-boy smirk.

Based on Lochte's history, I have a strong feeling this wasn't the first time he figured his good looks and personality could overcome bad choices. He figured it wrong. He let down his teammates and, in fact, an entire country. He also mocked the host country. At this time, it may not be a big deal to him that he did not get to meet President Obama and others at the White House, but many years from now, he will probably regret that his actions excluded him from being honored by the nation's top elected official.

Ryan Lochte, in compounding his bad choices, left Rio almost immediately after his drunken, exaggerated fabrication. I have been asked what this says about him, that he let his teammates face the music alone even though he was the primary instigator. I hate to say this, but it's very probable that those who manage Lochte's career deemed running away to be normal behavior, given the circumstances. It was likely the course of action they told him to take.

I would guess that when Lochte came to his senses and told those he perceived as being closest to him what he had really done, he was likely advised that staying in Rio would have resulted in dire consequences. He fled, pushing his teammates aside to try to save himself. I wonder if he still feels he made the right choice. Did he? Would you choose him as a teammate in your professional life? How about as a partner in your personal life?

ABOUT JAMES FEIGEN

James Feigen is interested in all of this because he was one of the members of the swim team that backed up Lochte's statement to the media, even though Feigen knew it was a complete fabrication. Maybe Feigen thought it would be like a scene from "The Three Musketeers" — all for one and one for all. It is one tenet of teamwork that individuals have each other's backs. Feigen did what he probably thought a good teammate should do. Unlike the musketeers, however, he still acted unethically, not courageously.

Being a good teammate doesn't make it OK to lie or do something else unethical. Rather, in this instance, being a good teammate might have meant taking Lochte to the side, being the voice of reason, and honestly helping him solve the problem. Feigen was protecting Lochte. I get that. But sometimes, the best gift you can give someone is to take away the safety net and let them fall and fail.

I might add that, immediately after the Brazilian police pronounced that Lochte had lied, an International Olympic Committee spokesman said: "Well, boys will be boys." When you're trying to keep up a front so as not to make matters worse, you often try to rationalize behavior. This statement is rationalization, pure and simple. It was just another person trying to protect Ryan Lochte from life.

As a sports ethics speaker who delivers keynote addresses across the nation, I often run into parents, coaches, and even officials unwilling to allow young men and women to grow up. A thirty-two-year-old Olympian who signs commercial endorsements and gets paid for competitions and appearances is effectively the CEO of his own sports promotion company. He is hardly a little boy.

ALCOHOL AND OTHER ETHICAL ISSUES

Lochte stated at one point that he had "yet to make up his mind" when it came to seeking help for his drinking. In my opinion, he needs counseling, but I'm not a psychologist. I am only someone who teaches ethics.

The thought process that goes into a man getting loaded, ripping apart a restroom, and then assaulting a security officer is affected either by alcohol, drugs, or just plain mental instability. At the very least, it appears that Lochte had a very real problem with alcohol abuse. His saying that he had yet to make up his mind about seeking treatment for alcohol abuse is both telling and disturbing. Lochte was, and possibly still is, unwilling to accept responsibility for his behavior. Until he does, he will be just like anyone else whose behavior is out of control. He will continue to be unstable and susceptible to further errors of judgment.

We must keep in mind that, right after earning the gold medal, Lochte was at the very pinnacle of his brand's value. But within a day or two, he had fallen to the lowest point of his career. He sold out his country, his team members, his family, and ultimately himself. He apparently still doesn't realize it.

Understand that prior to his Olympic meltdown, earlier in his days of competition, Lochte made other poor choices that are well-documented. But each time he did so, somebody stepped up to protect him from the consequences. What Lochte really needed was to learn lessons, not have others cover up his choices or handle his affairs to make his actions appear harmless.

Along those same lines, I'm certainly aware that Lochte went on the talk show circuit, where he promoted his appearance on "Dancing With The Stars" and other failed ventures, and where he made emotional pulling-at-heartstrings, hand-wringing statements. He even cashed in on his poor choices with a promotional cough drop deal. Is this bothersome? To an extent, it is, but, as I said above, Lochte's career is always being handled by promoters whose interests possibly lie more in making money than in encouraging Lochte to lead an ethical life.

We are in an age of reality TV where questionable or even unethical behavior is often rewarded because it elevates ratings. But reality TV isn't reality at all, and most people know that. Despite attempts to resurrect his image, Lochte will be remembered as a person who embarrassed a nation.

Unlike a television program, life ultimately demands of all of us that we do our best and be authentic. Apologies are only words unless they are backed up by good, ethical choices.

CHAPTER 28

LORI LAUGHLIN – OPERATION VARSITY BLUES

Who: Lori Laughlin, Mossimo Giannulli, William "Rick" Singer

Penalties: Conspiracy, Academic Fraud, Bribery, Wire Fraud

Results: Jail Sentences, Community Service, Losses of Reputation

In March 2019, a scandal broke that would bring into focus the hazy nexus where college athletics, academics, and recruiting meet; and the reputations of universities and the well-to-do would both pay a heavy price. On March 12 of that year, news outlets around the nation were suddenly in a frenzy over an indictment, handed down by the U.S. District Court for the District of Massachusetts.

The indictment and its supporting affidavit implicated some fifty individuals as participants in a criminal conspiracy to get *the children of wealthy people admitted into universities to which these students would not ordinarily qualify to attend.*

Among the defendants, one name would stand out, eventually coming to be the public face of the scandal. That defendant was Lori Loughlin. Loughlin, a one-time candidate for the non-official title of America's Sweetheart, began modeling as a child in the 1970s in southern California. As a teen in the 80s, she landed several television roles, including a recurring role in the series "The Edge of Night." However, Loughlin achieved lasting fame starring for eight seasons, from 1988 to 1995, in the successful sitcom "Full House" as Becky Donaldson, love interest and eventual wife of John Stamos' Jesse Katsopolis.

In real life, Loughlin married the founder of the Mossimo clothing brand, Mossimo Giannulli, in 1997. The couple would have two daughters. The elder sister, Isabella, or Bella for short, was born in September 1998. Olivia Jade was born one year later to the month.

Bella was the first of the Giannulli sisters to be ensnared in the scheme, the existence of which she likely had no inkling until it was already well in motion. At some point in their search for a university, Loughlin and Giannulli made contact with William Rick Singer, a failed basketball coach turned college admissions guru.

As owner and operator of The Edge College & Career Network, Singer served as an independent college counselor, ostensibly helping students gain acceptance to the colleges of their dreams – for an exorbitant fee. Had Singer's operation stopped there, no one would have committed any crimes. In addition to The Edge, Singer also operated a non-profit organization known as The Key, short for The Key Worldwide Foundation. This entity was integral to the scheme he would devise.

The crux of the scheme was that parents such as Loughlin and Giannulli would write checks payable to The Key, thus providing tax-free cover for their payments. The parents would also make payments disguised as contributions to a target school's athletics program. That university would then grant admission to the student.

According to the sworn affidavit, Singer's dealings with Giannulli and Loughlin began innocently enough around April of 2016. Via email, Giannulli told Singer that his goal for his eldest daughter was for them to find a "roadmap for getting her into a school other than ASU." Presumably, he meant the public Arizona State University.

As the ensuing emails and conversations make apparent, this was the opening Singer needed. In one email exchange, Singer stated that he could get Giannulli's daughter into the private University of Southern California. The plan would entail having *Bella pose as a coxswain in hopes of getting her a slot on the USC crew team.*

Smaller athletics programs such as rowing, water polo, and sailing would come to predominate this aspect of Singer's operation.

It is important to note that this scam involving more than 50 fraudsters and privileged parents essentially shut out qualified and disadvantaged or underserved potential scholarship recipients from consideration as legitimate student-athletes.

Another scheme described in the indictment involved Singer's use of a proxy to take entrance exams for students, but Singer applied the athletics scam to the Giannulli children. At Singer's request, Giannulli provided him with a photograph of his eldest daughter on an ergometer, mimicking the body position of a coxswain in action. The singer then used photo-editing software to superimpose this image onto that of an actual coxswain.

THE PLAN WORKED

With Bella admitted to USC, Singer then posed an obvious question. Referring to the younger Olivia, he asked that Loughlin and Giannulli let him know "if there is a similar need anywhere so we do not lose a spot."

Loughlin and Giannulli each responded that, yes, they would like Singer to acquire Olivia a spot as well. Singer simply repeated the scheme. Both daughters would gain admittance to USC *as members of the crew team* at a total cost of $500,000 from their parents.

The couple repeated their role as well. They again took a picture of their daughter simulating a rowing pose, and Singer again superimposed it onto a real coxswain. Singer then provided that picture and accompanying academic information to an assistant athletic director at USC, Donna Heinel, who would go on to plead guilty to wire fraud for her role in the scheme.

As one might expect, the recurring nature of the academically mediocre Giannulli children getting into the notoriously choosey USC drew attention. Specifically, the anomaly caught the eye of the girls' high school guidance counselor, who suspected that *neither child had ever participated in crew.*

Via email in April 2018, the unnamed counselor informed Giannulli that the senior assistant director of admissions at USC had been informed of the situation. But not to worry, the counselor assured him.

"I also shared," the counselor wrote, "that you had visited this morning and affirmed for me that [your younger daughter] is truly a coxswain."

In October 2018, with the scheme unraveling, Singer phoned Giannulli, stating that his foundation was being audited by the IRS. What Giannulli did not know was that Singer had already been compromised. The phone call was a ruse, orchestrated and recorded by the FBI, and it would not be the only one.

Giannulli incriminated himself in the first call, replying in the affirmative that he had indeed paid Singer and his foundation hundreds of thousands of dollars to get his daughters into USC. Loughlin would do likewise in a second phone call.

Loughlin would plead guilty to conspiracy to commit wire and mail fraud. She was sentenced to two months in prison, with two years of probation and 100 hours of community service. Giannulli would serve five months in prison for his role in the scheme.

In an interview on July 25, 2022, on Los Angeles' CW affiliate KTLA-5, it came to light that Loughlin had performed her community service at a food bank called Project Angel Food in LA. A tearful Loughlin spoke directly to the camera.

"It's been one of the most rewarding experiences of my life," said Loughlin. "They've welcomed me with such open arms at a time when I was feeling particularly down and broken."

Loughlin's rebound is laudable, though white-collar crimes often end with similar contrition. Perhaps a more cautionary example would be that of another celebrity caught up in the scandal, which the Justice Department code-named Operation Varsity Blues. Consider the case of actress Felicity Huffman, who pleaded guilty to mail fraud and received a fourteen-day prison sentence.

As is explained in the enlightening 2021 Netflix documentary "Operation Varsity Blues: The College Admissions Scandal," Singer assured Huffman that her daughter's scores would prevent her from being accepted to the university of their choice.

As it unfolded, she might have gained entrance anyway, had Huffman gone the ethical route. It all seems quite a high price to pay for the guarantee of prestige.

Rick Singer faces more than $1.5 million in fines and a jail sentence; several bribed college coaches, and officials were terminated.

CHUCK'S ETHICS REVIEW:

Comments

Some would call it creating a competitive advantage. Others might say it is a "privilege" being abused. Whatever term you give it, intentionally cheating is just not cool, though it happens every day. In this scandal, the arguments for what may or may not have taken place all have some level of truth.

If I'm extremely wealthy, worth, say, upwards of a billion dollars plus, I might find myself philanthropically giving money to my favorite institution of higher learning. Perhaps a gift of $30 million or more might get my name on the School of Business or the new wing of the medical school building.

So, here's the question: Let's say, I'm the person who made such a handsome gift. If my child didn't have the grades to qualify for regular admission, what are the chances my child would be denied entry into the university? Slim!

The idea of using whatever legitimate means available to give your kid a fighting chance to get into the school of choice is natural for a parent.

To be candid, in my extended family one child had marginal grades in high school and, although his school of choice was not top-tier, his acceptance was in doubt. Having friends in state politics isn't all bad. One letter from the state senator to encourage his acceptance into the school just might have been the tipping point to get him into his first choice. The point is that parents, being parents, naturally want to give their children advantages, whether that means admission into a college or university or a down payment on a first home.

Now for the big question: Is it acceptable to pay for advantage outside of commonly acceptable and legitimate means?

As in most cases of ethics, when we look at motivation, we can categorize actions into one of three legs on the "three-legged stool" of unethical conduct: Opportunity, Need and Rationalization. So, let's quickly dissect this case.

Loughlin wanted her kid to get into a prestigious school, based on the assumption that getting into the "in" school makes a clear difference later in life. I don't think it much matters unless that school is Harvard, Yale, or a school noted for a specific area of study that makes the degree special.

As a side note: I have a master's degree and never once have I been asked where it is from or anything about my academic background. The fact that I have one is sufficient. Perhaps the luster of a specific school is more important to the parent than the child, but in this case, I don't have facts to support that assumption on the part of Lori Laughlin.

OPPORTUNITY

Here's where the scandal gets interesting, as there were three options open to Giannulli and Loughlin:

1. **Academic excellence** — If your child has the grades, then the likelihood he or she would be accepted at a school such as USC is substantially improved. Is it only grades? Not necessarily. It might take extracurricular activities such as rowing crew and community involvement, combined with academics, to make for an attractive student. After all, the student is the inventory for the college or university, so it stands to reason you want the best inventory you can find. This young woman had mediocre grades and was never elite in a sport such as crew or volleyball or soccer. Other, much more qualified students were shut out.

2. **Great wealth** — If you were the child of an alumnus who has immense wealth and is a substantial donor, do you think that university would turn your application? I have answered the question above, and obviously, it is rhetorical. Laughlin and Giannulli are privileged and wealthy, but they didn't swim in those lofty waters.

3. **Find another way: cheat** — Now, let me be clear. It took more than just a parent or two to make this story happen. A fraudster was needed to create the opportunity for the parents to bite on the offer. While most of the focus was on the parents who took the bait, who were focused on meeting their needs, it took a con man to provide the foundation to make the scheme work. If the first two options aren't available, then cheaters will try to find another way to open the door to gain access to what they want. Someone had just the key!

RICK SINGER

For me, as much as the parents are the focus. I am interested to see how the three components of fraud were perpetrated by Singer — the "fixer." In general, to perpetrate fraud, three things must happen: promise, illusion, and trust. I call that the PIT. The fixer promised things. He appealed to the parent's desires that their kids gain entrance to prestigious schools, and they trusted him.

Singer, like those he defrauded, also had his NEED, OPPORTUNITY, and RATIONALIZATIONS.

In Singer's case, his three-legged stool meshed with the parent's three-legged stool and created the perfect storm. In fact, that's true for most frauds. Bernie Madoff, for example, had to have willing investors who believed his lies in order for the largest Ponzi scheme in American history to take place.

Singer played on the parents' need to support his need — money — and the rest has made these scandals infamous. There are two obvious lessons to learn from this fraud, which are true in sports, business, or life:

1. If it seems too good to be true, it likely is. Too good to be true generally means you are getting hoodwinked.
2. When you do something that is obviously dishonest, be aware there are consequences! My second book is entitled: "Every Choice Has a Consequence." The funny thing about consequences is that they tend to have ripple effects. I pity the kids of this entitled couple and the profound embarrassment they endured when it became clear that their parents had lied and that they would be faced with the ensuing humiliation.

Before I move on from these comments, let me touch on hypocrisy. The concept of privilege has been tossed about with abandon these days. No doubt, the wrist slap the participants in this scam received seems a major act of contrition to the elites of the inner circles, and it is maddening to see the sycophants run to their defense.

This scandal was not victimless. It excluded qualified, marginalized, and disadvantaged student-athletes from gaining consideration and entrance. It forever changed the arc of their lives. They had no privilege, no powerful friends, no bleating publicists or agents.

No matter the political leanings of these elites, they were fraudsters and hypocrites.

Nevertheless, I will say that history does not create one's destiny. I hope that the people involved in this scandal will find some positive lessons that could be life-changing. In that light, I care more about their actions than words and on-air tears.

The choice is theirs to make.

CHAPTER 29

TERRENCE WILLIAMS SCAMS THE NBA

Who: Terrence Williams, 18 former NBA players, Healthcare Providers

Offense: Defrauding the NBA Players' Health and Welfare Benefit Plan

Result: Fines and Jail Sentences

On August 26, 2022, former NBA player Terrence Williams pleaded guilty to conspiring with eighteen other former players and some medical professionals to defraud the league's healthcare plan of millions of dollars.

Williams' story, like his career, is one of unrealized potential. It is similar in many respects to the stories of countless other talented players at various levels of sport in general. His crimes, of course, are thankfully less common.

Terrence Deshon Williams was born on June 28, 1987, in Seattle, Washington. He was a standout athlete at Ranier Beach High School, as both a wide receiver in football and a point guard in basketball. At 6 feet, 5 inches tall, and 207 pounds, Williams was a commanding presence on high school courts. He was a four-year starter, helping his team to a state championship in 2003 and averaging 21.7 points, 8.9 rebounds, and 7.8 assists as a senior.

Williams then signed with the University of Louisville, where, under the tutelage of head coach Rick Pitino, he showed steady year-on-year improvement. He started twenty-one games as a freshman, scoring in double-digits 14 times.

Pitino would come to describe Williams' athletic abilities as "freakishly good," though still raw. Williams honed his game as a Cardinal, improving his shot-making, ball handling, and passing after moving to the wing. His 3-point percentage saw steady improvement each season, and Williams led Louisville to consecutive Elite Eight appearances in 2008 and 2009.

The already large Williams also added to his frame in college, growing to 6 feet, 6 inches tall, and 220 pounds. He retained his athleticism, though, enabling him to play as a swingman, moving seamlessly from power forward to small forward, and attracting interest among NBA franchises.

In the 2009 NBA Draft, the New Jersey Nets selected Williams with the 11th overall pick. He saw considerable court time in his rookie campaign, playing in 78 games and starting nine of them.

He averaged a respectable 8.4 points, 4.5 rebounds, and 2.9 assists that season, a predictable decline from his college years but a positive sign for his future.

Unfortunately, *Williams had issues off the court* that would, to an unknowable degree for outsiders, derail his career. Allegedly, he injured a teammate while dunking over him on the practice court. That stunt and his repeated tardiness perturbed his coaches.

New Jersey traded Williams to the Houston Rockets, but he got few minutes on the court there. Next was Toronto, but the Raptors used him less than the Rockets had. And so, it continued for a couple more seasons, until Williams finally found himself in the NBA's Development League.

Williams spent 2014 and 2015 bouncing between several international leagues, but he never found a permanent home. His final act as a player was, ironically, signing with the defunct AmeriLeague semi-pro basketball league. When it turned out that the league's operator, Glendon Alexander, was a scam artist, the league folded. With that, Williams was out of basketball. That ungracious ending to his playing career would not be the last the world would hear of Terrence Williams, however.

Beginning sometime in 2017, according to the Justice Department, Williams began a *complicated scheme to defraud his former employer*. Williams' scam was, at turns, simple and elaborate. His machinations had one target, though: the NBA Players' Health and Welfare Benefit Plan.

The health and welfare plan helps current and former NBA players get medical care, including wellness and dental services. Under the plan, players could petition the league for help with medical bills and receive reimbursement for services rendered.

With the average playing career spanning just four and a half years, often ending due to injury, it is not difficult to see the need for such health benefits.

"Williams led a scheme involving more than eighteen former NBA players, a dentist, a doctor, and a chiropractor, to defraud the NBA Players' Health and Welfare Benefit Plan of millions of dollars," stated U.S. Attorney Damian Williams in a press release. "Williams also *impersonated others to help him take what was not his—money that belonged to the Plan*."

From 2017 and continuing until his eventual indictment, Williams wove a tangled web of false medical claims, faked invoices, and pocketed reimbursements. He recruited other former players into the scheme, such as Anthony Wroten, Jamario Moon, Eddie Robinson, and Chris Douglas-Roberts, all of whom pleaded guilty to their roles in the conspiracy.

United States Attorneys alleged that Williams *procured fake invoices* for these and other players, which the players then submitted to the health and welfare plan. To do so, *Williams solicited help from medical providers.* Williams would then *demand kickbacks,* totaling approximately $300,000, from the players after the league reimbursed them.

Williams was also accused of using a fake email account to impersonate employees of the health and welfare plan. He allegedly fashioned the account to look like that of an administrative manager and then used it to intimidate ex-NBA player Douglas-Roberts into engaging with him.

In another fake email account scheme, Williams pretended to be that same administrative manager. He then used this tactic *to threaten a doctor who was participating in the scam,* telling the doctor he would contact authorities if he did not receive money, which he purported to be a fine of some sort. This incident alone netted Williams approximately $346,000.

In the end, Williams was undone by his own ineptitude. According to the U.S. Attorneys pursuing the case, Williams created fake letters attesting to the necessity of medical services, letters which the health and welfare plan would require periodically. The giveaway was that Williams' letters often contained grammatical errors. Some were formatted incorrectly or were missing letterhead and, in one instance, had the patient's name misspelled.

The players involved also *got greedy.* Invoices obtained by the prosecution showed that three of them, including Wroten, all had crowns on the same six teeth on the exact same day. In another instance, an invoice had a player getting crowns in Beverly Hills at the same time he was actually in Nevada. These inconsistencies naturally raised suspicion, the government alleged.

All told, Williams and his accomplices are alleged to have submitted claims to the league totaling $5 million, half of which went to the participants in the scheme.

As part of his plea deal, Williams agreed to pay restitution to the health and welfare plan to the tune of $2.5 million. He also agreed to forfeit more than $650,000 to the United States, and the worst for Williams may be yet to come.

Williams is currently awaiting sentencing, which the U.S. Attorney's Office for the Southern District of New York says is "prescribed by Congress." As such, Williams could be facing ten to twelve years in prison.

MEDICAL PROVIDERS FACE CONSEQUENCES

The players and medical professionals that Williams enticed into participating in his scheme face various penalties, which courts are still determining. What is clear is that Williams and his cohorts took advantage of a system designed to help former players like him lead normal, comfortable, healthy lives. But no one was minding the store.

Sometimes, it seems, the temptation of easy money can be overwhelming, especially when someone has already done all of the planning and much of the scheming ahead of time.

CHUCK'S ETHICS REVIEW:

Wasted Trust after a Wasted Potential

The fraudster's theme song could be titled "I'll find a weakness, I'll exploit the weakness, then I'll keep taking chances 'til I do something really stupid." As a sports ethics and business ethics speaker and ethics consultant, I have learned there is always something stupid a fraudster will do that becomes their undoing.

In 2009, in a case wholly unrelated to Williams, a wealthy financial advisor in the Nashville area who turned fraudster was sentenced to three years in jail plus a huge fine. He set up a Ponzi scheme where he smooth-talked investors out of about $14 million in 2022 dollars.

Like Williams, this man created fake documents to support his fraud. He even issued fake reports using phony documentation. Then, one day, this fool sent some fake documents to a new client who was supposedly invested in Fannie Mae and Freddie Mac funds. By that point, and with total disregard for the people entrusting him with their money, he let himself get sloppy with his arrogance, producing statements that read "Freddie Mae" and "Fannie Mac."

"Weird," thought one of the investors, who did some digging and then reported the incident to the FBI. The outcome was that the man was found guilty of perpetrating a massive fraud.

Because of his intimidation, disregard, and arrogance, Williams will be sentenced to prison as well. Of course, there is one positive: He'll probably be recruited for the prison basketball team.

Frauds consist of three components: A Promise, An Illusion, and Trust. Williams, either a scam genius or a lucky idiot, found himself uniquely positioned to accomplish a substantial fraud that will earn him the recognition that he likely did not expect early in his NBA career. Trust came from the NBA and his connection to that franchise. And, as long as he was smart when it came to documentation, he would have run his scheme, like the man above or like Bernie Madoff, for far longer. By making rookie mistakes, he burst the illusion, which caused the whole house of cards to come crashing down.

My concern, though, although folks may think these comments should be limited to Williams, deals with the lack of controls and procedures that should have been in place to protect the NBA Players' Health and Welfare Benefit Plan.

The number one reason a fraud can take place is trust. People responsible for the administration and protection of these benefit trusts and plans need to be vigilant. Yet, connected with players or former players of the NBA as they are, they can completely look past red flags and find themselves deceived.

I also need to add a strong dose of reality to the issue of NBA salaries. Obviously, we all know of the wealth of LeBron James and Steph Curry. However, in 2022, there were many players hovering in the annual salary range of $900,000 to $1 million. By any standard, these men are phenomenal athletes, but not league superstars. The average span of an average NBA player is about three years. They retire with decent savings, but they are by no means the wealthiest group of Americans.

When a man like Terrence Williams steals from a pension fund, he mainly steals from these souls.

NOT PROUD

I am not at all proud of my past, but the reality is, I defrauded retirement plans of clients who intimately trusted me. I could never have done what I did without that level of intense trust. It is easy to assume that the people you serve would be appreciative and never take advantage of a situation, but some do.

The responsibility of the fiduciaries of the NBA plan must go beyond trust. In fact, those people the players trust should be scrutinized even more, because that is one of the primary legs from which fraud can occur.

Williams was an opportunist who masterminded a massive fraud and drew others into his web. He and his co-conspirators will pay the price, but the lesson to be learned is to recognize how fraud happens, what to look for, and how to be vigilant in preventing it.

SECTION VIII
THE MONSTERS

CHAPTER 30

JERRY SANDUSKY AND PENN STATE UNIVERSITY

Who: Jerry Sandusky, Joe Paterno, University Staff, Numerous Victims

Offense: Sexual Abuse

Result: Life in Prison for Sandusky, Jail, and Terminations of Staff, Major Lawsuits

The sports scandal involving Jerry Sandusky not only ended the incredible coaching career of Penn State University head coach Joe Paterno, it almost brought down an entire collegiate football program. If that wasn't enough, Jerry Sandusky most probably ruined the lives of several young boys, now men, through his alleged sexual abuse.

During Sandusky's trial, his adopted son Matt claimed his father had sexually abused him as well, spilling the scandal over into Sandusky's family (The Patriot News, June 21, 2012).

The outrage of what happened follows a complicated and twisting path. The short version is that, in 1969, former Penn State defensive end Sandusky was hired as an assistant coach at Penn State. Sandusky went to work for Paterno, then a relatively young head coach.

By 1977, Sandusky had been named defensive coordinator in addition to being the linebacker's coach. Also, in 1977, Sandusky started a charitable organization called The Second Mile. The charity was organized with the noble intention of giving underprivileged children the opportunity to have better lives, and it included adult mentoring. The offices of the organization would be established in the nearby town of State College, Pennsylvania. The Second Mile charity continued until November 2011, when it was dissolved.

It would not be until news of the scandal broke that there emerged a better sense of what occurred during the 1990s.

Under sworn testimony before a grand jury, Victim 7 — the victims were not identified by name during proceedings or in the indictment — noted occasions in 1994 when he had showered with Sandusky in a Penn State locker room.

Victim 4 claimed repeated sexual encounters with Sandusky in 1996.

Victim 5 claimed to have been sexually abused by Sandusky in 1998 in the Penn State football locker room showers.

Victim 6 claimed he was hugged by Sandusky in the shower in 1998. The boy told his mother, who promptly reported the allegations to the university. The police investigated the matter, and on June 1, 1998, interviewed Sandusky, who admitted to showering with Victim 6. However, he defended the activity as harmless. In any event, the police specifically advised Sandusky not to shower with children anymore.

In an article that appeared on Fox News.com (November 15, 2011), in regard to his shower activity, Sandusky was quoted as saying: "I could say that I have done some of those things. I have horsed around with kids. I have showered after workouts. I have hugged them and have touched their legs without intent of sexual contact."

In July 1999, Jerry Sandusky retired as the defensive coordinator of Penn State, yet he still seemed to remain a fixture around the team and the facility.

Victim 3 claimed in his grand jury testimony that he was assaulted in the locker room showers by Sandusky in 2000. Even then, Sandusky was still granted access to all the football facilities despite not working there anymore. Also, in 2000, a janitor allegedly witnessed Victim 8 receiving oral sex from Sandusky in the locker room. The janitor reported this scene to his supervisor, but the event went unreported to campus security or athletic personnel. The matter was dropped.

Crucial to the grand jury report was Mike McQueary, a graduate assistant football coach, who testified to witnessing Sandusky sexually assaulting a young boy in the locker room showers in March of 2002 — three years after he supposedly lost all privileges.

McQueary reported the incident to head coach Joe Paterno the next day. Paterno notified athletic director Tim Curley. Curley and Penn State Senior Vice President Gary Schultz both went to Paterno's home. Paterno told them what McQueary had reported to him and advised them that, because McQueary had not provided details, they should speak directly to him, which they subsequently did.

Curley and Schultz reported the incident to Graham Spanier, who was president of Penn State at the time. McQueary later sent emails to three men — Curley, Schultz ,and Spanier — better detailing what he had witnessed.

There has always been speculation that perhaps McQueary was never clear on what he saw when he reported it. After witnessing this act, McQueary consulted his father and his father's boss, Dr. Jonathan Dranov, seeking their advice. As president of Centre Medical and Surgical Associates, Dranov was a mandated reporter in the state of Pennsylvania. Dranov testified that he questioned McQueary three times about what he saw, and each time McQueary kept going back to what he had heard.

Because McQueary didn't appear to have clearly witnessed a crime, Dr. Dranov and John McQueary recommended he talk to Paterno. But, as Dan Wetzel wrote in a June 12, 2012, article on Yahoo! Sports.com, according to NBC, "emails not only show McQueary was clear in his reporting of the incident (the Penn State officials originally insinuated he wasn't) but that the officials made the potentially criminal decision *to not turn the information over* to social services or law enforcement in an effort to be 'humane' to Sandusky."

There was also the rather obvious matter that McQueary reported the incident but did not attempt to stop it.

Upon recollection and under oath, Victim 9 testified before the grand jury that Sandusky had forced him to give and receive oral sex in the basement of Sandusky's home from 2004 to 2008.

Victim 10 claimed that, in 2007, he, too, was forced to have oral sex with Sandusky in Sandusky's basement. From there the crimes appear to only have escalated. Also in 2008, Sandusky purportedly forced Victim 1 to engage in oral sex with him more than twenty times. In 2009, Victim 1 told his mother what had taken place. She turned to the police demanding action. Finally, an investigation was unleashed by Pennsylvania State Police and the Attorney General's Office.

In September 2010, Sandusky resigned from duties at The Second Mile charity. The resignation was unexpected, and it was unclear whether this resignation was voluntary or forced.

After decades of getting a free pass, the clouds around Sandusky's behavior finally parted. On November 5, 2011, the grand jury charged Sandusky with forty counts of child molestation over a fifteen-year period. He was arrested but was soon released on a $100,000 bond.

News of the case exploded, both nationally and internationally, and almost immediately began to divide the Penn State campus as to who had ultimate responsibility.

On November 6, 2011, Paterno issued a statement admitting to knowledge of McQueary's eyewitness event, but he went on to say that McQueary did not seem to be very detailed in his reporting.

In his statement, Paterno said: "... I was informed in 2002 by an assistant coach that he had witnessed an incident in the shower of our locker room facility. It was obvious that the witness was distraught over what he saw, but he at no time related to me the very specific actions contained in the Grand Jury report. Regardless, it was clear that the witness saw something inappropriate involving Mr. Sandusky. As Coach Sandusky was retired from our coaching staff at that time, I referred the matter to university administrators."

Amid protests both pro and con, on November 9, 2011, the university board of trustees fired Paterno from his coaching duties, and a stellar coaching career came to an ignoble end.

On November 30, 2011, an additional accuser came forward claiming to have been sexually assaulted more than 100 times. He filed suit against Sandusky and The Second Mile. This claim was followed on December 7, 2011, by another ten accusers coming forward. Joe Paterno passed away shortly after his firing, on January 22, 2012, at the age of eighty-five.

On October 9, 2012, Sandusky was convicted and sentenced to thirty to sixty years in jail. He is currently held in a maximum-security prison and not allowed contact with the other inmates.

According to court documents that came to light in 2016 (USA Today, July 12, 2016), another man, identified as John Doe 150, alleged in a 2014 deposition that in 1976, when he tried to tell Paterno about Sandusky's inappropriate sexual contact in a shower. Paterno allegedly said, "I don't want to hear about any of that kind of stuff, I have a football season to worry about." In fairness, Paterno is not here to address this allegation, and it has not been corroborated by any other witnesses.

McQueary was vilified from both sides, as both a whistleblower and as someone who stood by and did nothing as a young boy was being sexually assaulted. McQueary has said he himself was abused as a child. Sandusky's wife defends him to this day. Penn State has removed Joe Paterno's iconic statue from view on campus.

In March 2017, Curley and Shultz pleaded guilty to endangering the welfare of children. They served jail time and house arrest. Both men testified at Spanier's trial. Spanier was found innocent of conspiracy but was found guilty of endangering the welfare of children. He served two months in prison.

The Penn State football program came very close to receiving the "death penalty." As it was, the NCAA initially stripped Penn State of all wins between 1998 and 2011 and instituted a number of other sanctions, though the NCAA restored the wins and reduced the sanctions in 2013. Sandusky's victim's soldier on, trying to live their lives as normally as possible.

CHUCK'S ETHICS REVIEW:

Sandusky: Purveyor of Perversion

In this terribly sad scandal, layered with one tragedy piled on the next, we have to start with the legacy of Sandusky's superior, Joe Paterno. We cannot blame a coach or athletic director in one case, and then overlook the responsibility of the same people in another case.

As head coach, Paterno had a head coach's responsibilities. Knowing what we know today, I would have to fall on the side of Paterno being fired. I regret to say it, but it's the truth we must live with if we are to be honest.

It seems painfully clear that there was a pattern of repulsive behavior on the part of Sandusky.

Paterno should have recognized this pattern in the ex-coach, who was allowed to hang out on campus and use the school's athletic facilities at will long after his retirement. He should have listened more closely when rumblings of Sandusky's misbehavior reached his ears, which it most certainly must have.

Once McQueary reported a specific incident to him, Paterno should have done something. He should have made sure that the people the head coach reported the matter to — the athletic director and the vice president, not to mention the university president and campus law enforcement — followed through and stopped Sandusky, prosecuting him for the crimes he committed. Paterno should have been more than a quiet bystander on the sidelines while children's lives were ruined.

Sandusky retired from Penn State in 1999, and yet he was still a fixture around the locker room and facilities. In fact, he committed crimes in the locker rooms long after he retired. Although there were hints of a problem, it's almost as if the athletic department was allowing Sandusky to keep his privileges to allow him to maintain a connection to his former identity and to let him hang out.

I have to be careful here because it is dangerous to refer to these two coaches in the same sentence, but the late coach of the University of North Carolina at Chapel Hill, Dean Smith, kept his office long after his retirement, even while he was dealing with Alzheimer's and dementia—the UNC administration out of respect and admiration.

In Sandusky's case, there was deference to his past service, but there were also the hints of those hidden, hushed problems. Having an office is one thing; going into the locker room to carry out abuse is worse than fiendish.

NO ONE STEPPED UP

We need to acknowledge that, on several occasions, the local police were notified as to Sandusky's possible behavior, but their investigations were inconclusive. However, we have to understand that the university had tremendous power and standing in the community, and the local police — perhaps in deference to their counterparts in the campus police force — may not have wanted to rock the boat.

Did this dynamic exist only at Penn State? Hardly. I think you would find this true at almost all major universities; I really don't care where you go. If you are sitting there at the University of South Carolina or Arkansas or New Mexico, if the issue was not so absolutely blatant as this sandal, if it was just something that was alleged, the police departments associated with the cities would tend to back off a little. Like it or not, local police curry a lot of favors — game day tickets, special invites to banquets, etc. — from universities and campus police friends in exchange for preferential treatment. Moreover, campus law enforcement will sometimes hush up crimes to protect the reputation of the school. They sometimes convince victims not to prosecute. School officials will sometimes compensate victims outside the court system so as not to draw attention to the crime. They worry that, if a rape or robbery gets reported, current students will fear for their safety, future students won't come here, and alumni won't give as much money.

I am quite confident there have been many situations where problems have been swept under the table, and the police have looked the other way. It is an ingrained, cultural thing between universities and town police departments.

We cannot overlook the internal winks and nods, either. We might ask why the university would not listen to McQueary and do something about it, or at least conduct a rigorous investigation. Curley and Shultz initially decided to report the McQueary incident to child protective services, but then they backed off and decided to try to handle it internally. They involved university president Graham Spanier in this decision, and together they made wrong choices, not just ethically but legally. All three men paid the price for it.

You have to understand that this was a fraternal organization. I am not saying it is a fraternity but a fraternal organization. When you see someone doing something wrong, what do you do? You either sound the alarm or you try to correct the behavior. McQueary, having been abused in the past himself (according to his own testimony), might have seen something that clouded his judgment or stopped him from acting or even reporting the crime correctly. It was a kind of trigger.

It doesn't strike me as much different than some of the abuse that has occurred in the Catholic Church. What do you do there? If you are on the inside of the church hierarchy and you see a priest abuse a young boy, do you report it to the police, conceivably risking your position in the clergy, or do you keep it among the ranks? We know what has typically happened: Church officials counseled the priests or transferred them, but the matter was hidden from the public and swept aside. I need to say, of course, that these offenses have been committed by a small percentage of the Catholic clergy. We also know that it is not just a Catholic problem. Virtually all religions have had predatory clergy members accused of such abuse.

In any case, McQueary reported it as best he could, and Paterno's superiors chose to downplay it and brush it off, which put McQueary in a bind. Not only did he relive his own past trauma, but nobody seemed to want to believe what he saw could be true.

TURNING THEIR BACKS

There is something here that is ethically very troubling. Along the way, many people had the opportunity to stop Sandusky's predatory behavior, and no one did. It bothers me whenever I review the case, and frankly, this might be a mystery we never fully understand.

If I were a betting man, I might imagine that Jerry Sandusky, even while he was engaged in predatory behavior, would not come across as an ogre. He was probably a very likable person. You know … "one of the guys." After all, he started a charity that helped children. He was probably able to connect with people very well. He got away with this horror for many years. My feeling is that, while he had an incredibly dark side, the other side was one that was quite charming and lulled people into falsely thinking he was great.

Here's another question that goes right to the heart of our society and the way we look at gender these days: What if Jerry Sandusky had been suspected of abusing young girls, not young boys? I think the case would have been investigated differently. If you are a male sexual predator, as was Sandusky, I think there would be the clear assumption that he was exercising power, that he needed to feel dominant.

Had he abused females, he might have been seen in a different light — as would his victims. The idea of crimes being committed by men against boys in a football locker room creates uneasy feelings many in sports might be hesitant to explore. Sexual abuse against boys and young men is woefully underreported and minimized. Young male victims are shamed and stigmatized; young female victims are more easily believed and helped.

Sexual abuse is sexual abuse, with the victim feeling great embarrassment along with it. Several psychologists I have spoken with are concerned that, in the midst of all of the empowering of girls, which was long overdue, boys are often forgotten or demeaned in the childhood equation.

Boys boast that they are strong, so how can they justify in their minds that they were weak enough to allow this monster to violate them? The boys whom Sandusky victimized were under his control and power. He was a coach and an authority figure in his charity — a father figure even. It wasn't as if he was a male coach for a female basketball team; his access was to young males.

Had he abused females, the question might have been: How could he have had access to do that? In this case, he was in a locker room setting with many young boys, and he is a male sexual predator. Sex is not the issue that drives this; it's power.

WHAT IS THIS INCIDENT ABOUT?

This case is not solely about Sandusky's sexual abuse, and it would be a mistake to let it go at that. To me, on a far broader level, this case demonstrates a number of failures — a failure to recognize that, within a large organization, something was wrong; a failure to vigorously right that wrong; and a failure to protect the innocent. It was a failure of ethics.

I think the circumstances of this case scream that, despite multiple allegations over the course of many years, no one was willing to recognize that there was a really serious problem here. The question from an ethical perspective is this: Was the organization's need to win and keep everything in-house greater than its willingness to be transparent and above board? That is a serious question that is applicable to many situations, both within and outside of sports.

Sometimes when problems are hidden for a very long time, they damage many lives before they're brought to light. Who knows how many victims Sandusky abused, all while the athletic department had at least some inkling that there might be a problem?

With that, we must come full circle to Paterno and his inner circle. Many Penn State fans were angered when Paterno was fired. They felt he was just as much of a victim. I understand that fans, by their nature, are passionate. Vicariously, they win when their team wins. When a team does well, you want to continue this process. You don't want anything to interfere with your joy as a fan.

Paterno was much more than just a coach; he was an icon. Though many fans thought he should have retired before this, they did not want to see him forced out of coaching. They felt he had earned the right to retire on his own schedule. All of a sudden, everything was turned around for them. If you have idolized a coach or a leader, and he or she is so connected to an organization and is then ousted, then that completely changes your experience as a fan. If I'm a die-hard fan, I don't want that.

One thing we know for sure: Every child Sandusky victimized will forever be affected by his abuse. These kinds of scars never go away. The victims can never escape them. Every adult who knew about or suspected what was happened was, at least in part, responsible for this tragedy.

CHAPTER 31

LARRY NASSAR AND A CULTURE OF ABUSE

Who: Larry Nassar, USA Gymnastics, Michigan State University

Offense: Sexual Abuse of Young Athletes, Pornography, and Subsequent Cover-ups

Result: Life imprisonment for Nassar, Lawsuits, Terminations, and Jail Sentences

Monsters are created when ethical behavior is treated as a joke, and ethical training is, at best, an afterthought. The creation of Larry Nassar was a group effort. Let us make no mistake about that.

The scandal surrounding Larry Nassar, who is now behind bars for the rest of his life for sexually abusing female athletes, has engulfed not only USA Gymnastics but also Michigan State University and the FBI.

More than 500 survivors, including Olympic medalists Simone Biles, Gabby Douglas, and Aly Raisman, have reported that the longtime physician for the national women's gymnastics team, molested them while treating them for pain.

The Indianapolis Star newspaper broke the news of the allegations against Nassar in a Sept. 12, 2016 article. One of the women the newspaper interviewed for the article, who asked that her name not be revealed, was a member of the 2000 U.S. Olympic Team. In a lawsuit she had recently filed in California against Nassar and USA Gymnastics, she stated Nassar began abusing her when she was twelve or thirteen years old.

The other woman the paper spoke with, Rachael Denhollander, filed a complaint against Nassar with the MSU Police Department in August 2016. She alleged Nassar, a faculty member, and physician who treated university, high school, and club-level gymnasts, sexually assaulted her in 2000 when she was fifteen. Michigan State told the Indianapolis Star that it suspended Nassar following the criminal complaint. The university fired him a week after the paper's expose, and university police arrested him two months later.

In July 2017, Nassar pleaded guilty to three child pornography charges after investigators found he possessed thousands of sexually explicit videos and photographs of minors. In December of that year, a judge sentenced him to sixty years in federal prison. Meanwhile, more and more Nassar survivors were coming forward.

In November 2018, Nassar entered a guilty plea in the sexual abuse of seven girls he was treating for gymnastics injuries. The following January, Judge Rosemarie Aquilina sentenced Nassar to 175 years in prison on seven counts of first-degree sexual misconduct in Ingham County, Michigan.

The following month, a judge sentenced Nassar to forty to 125 years in prison for three counts of criminal sexual misconduct in Easton County, Michigan. He had earlier pleaded guilty to the charges.

But the fallout from the Nassar scandal did not end when he went to prison.

CONSEQUENCES FOR MICHIGAN STATE

In an article published on Jan. 18, 2018, The Detroit News reported at least fourteen Michigan State University representatives heard accounts of Nassar's misconduct with female athletes in the twenty years before his firing. In May of that year, MSU settled lawsuits by more than 300 Nassar survivors. The total payout was $500 million.

United States Education Secretary Betsy DeVos announced in September 2019 that Michigan State would pay a $4.5 million fine as part of a settlement with the federal government for the university's non-response to reports of Nassar's sexual abuse. The settlement also required MSU to overhaul its Title IX compliance procedures.

The only MSU employee besides Nassar, who served prison time in the wake of the scandal, was his supervisor, William Stampel, dean of the MSU College of Osteopathic Medicine.

In June 2019, a jury found Stampel guilty of neglect of duty and misconduct in office after investigators concluded he sexually harassed female students and failed to monitor Nassar properly. A judge sentenced him to a year in prison.

In August 2020, a judge sentenced former MSU gymnastics Coach Kathie Klages, who also oversaw the Spartans youth gymnastics program, to ninety days in jail for lying to police during the Nassar investigation about her knowledge of sexual abuse allegations against him during the 1990s. However, in December 2021, the Michigan Court of Appeals overturned her conviction, stating her 2018 interviews with authorities were not crucial to the investigation. Former MSU president Lou Anna Simon also was charged with lying to police during the Nassar probe. A judge dismissed the case in May 2020.

Michigan State's interim president, John Engler, who took over when Simon resigned from her post in January 2018, turned in his own resignation one year later — allegedly under pressure from the MSU Board of Trustees, according to a Detroit Free Press article.

Engler had previously told The Detroit News that the survivors of Nassar's abuse were "enjoying" the publicity.

USA GYMNASTICS FALLOUT

In September 2018, authorities arrested Debra Van Horn, a former sports medicine trainer who had worked for USA Gymnastics for three decades, after a grand jury indicted her on one count of second-degree sexual assault of a child.

According to the Associated Press, Walker County, Texas District Attorney David Weeks had previously stated Van Horn was "acting as a party" with Nassar. A judge dismissed the charge in January 2020.

Authorities arrested former USA Gymnastics President Steve Penney after a Texas grand jury indicted him on tampering with evidence charges in the Nassar case.

Penney allegedly ordered the removal of documents from the Karolyi Ranch near Houston, the location of a gymnastics training facility for Olympic hopefuls. Dozens of gymnasts said Nassar molested them there. The facility closed in early 2018. The charges against Penney were later dismissed due to "insufficient evidence to prosecute," according to court documents.

In December 2021, USA Gymnastics and the U.S. Olympic and Paralympic Committee reached a $380 million settlement in a lawsuit filed by Nassar survivors. The organization has pledged to provide better protection for athletes.

FBI INVESTIGATION COMES UNDER SCRUTINY

A July 2021 report by the U.S. Justice Department's inspector general stated the FBI made many grave mistakes in the Nassar investigation. The inspector general became involved due to allegations that the FBI didn't respond quickly enough to complaints about Nassar in 2015.

Although USA Gymnastics reported the incidents to the FBI, the bureau did not investigate until fourteen months later. Lawyers for survivors stated more than one-hundred girls and women reported that Nassar abused them during that period. In April 2022, the attorneys announced they were seeking $10 million each in damages from the FBI for thirteen clients.

However, in May of the same year, the Justice Department said it did not have enough evidence to file criminal charges against two former FBI agents — one who had been fired and another who had retired — suspected of lying to internal investigators.

COURT REFUSES TO HEAR NASSAR'S APPEAL

In June 2022, the Michigan Supreme Court rejected Nassar's final appeal of the 175-year sentence handed down by Aquilina. Nassar's lawyers argued he was entitled to a new sentencing hearing because of Aquilina's remarks, including her calling him a "monster."

However, the state's highest court stated in its order that, although it had concerns about Aquilina's statements, she based Nassar's sentence on an agreement between attorneys for the state and the defense.

DENHOLLANDER POSTED ABOUT THE ORDER ON TWITTER.

"Almost six years after I filed the police report, it's finally over," she said.

As an ethics speaker and consultant, I can say with certainty that the scars caused by this monster will last a lifetime for each one of the victims. It is not over, only lurking beneath the surface.

CHUCK'S ETHICS REVIEW:

Nassar: The Spider and its Prey

Larry Nassar is a monster, and he will spend the rest of his life in prison. We could spend pages guessing the psychological motivation behind Nassar's actions, but that's not my focus. Rather I'd prefer to focus on three questions, the answers to which will determine the fate of those who surround him.

Think of Nassar like a spider whose craft and stealth can create a web so powerful that it catches prey of all sorts. Of course, Nassar's primary prey was young women in the gymnastics program.

He was the spider, clothed as a trustworthy doctor who could lure the youngest victims into his web, and they could be caught without even knowing what was happening. His actions were so deceptive, he could torture their psyches for a lifetime.

However, even the craftiest spider cannot create a successful web without having something to attach the strands. It is critical to remember that point, whether you are the AD of a school in the SEC, the CEO of an accounting firm, or the shift manager in an electric vehicle factory. The helper with the web, the enabler, is where the three questions must come into play.

Nassar's web was attached to the university, its support staff and those connected with his actions, as stealthy as they might have been. Here are the three primary questions to be asked of everyone connected, and to be clear, the answer to each is critical when dealing with someone who has been a perpetrator of crime for some time.

Question One: What did you know?

Question Two: When did you know it?

Question Three: What did you do about it?

For a second, ignore Nassar completely and rather ask yourself, what if you were one of those caught in his web, someone who supported his web unknowingly and then was informed about the nefarious actions of which he was initially accused?

HOW WOULD YOU ANSWER THE THREE PRIMARY QUESTIONS?

This scandal isn't just Nassar (It is never just "a Nassar.") that creates such an elaborate web. It needs help to thrive. This is an ethical issue that occurs over and over again.

The spider starts to weave its design, and something might seem a bit off at first. You choose to ignore the feeling. Without raising the slightest concern, even the slightest doubt, you become connected at the periphery, never having intended to cause harm.

Here is where the challenge is for almost everyone caught in the web. You hear gossip that there may be a problem, but you are connected so intimately to the spider that you can't believe it.

How could there be a problem with your colleague and pal Larry Nassar? Surely, it's a mistake, you believe — not true of a medical professional, a healer. Nevertheless, you, as the slightly suspicious observer, fail to take it seriously immediately. Ultimately the web catches you as well. The spider continues its activity, catching more and more victims. Then one-day reality hits, and the answers to the three questions catch you in the web.

That is what happened in this case. Whether or not the web was sufficient to create a prison sentence for those who stood by and did nothing, the stickiness of the web still trapped them, costing much in the way of reputation and legal expense.

In today's world, the expectation is that, when made aware of an unethical action, anyone even distantly involved should acknowledge that awareness and then take action to — at a minimum — report the purported action.

While it may not be up to you to take legal action or to report the crime, to raise doubts keeps you from being caught in the spider's web.

AN EXAMPLE OF REPORTING

I was recently consulting with a former CPA who was facing a jail sentence for a felony conviction. His story was sad and disturbing.

He was a CPA and chief financial officer of a fairly large company. He believed the chief executive officer and chief operating officer were both doing something shady. As he couldn't stand the idea of being a part of their illegal scheme, he quit. The next CFO did likewise, suspecting the same thing. The third CFO joined the CEO and COO in the illegal activity, and now all three CFOs are in prison.

When he shared that he was entering prison even though he had walked away, I asked why? His response was inciteful and clear. As part of their investigation, the Department of Justice asked him why he quit. His response was that he suspected something and did not want to be a part of their unethical and potentially illegal activities.

The DOJ interrogator asked, "Oh, so you knew something and didn't report it? What did you do about it?"

"I quit," he replied.

It was not good enough. If you know something is wrong and fail to report it; then you have conspired to make it happen.

He was given an option — take a plea deal or take his luck with a jury. Trust me here. When the federal government is coming after you, take the plea; the outcome is usually far better. He pleaded to one count of conspiracy, which meant he became a convicted felon and lost his license as a CPA.

The consequences of failing to properly answer the DOJ's questions were significant.

Nassar shattered many lives. He was a serial abuser and pedophile. The young women and men caught in his web will never be completely healed. All of the collected legal fees that have gone to their therapies can never fully compensate them for their pain.

However, the crime all of those around Nassar committed, those who enabled him to continue with his abuse even though they suspected something was not quite right, was very nearly as bad.

What did they know? More than enough to be suspicious and say something. When did they know it? Some had a sick feeling and nagging doubt for years. What did they do about it? Pathetically little.

There will always be spiders like Larry Nassar, and they are despicable. What makes them powerful are the people who help them weave their webs. He had plenty of help for far too long.

ABOUT THE AUTHORS

CHUCK GALLAGHER

"Ethics in sports is a serious matter, but talking about it doesn't have to be 'a losing proposition.'" – Chuck Gallagher

Chuck Gallagher learned his lessons about ethics, choices, and consequences the hard way, but now he shares his experiences so that others do not have to go through what he went through. You may have seen Chuck on TV or heard him on CNN, CBS, NPR, or other sports radio programs.

Chuck's insights are sought after for his strong position on sports ethics, business ethics, and ethical choices. His focus is ethics, but his passion is empowering others. His unique presentations and consulting on sports ethics clearly demonstrate that he brings something to your team or organization that is not often found in speakers, authors, and consultants.

Chuck, a former senior vice president of sales and marketing for a public company, is currently president of SportsEthics.com. It was the school of hard knocks that provided a fertile training ground for Chuck's lessons in success. In the middle of a rising career, Chuck lost everything because he made some bad choices. He has since rebuilt his career and his life back to immense success.

Chuck shares his life journey with his clients — the consequences of his unethical choices and how life gives you second chances when you make the right choices. He connects the dots between behavior, choices, and success. Chuck gives his sports clients what they need to turn concepts into actions and actions into results. He offers tested and time-proven methods that can enhance personal and professional performance. Yet he keeps it real and honest and fun. He will have your group asking for more because he knows that what is discussed today will yield results tomorrow!

Virtually every sports scandal, large or small, is caused by bad ethics off the field. Bad ethics destroys athletic careers. Whether you're an athlete, coach, athletic director, association, trainer or anyone involved in the world of sports, Chuck's courses are for you.

While Chuck ran track in high school, the allure of business and speaking became front and center for him in college. Chuck and his family live in South Carolina.

chuck@chuckgallagher.com

BRUCE H. WOLK

Writer and marketer Bruce H. Wolk earned an M.B.A. in marketing and management from Fordham University in New York. He writes for magazines, newspapers and online publications, and is a published author.

Bruce co-wrote Monday Morning Ethics with Chuck Gallagher and, day-to-day, he is responsible for the marketing for SportsEthics.com. Bruce is at work on a new sports history book about the lifelong friendship between two basketball players.

Bruce has an enduring love of sports, having played and coached soccer and run marathons. While in the corporate world, Bruce organized a national promotional program with Minor League Baseball and helped sponsor events in collegiate wrestling, high school and collegiate volleyball, road racing and competitive rowing events. Bruce and his family live in Colorado.

bruce@brucewolk.com

Printed in the USA
CPSIA information can be obtained
at www.ICGtesting.com
CBHW071713050424
6341CB00005B/2